BUSINESS
explained

CITY OF WOLVERHAMPTON COLLEGE

D1347641

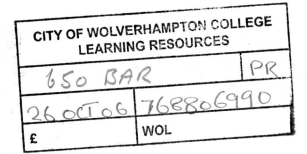

CITY OF WOLVERHAMPTON COLLEGE
LEARNING RESOURCES

650 BAR   PR

26 OCT 06   768806990

£   WOL

Orders: please contact Bookpoint Ltd, 130 Milton Park, Abingdon, Oxon OX14 4SB. Telephone: (44) 01235 827720. Fax: (44) 01235 400454. Lines are open from 9.00 – 6.00, Monday to Saturday, with a 24-hour message answering service. You can also order through our website: www.hodderheadline.co.uk

British Library Cataloguing in Publication Data
A catalogue record for this title is available from the British Library

ISBN 0 340 78254 4

First Published 2003
Impression number   10 9 8 7 6 5 4 3 2 1
Year   2008 2007 2006 2005 2004 2003

Copyright © Stephen Barnes 2003

All rights reserved. This work is copyright. Permission is given for copies to be made of pages provided they are used exclusively within the institution for which this work has been purchased. For reproduction for any other purpose, permission must first be obtained in writing from the publishers.

Cover photo from Photodisc
Artworks by Jeff Edwards.

Typeset by Dorchester Typesetting Group Limited
Printed in Great Britain for Hodder & Stoughton Educational, a division of Hodder Headline, 338 Euston Road, London NW1 3BH by J. W. Arrowsmiths Ltd, Bristol

Contents

Acknowledgements

The author and publishers would like to thank the following for permission to reproduce copyright material:

'Seven-S' Framework (p. 13) from THE AGE OF UNREASON by Charles Handy published by RH Business Books. Used by permission of The Random House Group Limited.

Yorkie promotional material (p. 25) reproduced by kind permission of Nestlé Rowntree.

Porter's generic value chain (p. 31) and Porter's generic strategies (p. 46) adapted with permission of The Free Press, a Division of Simon and Schuster Adult Publishing Group, from COMPETITIVE ADVANTAGE: Creating and Sustaining Superior Performance by Michael E. Porter. Copyright © 1985, 1988 by Michael E. Porter. All rights reserved.

The 'tree model' for core competencies (p. 54) reprinted by permission of Harvard Business School Press. From COMPETING FOR THE FUTURE by G. Hamel and C. K. Prahalad. Boston, MA 1994, p. 254. Copyright © 1994 by the Harvard Business School Publishing Corporation; all rights reserved.

Porter's five forces model (p. 76) adapted with permission of The Free Press, a Division of Simon and Schuster Adult Publishing Group, from COMPETITIVE STRATEGY: Techniques for Analyzing Industries and Competitors by Michael E. Porter. Copyright © 1980, 1998 by The Free Press. All rights reserved.

Kotler's product levels (p. 119) from MARKETING: AN INTRODUCTION, 1st edition, by Kotler, ©. Reprinted by permission of Pearson Education, Inc., Upper Saddle River, NJ.

Routes to creating new value (p. 136) reprinted by permission of Harvard Business Review. Adapted from 'Creating New Market Space' by W.C. Kim and R. Mauborgne, January/February 1999. Copyright © 1999 by the Harvard Business School Publishing Corporation; all rights reserved.

Four diagrams (pp. 237-38) from UNDERSTANDING ORGANIZATIONS by Charles Handy (Penguin Books 1976, Fourth edition 1993). Copyright © Charles Handy, 1976, 1981, 1985, 1993, 1999.

Pine and Gilmour's progression of economic value (p. 266) reprinted by permission of Harvard Business Review. Adapted from 'Welcome to the Experience Economy' by B.J. Pine and J.H. Gilmour, July/August 1998. Copyright © 1998 by the Harvard Business School Publishing Corporation; all rights reserved.

Every effort has been made to obtain necessary permission with reference to copyright material. The publishers apologise if inadvertently any sources remain unacknowledged and will be glad to make the necessary arrangements at the earliest opportunity.

Introduction

This book explains how business works. Written at undergraduate level, it provides a complete subject overview. It is unlike other business texts because:

- it identifies and explains the basic concepts that underpin business as a field of study;
- it explains strategy and all the main functional areas (marketing, operations, human resources and finance) showing how the same key concepts clarify and unify each theme or module of study;
- it explains and discusses a full agenda of cutting-edge ideas that are subjects of research and debate in the early 21st century.

The aim of this book is the empowerment of its reader. There is a danger that courses in business and management come to seem like a series of self-contained modules with little to link their themes. Lecturers know that this is not the case but this book explicitly shows how a common subject 'wiring' connects and illuminates each and every topic.

Which concepts found in marketing are also at work in finance and accounting? How exactly are the ideas in operations also useful in considering human resources? How can the principles of strategy be used to solve problems in all other topic areas? *Business Explained* answers these questions while providing a clear summary of key course material. A wide range of academic references are carefully explained. Nothing important to understanding business strategy and management has been left out but, equally, detail has not been allowed to blur the essential ideas.

The book can be used in different ways. You may wish to read it as a whole. This will provide a full introduction to the subject and act as a foundation for all optional modules. Alternatively, each section provides a complete support system for specialist courses while individual chapters will form a baseline for specific lectures and seminars.

Part A *Basics explained* takes a firm grip on the 'big ideas' that run though business courses. In Part B *Strategy explained*, we go to the heart of this complex area and make sense of the major perspectives. The same ideas are applied in Part C *Marketing explained* where the classic models are outlined and evaluated. The material in Part D *Operations explained* forms a closely knit whole that makes a useful introduction to Part E *Human Resources explained*. Then in Part F *Finance explained* we tackle all the concepts that students often find problematic while showing that they are only the quantitative expression of human decisions. Finally, Part G *Agenda explained* explores key strands of new thinking in the subject. These are diverse and exciting but combine intriguingly to reveal the emerging paradigm for business today – less bureaucratic and more creative, less mechanistic and more biological.

PART A

BASICS explained

1 How business works

Choice and opportunity cost

All human beings make choices. As involuntary seekers of satisfaction, we aim to move from the circumstances we are in towards circumstances that we anticipate will be more desirable. This means making choices – or decisions – about the best use of the resources at our disposal.

These resources take many forms, but they are limited in their availability. The key resource constraint varies: it may be land and natural resources; it may be the existing products of human labour; it may be people and talent; or it could simply be time. In any event, no resource is either limitless or 'free'. Indeed, a crucial realisation in the late 20th century was that even the gifts of nature require stewardship and choices about their most appropriate use.

Virtually every resource has more than one possible use. It follows that the most basic 'cost' when using a resource is the value of its next-best use. This is the baseline against which every decision about resources can be compared. In making a choice, which next-best opportunity was *not* grasped? This opportunity cost lies behind every human decision.

Sometimes the choice is decisive and its opportunity cost seems safely far behind. For example, we may have bought an item in a sale and been charged less than half the price we would have been prepared to pay. In other cases, a choice is made by the narrowest of margins and the opportunity cost is an almost painful reminder of what might have been. For example, we forego a holiday in order to repair the house – and think often of the holiday missed. All too often, the opportunity cost of a decision rises over time until the original choice is overwhelmed. We might take the car, run into worsening traffic jams and wish that we had gone by train. Sometimes the decision can be reversed and sometimes it cannot.

Adding value

All decisions about resources aim to add value. People as individuals and people as members of organisations are engaged in a constant effort to combine resources so that the outcome is more valuable than its constituent elements. Put another way, resource decisions aim to ensure that the value of outputs exceeds the corresponding cost of inputs. This requires skill and ingenuity. To keep ahead of opportunity cost also often requires originality and creativity.

Adding value in this sense means the value attached to a product by buyers in the market. The process of manufacturing a computer has an obvious effect on adding value. Customer service in the form of expert advice is also likely to add value. Equally, the friendliness and courtesy of retail staff may add further value.

CITY OF WOLVERHAMPTON COLLEGE

It is important to recognise that value in the market is extrinsic and not intrinsic. In other words, the value of a product is based on what people will pay and not on what someone thinks it is worth. This is why prices sometimes seem to defy common sense. For example, an antique dealer may find that simply cleaning the dust from a piece of furniture adds very substantially to its value. By contrast, the presence of dust can actually add value to vintage wine! It is perceptual and psychological factors of this sort that make product packaging such a potent source of added value.

Billy'z Café

Billy'z is a café on the sea front of a small Cornish surf resort. It opened in 2000, its competitors a traditional beach café and a fish and chip shop. Billy'z is different. Its customers are young professionals on weekend breaks from London and the big cities. Others are surfers, and others again are walkers on the South West Coast Path.

Cappuccinos froth out of brilliantly coloured mugs. R&B music provides a gentle but chiming ambience. There are small clasps of flowers on the Italian aluminium tables. The walls are sea-blue and sand-yellow, half and half.

Billy'z menu is not cheap. There are no chips or burgers. But there are croissants and late breakfasts, pizzas and salads. And there are interesting other customers.

Just temporarily you join a family, busy in the kitchen. Students help out with cooking and waiting. Staff wear free-size navy T-shirts emblazoned with the orange Billy'z logo. Customers can buy the same.

Meanwhile, through the one picture window, there is the vast Atlantic – all endless arrivals, wave after wave, breaking into endless surf.

This is added value.

Source: Interview by author

Specialisation and exchange

Specialisation and exchange are the motive forces that drive millions of decisions every day. What proportion of the goods and services consumed is produced by consumers themselves? In an industrial society such as Britain's, the answer might be 1 or 2 per cent. The great bulk of products consumed is the specialised output of other people that has been traded for money.

Virtually everyone is a specialist. Most people do not even produce a single whole product. Instead, they make repeated (often very small) contributions to the making of one or more products. In this way they can be very much more productive than if they were obliged to spread their talents across many different and diverse tasks. Through their work, people generally add value at the highest rate of which they are capable since, unsurprisingly, this earns the greatest rewards.

Consider the rush hour in a city like London: trucks on the motorway, cars at every road junction, trains approaching their terminus, planes waiting to land. Then think of the letters, faxes, phone calls, e-mails and internet searches that are continuously making and remaking an inconceivably complex web of communications. This is all the signature of exchange that makes possible specialisation.

Demand

The force to which every producer responds is customer demand. As households produce less and less for themselves, they demand more and more of others. Some demands can be regarded as needs. Everyone needs the essentials of basic food, clothing, warmth and shelter. However, most demands are simply wants: a vast array of goods and services ranging from haircuts to holidays, and from soft drinks to family cars. These are the demands of final consumers; but in meeting consumer demand, there are many intermediate demands from producer to producer, from business to business. A firm that makes cars, for example, will demand parts from many suppliers, as well as expert services such as computer programming or market research.

If demand is the engine for business activity, then firms must analyse and understand the nature of the markets they can profitably serve. This involves a matching process as the firm aligns its internal strengths with the external opportunities identified. Once a market has been targeted, then available resources can be focused on meeting that demand and generating added value.

However, the pattern of demand is like a weather map – constantly changing. Sometimes the direction of change is clear (e.g. an expanding market for mobile phones), but often the true pattern is obscured or a clear trend has yet to emerge. A combination of detailed market research and intuitive flair is then required. Recognising market change early is a key route to business success (e.g. the launch of First Direct as a telephone banking service in 1989).

Markets

Wherever and however these many sources of demand can be met, a market exists. If there is a potential for exchange, there is a potential market. As an economic mechanism for exchange, a market allows sellers and buyers to trade at an agreed price. This is only possible if the buyer's highest price exceeds the seller's lowest price. In other words, there must be a basis for the 'swap' that a market implies. The transaction can only take place if, through the decision to exchange, both sides consider that they will make a gain (see Chapter 4). The buyer believes that the best possible value for money has been obtained. The seller believes that the best possible profit has been realised. Both sides are satisfied that they have kept ahead of opportunity cost in the use of their resources.

Profitable business activity means making a systematic financial gain through the action of markets. And the same basic principle extends into the not-for-profit sector. A publicly owned service must still demonstrate net gain in the use of the resources that are its inputs. Likewise, a charity must achieve a sufficient level of income relative to the costs that it incurs.

Competition

Profitability, however, invites challenge. Decisions that aim to add value ahead of opportunity cost face two basic problems. The first is competition. Unless everyone else is prevented in some way from making rival decisions, then any route to adding value is liable to the competitive impact of other routes. And what looks initially like 'another way of doing things' may, if sufficiently successful, become the new and dominant way in which things are done.

Where a market is open to competition, it is said to be contestable. The greater the profitability and potential market size, the greater will be the attractiveness of the market to competitors. To act as protection for their markets, firms erect barriers to entry, but these are rarely secure. Legal protection is possible – for example, in patents and licences – but most firms must rely on their own internal strengths, such as speed of innovation or the reputation of their brand.

Uncertainty

The second problem is the threat of uncertainty. Every decision is based on expectations about the behaviour of variables. Some of these variables relate directly to the elements of resource combination. For example, in opening a new hotel, both the reliability of suppliers and the morale of staff remain unknown. Others variables are embedded within the market and its environment. Will the resort become more or less fashionable? What will be the room occupancy rate? Will a new access road be built? These sources of uncertainty both pose risks and offer opportunities. A critical part of the skill when making resource decisions is the evaluation of uncertain variables.

Further uncertainty is represented by the behaviour of the economic environment. The level of taxation, the rate of interest and the value of the currency can all change without warning. More crucially still, the economic climate and corresponding level of general spending are subject to cyclical change, the profile and timing of which are extremely difficult to forecast.

For all these reasons and more, every producer participating in the market faces a chronic exposure to risk. It is not surprising that the English interpretation of the term *entrepreneur* is risk-taker. The only certainty in business is that nothing is certain. Small firms regularly founder or make fortunes. Large firms can seem one year like great ocean liners in the reliability of their profits and then, without warning, experience the fate of the *Titanic*.

The main antidote to risk is strategy (see Chapter 12). This expresses a scheme of action to reach shared objectives. In formulating strategy, managers set the direction of decision making to target their market in such a way as to counteract competition and to exploit the economic environment. Flexibility is essential in responding to changed conditions and unexpected events. Ultimately, there is no guarantee of success or even survival. As the speed of change accelerates, the nature of change has become more complex and less predictable. Rosabeth Moss Kanter (1989) observes, firms must be 'fast, friendly, focused and flexible'.

Summary

Undoubtedly everyone is a manager of resources. Every day every individual and every organisation try to manipulate the resources at their disposal in such a way that value is added. Business management is therefore concerned with:

> **making decisions about the use of resources with an opportunity cost in order to add value within a competitive and uncertain environment.**

2 The idea of management

Overview

The notion of management as a self-conscious process is derived from the Industrial Revolution. With the onset of the 20th century, the practice of management was shaped by the quickening forces of competition and the widening application of scientific method to human affairs.

The post-war years saw a high water mark of faith in scientific decision making. As the 1960s came to a close, question marks hung over the mechanistic model of business management.

Attention began to focus on the 'softer' qualities of human interaction and the springs of employee commitment. The global success of Japanese companies and the rapid advance of economies in the Pacific Basin proved a catalyst to new thinking. By the 1990s, the traditional 'command-and-control' hierarchies of Western countries were in significant retreat and a more organic paradigm for management was in the making.

The emergence of management

The Role of Management ←

The manager is the dynamic, life-giving element in every business. Without his leadership 'the resources of production' remain resources and never become production. In a competitive economy, above all, the quality and performance of the managers determine the success of a business, indeed, they determine its survival. For the quality and performance of its managers are the only effective advantage an enterprise in a competitive economy can have.

The emergence of management as an essential, a distinct and a leading institution is a pivotal event in social history. Rarely, if ever, has a new basic institution, a new leading group, emerged as fast as has management since the turn of this century. Rarely in human history has a new institution proven indispensable so quickly; and even less often has a new institution arrived with so little opposition, so little disturbance, so little controversy.

Management, which is the organ of society specifically charged with making resources productive, that is, with the responsibility for organised economic advance, ... reflects the basic spirit of the modern age. It is in fact indispensable – and this explains why, once begotten, it grew so fast and with so little opposition.

Source: Peter Drucker The Practice of Management *(Heinemann, 1955)*

Resource management is a natural, even involuntary human activity. People want to get the most from what is available, yet until the 19th century little systematic thought had been given to that process of optimisation or 'getting the best'. The catalyst for change was, of course, the Industrial Revolution. Until the new technologies of the late 18th and early 19th centuries became available, almost all business enterprise was small-scale in operations and local in the markets served. The application of steam power to machinery and the development of faster, more reliable communications meant that many goods could be mass-produced and distributed to national and even international markets. This implied much larger-scale organisations, where the combination of resources was more complex and where much larger numbers of people were employed in one place. In many ways, industrialisation marked a complete break from the informal domestic patterns of work that had characterised the pre-industrial economy.

Mechanised mass production in a factory setting implied rules and procedures that mirrored the nature of machinery itself. Until well into the 20th century, the jobs of many employees represented little more than 'machine-shortfalls'. People were pairs of hands employed to perform specialised tasks that had not yet been mechanised. To most employers, it therefore made sense to regulate jobs and workers, as far as possible, in the same style as they regulated their machines. Moreover, mass production is generally based on the achievement of lowest possible cost. This suggested offering workers the lowest possible remuneration that was consistent with an adequate supply of labour.

The classic model for capitalism was the owner-entrepreneur. This individual might own the entire business outright or combine his own capital with what he could raise from partners or the sale of shares. He then directed the enterprise – usually with absolute authority – and expected managers and workers alike to perform their allotted tasks according to a literal or near-literal book of rules.

The principle of limited liability (introduced in Britain from 1855) meant that large numbers of smaller investors could, with relative safety, subscribe to issues of shares. The willingness to supply capital to these large public companies was further supported by the Stock Exchange, which ensured reasonable liquidity (potential to raise cash) for securities after they were issued. There now emerged the so-called divorce between ownership and control. Shareholders were legal owners of their company, yet were mostly lacking the inclination or expertise to run their business in person. Instead, boards of directors were elected to act on the shareholders' behalf and themselves appointed subordinate managers who, in practice, appointed their own subordinates in an extending chain of command. In this way the classic hierarchical corporation was constructed and management became a profession.

This last development was relatively slow. Throughout the 19th century, decision making was assumed to be the product of experience and native intuition. This approach meant that the 'machinery' of human organisation was often far less efficient than the actual machinery that it mimicked. One of the first serious efforts to close this gap was launched by FW Taylor from around 1885.

Scientific management

What the workmen want from their employers beyond anything else is high wages and what employers want from their workmen most of all is low labour cost of manufacture . . . the existence or absence of these two elements forms the best index to either good or bad management.

FW Taylor (1856–1917)

Taylor was a qualified engineer who aimed to transfer the success of scientific method in predicting the behaviour of physical objects to improving the performance of human beings. In particular, he wanted to combine the scientifically optimised specification of jobs with the scientific selection and training of workers to perform those jobs. With meticulous attention to the benefits of specialisation, Taylor would divide a process into its component tasks and conduct scientific research into the most productive way that the task could be performed. The selected worker was then trained and equipped accordingly and rewarded in proportion to output.

This application of mechanical reasoning to the organisation of work was hugely successful in improving productivity. Though bitterly opposed by trade unions, 'Taylorism' spread rapidly in America, was adopted enthusiastically in Japan and was admired by both Lenin and Mussolini. *Principles of Scientific Management* was published in 1911 and has been hugely influential ever since.

By the start of the 20th century, very large organisations were emerging in both the private and public sectors. This trend was driven by rising population, access to ever larger markets and the economies of scale. Increasingly, the efficient management of large organisations became a priority.

Among the first to exploit rigorous division of labour, repetitive production lines and economies of scale was Henry Ford (1863–1947). A combination of ruthless Taylorism and flair in recognising a mass market lay behind the phenomenally successful 'Model T'. The Ford plant at Highland Park, Detroit, was an ultimate expression of mechanical logic. The production process, the shop-floor jobs and the role of management itself were all mechanical and routine-driven. Neither questions nor original thought were wanted: standardisation was the goal.

Early theory of management

Henri Fayol (1841–1925) was a French mining engineer who became managing director of Commentry-Fourchamboult-Décazeville, the mining company where he spent his whole working life. From 1900, his lectures on management attracted widening interest and, in 1916, his classic *General and Industrial Management* was published. Arguably this was the first book ever written on the challenge of management as an organisational role. Indeed, one reason for its importance is simply that it recognised management as critical to the success of any human undertaking.

The *activities* identified by Fayol were technical, commercial, financial, 'security' (protection of people and property), accounting and managerial. There was no doubt about the central importance of the managerial function in driving forward the organisation. As Fayol said: 'The management function is quite distinct from the other five essential functions.'

He then describes the generic *elements* of management as:

1 Forecast and plan
2 Organise
3 Command
4 Co-ordinate
5 Control

This functional model of an enterprise, which stresses its separate activities, has been very influential. Most organisations have established specialised functions such as production, sales, personnel and accounts. These have been mostly centralised to some degree, with authority expressed through a hierarchy and descending chain of command.

The theory of the organisation as a well-oiled machine was developed by the German, Max Weber (1864–1920) in his analysis of bureaucracy. His 'rational–legal' model stressed jobs with clear boundaries of discretion arranged in a hierarchy and driven by rules. Such an organisation operates with precision and objectivity and has been the template for many public and private sector bodies. Its strength lies in its design for consistency and efficiency. In practice, however, the model has been prone to becoming cumbersome and wasteful. Bureaucracy in itself is a neutral concept, but is often used as a pejorative term. A key factor has been the expectation that people work as though they were part of a machine.

The paradigm is challenged

A 'scientific' style of thinking about management gathered momentum during the mid-20th century. The Second World War not only quickened the pace of technological advance, but also saw the development and application of new mathematical techniques in the management of people and materials. As part of the same intellectual current, there was an increased interest in planning of all kinds. Events in the future, it was believed, could be made more predictable and more likely to conform with objectives if they were rationally planned.

The current of scientific decision making was still running strongly in the 1960s when it met its first serious challenge. Stirrings of the environmental movement and disenchantment with the rationalist ethic of big business among the young set an agenda of questions that remained active for the rest of the century.

Drucker (1954) had argued that mathematical techniques of problem solving could not assist the critical managerial role of asking the right questions. Effective strategic management depended more on the quality of questions than on the accuracy of answers. Herein lay a danger in the *linear* thinking on which so many managers had come to rely. Designing and implementing a sequence of cause-and-effect events successfully could come to fill the whole picture. The risk that the entire sequence is addressing the wrong problem or ignoring its own interactivity with other variables is easily missed.

Mintzberg (1973, 1975) launched a powerful critique of scientific decision making. He found that managers did not work through a series of logical steps but were engaged in a continuous and often intuitive process of shaping and configuring events. Similarly, he described strategy-making less in terms of cerebral reasoning and more as a crafting process that was emergent and creative. He argued that the scientific approach failed to achieve a holistic understanding of problems and drove out the 'soft' values of human concern.

Meanwhile, the view that business could be dehumanising was not new. Indeed, Adam Smith had warned that dull, repetitive labour could stunt human intelligence and imagination. Numerous writers and novelists had attacked mass production for its deadening effects on the workforce and the cultural impoverishment of its products. And pioneers of the Human Relations School of management – such as Elton Mayo in the 1930s and Abraham Maslow in the 1940s – had analysed and illustrated the need to address the higher, more complex needs of people at work.

Yet these insights had been slow to be adopted and were often perceived as second rank to the imperatives of the quasi-scientific management. In most workplaces of the Western world there was still a dualistic, if not antagonistic, model for industrial relations. In many ways the interests of business managers and the mass labour force remained as clearly opposed as ever.

'The power of the Pacific'

In the end it was the sheer force of competition from Japan and the Far East that precipitated real change, especially in the US and the UK. By the early 1980s many Western countries found their home markets under assault from Japanese imports, and their traditional export markets challenged by the emergent economies of the Pacific Basin. Energetic rebuilding of Japanese industry after the war was based on productivity, quality and market orientation. These ideas were linked by the engagement of all levels in the workforce in a unified commitment to the organisation's success. Many Japanese firms had a closer cultural 'knit' than their Western counterparts, with shared values from the boardroom to the shop floor.

Meanwhile, Peters and Waterman's *In Search of Excellence* (1982) became the best-selling business book of all time. It studied a range of US companies achieving 'excellence' and looked for common factors. Although many of the chosen firms later declined, the key success factors identified were telling. These included closeness to the customer, simple structures, unifying values and 'a bias for action'. It was also found that successful firms 'stick to the knitting'. This was the idea that a business must focus its resources and energies on doing what it does best and avoid peripheral activities.

Meanwhile, Pascale and Athos (1981) had produced – with help from Peters and Waterman – the 'Seven-S' framework (see Figure 2.1) which used a molecule-style graphic to highlight the key factors in management.

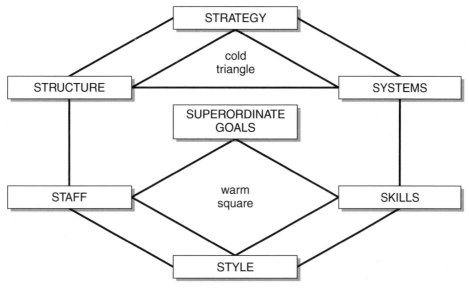

Figure 2.1 The 'Seven-S' framework

Particularly significant was the distinction between the 'hard S' factors (strategy, structure and systems) and the 'soft-S' factors (style, shared values, skills and staff – taken much more seriously in Japan). Shared values, or 'superordinate goals', later became a key subject of interest. Pascale noted that Westerners tended to see the 'soft-S' factors as mere froth. 'That froth has the power of the Pacific,' he remarked.

The impact of the Japanese example was increasingly felt in most parts of the world. Business management was increasingly driven by the pursuit of lean production. This meant finding and implementing every possible way to make most efficient use of resources and to maximise the value of their output relative to the cost of their input. In this task the workforce gradually became not the instruments of production, but the instigators of productivity. Simultaneously there was a new emphasis on quality. This involved not simply a major shift upwards in quality expectations and standards, it embraced a basic relocation of responsibility for quality from managers to workforce. 'Right first time' was the new mantra. Finally, there was a vigorous move to focus on the market and the customer. This is logical since it is in the marketplace that production cost and production quality are expressed in terms of price and value. Understanding what gives rise to customer value in the target market and generating that value at lowest cost became the new highway for management objectives.

From machine to living organism?

The century began with the image of the human organisation as a machine. It ended with that image deconstructing and a new vision of the firm as a living organism. The science of scientific management had been essentially the Newtonian mechanics of cause and effect. A new science began to reveal unexpected complexity and unpredictability, chaos and creativity in natural systems of many kinds, with important implications for the systems of human organisation.

It was not that the 'hard' theory of strategy and quantitative methods was wrong. On the contrary – it offers a wealth of insight. But it began to be clear that, as Handy (1989) puts it, the 'cold triangle' of structure, strategy and systems has a highly complex interactivity with the 'warm square' of style, shared values, skills and staff. Moreover, the beginnings of a new synthesis have made some important departures from the traditional language and structures of management. This has reflected some new realities both outside and inside the firm. First, there has been, over the past 20 years, a vast unleashing of market forces (see Chapter 4) with business thinking now permeating almost every area of human organisation. This has brought greatly increased competitive pressures to bear on management decisions. Second, the speed of technological change, already fast, has arguably quickened while the technologies themselves have radically accelerated the unfolding of events in business. The result has been that the old structures and systems of management begin to look like the tools of an earlier period.

One way to understand the changes in management of recent years is to imagine the 'hard', geometric structures of a machine giving way to the 'soft', non-linear forms of nature. Hierarchies have first become flatter and then begun to resemble more closely a network. Once self-contained functional departments are becoming communicative and mutually dependent. Planning is giving way to responsiveness, while assets are becoming less 'fixed' and more contingent. Even products are tending to deconstruct and dissolve into experiences as markets configure and reconfigure ever faster. Today's organisation needs intelligence to survive. Responses that lack sensitivity and holistic intelligence are increasingly penalised.

3 Specialisation

Overview

In every process of adding value, the principle of specialisation is a critical driver. There are two essential reasons. First, the factors of production – land, labour and capital – are made greatly more productive if used in a specialised way. Second, the surplus output generated by specialised firms and individuals requires markets to allow exchange and the setting of prices. Markets provide a continuous verdict on the amount of value added and thus inform business decisions.

Specialisation

Flint Mining

One of the most important economic breakthroughs in history was the discovery of farming around 10 000 years ago. Marking the start of the Neolithic period or New Stone Age, the first farms were established in the river valleys of the Near East and spread gradually to Europe. The settled production of food enabled the earliest towns to emerge with markets in quite a wide range of products.

In Neolithic Britain, one of the most valuable raw materials was flint. Boulders could be broken up and fashioned into weapons and tools of all kinds. By the later centuries of this era (*c* 2500 BC), an elaborate flint-mining industry had developed. At Grimes Graves mine in Norfolk there were 300 shafts, with some reaching to 12 metres (40 feet) in depth.

The miners needed to work in teams with clear tasks for each group. When the shaft had been sunk, radial tunnels were excavated to exploit the seam of flint-bearing chalk. Using antler picks, about six men would hack out the flint stones. These were broken up into large chunks and carried by another team up a series of ladders and platforms using skin sacks. On the surface, yet another team worked at cutting and chiselling the stone into useful implements. Few of these were for local use and the majority were traded with distant communities.

Why does a doctor not clean the surgery waiting room? Why does a hotel manager not prepare any meals? And why does a bus driver not service his own vehicle? The answer to these questions – at least in principle – was resolved very well by Neolithic tribes about 5000 years ago. If every worker concentrates on the task for which they are most suited or in which they are most skilled, then their output will be higher and the flow of new value created will be correspondingly greater.

In very basic subsistence economies, people provide most things for themselves. There is little exchange and everyone needs a wide range of practical skills, but the benefits of specialisation cannot be achieved and living standards are likely to be very low.

Dividing up work so that each person specialises in one particular job is called the division of labour. For many centuries it was practised by trade – workers became carpenters, miners, weavers, spinners, millers, bakers and so forth. Many modern surnames such as Sawyer, Cooper or Dyer have their origins in different crafts or trades. This type of specialised production system has a vital economic consequence in the form of markets and exchange. Each specialised producer deliberately generates an output that is far in excess of his or her own needs. Most of what is produced can be termed a surplus – that is, surplus to personal needs. But its economic value can only be released through trading with other people who themselves have a surplus of different products. Today, we tend to think of trade as being with other countries, but the word 'tradesman' expresses the idea of trade as an everyday local activity.

What are the mechanics of specialisation that so powerfully increase output? The classic factors are:

- workers can concentrate their time and energy on the tasks for which they have the most aptitude
- staff gain high levels of proficiency in one type of task, so raising their productivity
- the application of technology to jobs becomes worthwhile as floorspace, tools and other equipment can be used intensively rather than on an occasional basis
- the time wasted between tasks is reduced as one person can remain in one place and be focused on one process.

If economic specialisation means exchange, then the organisation of a market becomes essential. Historically, this meant a place where tradespeople could gather and where their produce could be bought and sold. Later, these places became towns, and many parts of the market moved into permanent shops. Business as an organised activity began in this way.

Early traders tackled the process of exchange through barter – one product was exchanged directly for another. So, sheep might be exchanged for hens or wool might be traded for butter. The introduction of money as a medium of exchange overcame the clumsiness of this system. Economic value could be divided, stored and spent as and when required. Prices could be quoted and accounts could be kept. Much later, from the 17th century, banks became keepers, lenders and issuers of money and an organised market in money itself was able to develop.

A really revolutionary extension to this principle of specialisation began to happen just over 200 years ago. New technologies allowed production to move from homes and workshops into purpose-built factories. Mechanisation meant that many production processes could be broken down into a series of prescribed and fairly short tasks, each of which became a specialised job or 'trade' itself.

This industrial revolution was not just a change in technology and patterns of work. It also greatly extended the use of markets and money-based exchange. One employee who put the heads on pins was still producing a kind of surplus that his employer would sell. Payment of wages in money then allowed him to buy the highly specialised output of other workers and firms. It was also during the 19th century that 'globalisation' began. Improved transport and trading systems meant that a factory worker in England could buy the output of sheep farmers in New Zealand, cotton plantation workers in America or tea-growers in Sri Lanka.

Pin-making

This is a famous extract from an early book about Economics, *The Wealth of Nations* by Adam Smith. It was published in 1776.

> To take an example from a very trifling manufacture . . . the trade of pin-maker. A workman not educated to this business . . . nor acquainted with the use of the machinery employed in it . . . could scarce, with his utmost industry, make one pin in a day and certainly could not make twenty. But in the way in which this business is now carried on, not only the whole work is a peculiar trade, but it is divided into a number of branches of which the greater part are likewise peculiar trades. One man draws out the wire, another straightens it, a third cuts it, a fourth points it, a fifth grinds at the top for receiving the head: to make the head requires two or three distinct operations; to put it on is a peculiar business, to whiten the pins is another; it is even a trade by itself to put them into the paper; and the important business of making a pin is, in this manner, divided into about eighteen distinct operations, which, in some manufactories, are all performed by distinct hands.
>
> I have seen a small manufactory . . . where ten men only were employed, and where some of them consequently performed two or three distinct operations, but though they were very poor, and therefore but indifferently accommodated with the necessary machinery, they could when they exerted themselves, make among them about twelve pounds of pins in a day. There are in a pound upwards of four thousand pins of a middling size. Those ten persons, therefore, could make among them, upwards of forty-eight thousand pins in a day. Each person, therefore, might be considered as making four thousand eight hundred pins in a day. But if they had wrought separately and independently, and without any of them having been educated to this peculiar business, they certainly could not each of them have made twenty, perhaps not one pin in a day. . . .

Today people are more specialised in their work than ever. A skilled computer operator may literally be using no more than a mouse to add value and earn a living, yet the movement of that mouse in exchange for electronically stored money allows her daily life to depend on the different skills of innumerable workers scattered all over the world. Although direct markets for face-to-face trading still exist, most goods and services are now bought and sold anonymously through superstores, catalogues, telecommunications and the internet.

There can be no doubt that the Industrial Revolution triggered an explosive growth in total output. Population began to increase rapidly, but the new specialisation, combined with advancing technology, still allowed an unprecedented growth in income per head. This continued throughout the 20th century and looks set to advance still further in the new millennium.

A rising standard of living

England, Wales and Scotland 1800–2000

	1800	1900	2000
Population (millions)	10.7	36.6	58.5
Output value (£m at 2000 prices)	5 617	76 888	578 319
Output per capita (£)	525	2 101	9 886

Sources: Based on BR Mitchell, British Historical Statistics (Cambridge University Press, 1988); Annual Abstract of Statistics (ONS, 2001)

Business organisation

Specialisation today extends into the heart of business activity. Almost every firm adopts some form of internal organisational structure that is based on specialisation. The typical pattern is based on business functions: marketing, operations, human resources and finance, for example. Specified managers with specialised knowledge take responsibility for a given function and then employ a hierarchy of specialised staff to undertake the allotted tasks.

Different dimensions to specialisation are found in product divisions, trading branches and stand-alone business units. In all cases, the aim is to use resources more effectively in adding value. Not only is efficiency usually increased, but expertise and knowledge accumulate (see Chapter 33). This is an important factor in achieving a competitive position in the marketplace.

In the external relationships between firms, specialisation is also crucial. Every firm performs a complex series of value-adding activities that form a network of linked operations. If we think of a production sequence extending from the original procurement of basic resources through to the delivery of a final product, then the operations of most firms represent only one stage in the overall process. 'Upstream' there are other firms supplying, for example, materials, components and service inputs. 'Downstream' the firm itself supplies the inputs of its customers who may typically be responsible for finished goods, distribution or installation services. In this sense, each firm is a specialised network of activities that makes a specialised contribution to the larger productive stream.

Significantly, the 'gaps' between the stages in this stream are tending to be tightened and made more seamless. Fewer firms are adopting the vertically integrated structures where very long, or even complete, streams of productive activity were carried out by the same enterprise. Instead, more specialised organisations are finding mutual advantage in improving the connectedness of successive operations, bringing reductions in cost and improvements in quality (see Chapter 23).

Playing to strengths

During the 20th century, many successful firms greatly increased the scale and scope of their operations. Not only did the output of their core activities increase, but many diversified activities became bolted on by design and by accident. Diversification was popular because it spread risk across different types of business. Competitiveness could be achieved by applying the generic skills of management and supplying co-ordination from the centre.

In practice, many diversification strategies led to inefficiency, compromise and loss of competitive edge. The organisation could lose its sense of direction and purpose. Co-ordination could be lost. Staff morale and motivation could decline. As a result of haphazard expansion, including acquisitions, some large firms became ungainly giants that were extremely difficult to manage while failing to exploit their own greatest strengths.

In the face of growing international competition, especially from Japan, the early 1980s saw the start of a major rethink. This was crystallised by Peters and Waterman (1982), who urged firms to 'stick to the knitting'. The essence of this advice was the finding that Chief Executive Officers (CEOs) and senior managers should keep the organisation sharply focused on those activities in which it had a clear competitive strength. Blurring of this focus was dangerous because it allowed resources to become absorbed in activities where the firm fell short of excellence. Again, specialisation was a key factor in achieving superior returns. A firm, like an individual, should play to its strengths.

This principle has wide implications that extend through all the activities of a firm and also enter its relationships with other firms. The key to the concept lies in the idea of opportunity cost. Every existing use of resources is shadowed by its next-best alternative use. Provided that the value of the outcome of an existing use is greater than that alternative, then there is no necessary cue for change. But it is almost inevitable that in the complex operations of any but the smallest firm there will be a good many activities that do not pass this test.

As the core activities of a business expand, an extensive range of support activities is likely to emerge. These might vary from computing and financial services, to the welfare functions of a personnel department, to the provision of canteens and gardens. Some of these services are likely to carry proprietary significance for the firm – for example, technical expertise in operations, research and development, creative design or quality of customer service.

However, there are often other activities where the firm is just an average or even below average performer. Typical candidates include transport, training, catering and large areas of marketing such as market research, brand development or just fielding telephone calls. Where such activities can be isolated and detached without damaging other parts of the total enterprise then there is a strong case for outsourcing. Sometimes the same logic may extend to selling selected parts of the enterprise. This allows other specialist firms to carry out those tasks more efficiently and often to a better standard. Resources are then released from relatively ineffective uses to be injected into core activities where the firm has a distinctive and competitive position.

An alternative approach may be to seek a partnership or alliance with another firm whose needs are in some way complementary. For example, a business supplier of industrial components might recognise that one of its own technical breakthroughs has the potential to make a successful consumer product; but such a firm might lack the required marketing skills and distribution links. Rather than trying to develop its own capabilities of this kind, it could be far more effective to form an alliance with an established consumer goods company that would take on the relevant functions and retain an appropriate part of the total profit generated.

4 Markets and market forces

Overview

The gains from specialisation depend on firms and individuals producing a surplus of output relative to their own needs. In a modern economy this 'surplus' usually represents the whole of the relevant output. It is therefore essential that well-developed markets exist so that goods and services can be traded for mutual benefit.

What is a market?

A market is any medium of communication that allows sellers and buyers to agree on a transaction at a price. Traditionally, this involved face-to-face contact, but today markets also operate by post, telephone and the internet. The essence of a market is that it allows 'swaps' or transactions to be agreed at such a 'rate' or price that both parties experience a gain. The size and nature of these gains are at the very heart of business as a subject for study.

The term 'market' is also used in a wider sense to mean the potential for selling and buying a given product. In this sense, the term refers to the existence of sellers or buyers who are likely to wish to trade. An 'active' market implies plentiful sellers and buyers who agree frequently on transactions. An 'inactive' market suggests the reverse.

The idea of demand

We have seen that the driving force in every market is a desire to exchange. The expectation is always of mutual advantage. This principle is no different whether the swap is direct or whether money is used as the medium of exchange.

As buyer and seller confront each other in a market, it is important to analyse the chain of reasoning that makes the transactional mechanism work.

No transaction – and no business enterprise – can occur without a need or want being experienced by someone. A need or want is said to be a demand for a good or service. Economists distinguish between needs as a demand for essentials (such as food, clothing and shelter) and wants as the demand for everything else. In business, the distinction is of no practical importance: demand is desire by one or more customers to buy a product. However, demand on its own can exist without the means to pay. A luxury car manufacturer, such as Porsche, knows that many consumers would like to buy their product in principle but lack sufficient funds. Only the demand that is backed by money and thus empowered in the market is called effective demand.

The counterpart to demand is, naturally, supply. When a firm uses resources to produce goods and services for the market it is responding to an opportunity for gain. If there was nothing a firm could produce that would command more value in the market than the sum of its costs, then that firm would cease to produce or trade. But where a market allows the chance to produce and trade at a profit, then business enterprise will be quick in offering to supply. However, just as demand is only made effective by the availability of spending power, so supply needs backing with finance. This will normally be forthcoming where there is the expectation of sufficient profit.

PineLine 1

PineLine supplies new pine furniture through the internet and warehouse-style shops. Its three main, standard flat-packed products are:

- chairs at £25
- tables at £60
- bookcases at £35.

PineLine faces a competitive market where there are few barriers to the entry of other firms. However, the company stresses its quality of timber and fittings, easy assembly and fast delivery.

How markets work

The next step is to consider exactly what happens when a buyer meets a seller in the market. Each side has something to offer the other, but at a rate of exchange or *price*. Sellers can have a variety of motives, but these will always include the basic objective of gain or profit. It therefore follows that the price agreed must exceed the costs of bringing that product to market.

The buyer's logic follows the same pattern but is more difficult to measure. How much is the anticipated stream of satisfaction to be derived from the product worth? It is clear that the price agreed must be less than this value so that the consumer enjoys a surplus that is the counterpart to the producer's profit.

PineLine 2

Consider a PineLine customer who is weighing up the cost and benefits of buying a chair.

The direct cost of a standard chair is £15 and the selling price is £25. The company allocates £5 to cover overhead costs, leaving a net profit of £5 or a 20% margin.

Suppose that the customer estimates the value of the product to herself as £30. Since the producer's total cost of bringing the chair to market is £20 and the customer's valuation is £30, it follows that a transaction could only go ahead in the price range £20–£30.

It is now important to focus on the price mechanism that is at the centre of any transaction.

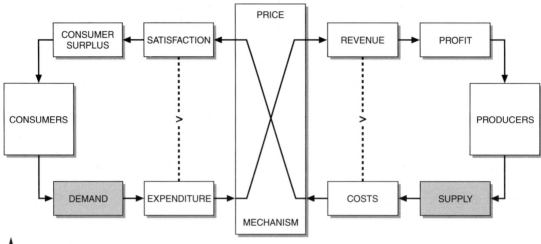

Figure 4.1 The price mechanism

The producer has incurred costs that are intended to be the generator of consumer satisfaction. The consumer is considering expenditure that would form sales revenue for the producer. To meet the conditions of producer and consumer, the price agreed must be higher than the producer's costs, yet less than the consumer's valuation of the product. The level at which price is finally set divides the surplus value between producer and consumer.

Opportunity cost

The scenario analysed so far has exposed the necessary but not the sufficient conditions for a transaction to take place. In an open market economy, the possibility of profit attracts competitors. These firms will also offer products to the target market. The set of competing products on offer to the consumer will, to a greater or lesser degree, be substitutes for one another. Each product will carry a different combination of cost and value in the market, and its price will allow the producer and consumer different levels of surplus.

We have seen that every decision in business is shadowed by its opportunity cost. It follows that a consumer's test for purchasing a product is more severe than simply the requirement that perceived value exceeds price. In addition, the level of value anticipated must exceed the value offered by the *next-best substitute* purchase. In other words, like any other decision, a purchase must have an anticipated value greater than its opportunity cost.

PineLine 3 ←———————————————————————————

The customer now considers the next-best alternative chair. Made by Big Pine, this is also priced at £25 but is valued by the customer at only £28. The PineLine chair, therefore, offers a higher value in terms of consumer surplus (£5 against £3) and a purchase is made.

The same principle applies to production. The output of goods and services requires the commitment of resources with an opportunity cost. It follows that the return earned from the sale of any product must not only be positive but also exceed the potential return from the next-best use of those resources. Of course, in the short run, a firm may be obliged to continue producing when this underlying condition no longer holds. This is only because the negative outcome of ceasing production immediately is greater than the short-run suboptimality of continuing.

PineLine 4 ←———————————————————————————

If costs at PineLine were to rise and price was increased to say, £28, then the consumer in this example would find that the decision to buy a PineLine chair (now only yielding £2 in consumer surplus) had been overtaken by its opportunity cost (£3 in consumer surplus). More consumer surplus could now be obtained by switching to Big Pine. Sales of chairs at PineLine would be likely to fall.

This kind of situation often occurs in business. A range of exit barriers confront a firm wanting to withdraw from any process of production. These include such costs as spending on assets that cannot be recovered on withdrawal, as well as a wide range of displacement expenses varying from redundancy costs to the disposal of stock.

The implication is that the failure of a product to exceed the opportunity cost of its resource requirements must be by a sufficiently large margin to overcome these exit barriers. Nevertheless, in the longer run every product must earn its continued production by generating returns ahead of opportunity cost. In dynamic markets, a marginal failure to meet this condition can rapidly become a major sacrifice of potential profit. Indeed, the 'marginal failure' can be a critical signal to management that should prompt radical decisions. Missing such signals is a common source of business decline.

Why do firms expand and contract?

The market mechanism has a larger role in allocating and reallocating resources. Very small changes of cost and value can sway a decision in the market. When one decision sways, others almost always follow. As levels of surplus and opportunity cost shift, then real resources such as plant and people are soon shifted in their wake.

In one sense the marketplace is like a continuous election. With every purchase a consumer makes a choice, or casts an 'economic vote' – and competing products are the 'candidates' for election. But this is not like the political world where a candidate can win and then enjoy a term of office.

Instead, every candidate must fight daily for re-election as consumer spending ('voting') decisions follow complex changes in the market.

When sales are increasing, a product usually earns an increasing value in total profits with strengthening rates of return. In effect, the product becomes a 'hot spot' of business opportunity that will attract increased financial support and investment in its future.

By contrast, a product fails the market test when it earns a rate of return below the opportunity cost of the resources needed for its support. Where this is short term or likely to be reversed by more favourable conditions in the future, then the product will usually survive. But any sustained failure to meet this basic business test must lead to decline and withdrawal.

Of course, this has implications beyond the product itself. The dedicated resources deployed for the output of that product are indirectly up for election in the same economic ballot. And if those resources represent the whole or a critical part of that firm, then the business as an entity is at stake.

What emerges from this picture is often called the profit signalling of resources. When a product begins to earn less than its long-run opportunity cost, then that product's hold on resources weakens. An alternative deployment has now become more profitable and, as such, exerts a 'pull'. In business terms this may reflect a strengthening of demand for one product and a weakening of demand for another. Or it may mean that unit costs of one product have risen and for another product have fallen. Either way, relative rates of return have changed in value and the pattern of resource allocation will come under pressure to shift in the same direction.

At first, there is usually some resistance to resource reallocation, and existing patterns of production are protected by a certain amount of inertia. But as time passes or the relative performance gap widens, then pressure builds for a change in resource use.

This may mean that a firm will produce less of one product and more of another. It may imply that a whole division or sector of a firm be sold or closed while another is expanded. And it may mean that an entire business must find new ownership or close completely, so allowing all the resources to find a more profitable use.

The patterns described, and many more complex permutations, are emerging and being enacted all the time. The dynamism of markets with constantly shifting patterns of supply and demand is reflected by an ever-changing allocation of resources. This is expressed and transmitted through the countless purchasing decisions of consumers over every 24 hours in every part of the world.

Cadbury's Dairy Milk

Originally launched in 1905, Cadbury's Dairy Milk is the oldest name still to feature among the UK's top twenty chocolate confectionery brands. The Dairy Milk brand has been periodically revamped, but the proposition of whole-milk goodness and the distinctive purple and gold livery have remained.

As leader in the market for chocolate in moulded blocks, Dairy Milk is continuously succeeding in meeting the terms imposed by the price mechanism. Every day over one million consumers judge that the value (or consumer surplus) offered by Dairy Milk exceeds both its price and the opportunity cost threshold of its nearest competitor. Cadbury-Schweppes experiences these decisions as sales, with a level of profitability that exceeds the projected returns of the next-best use for the resources required for continuation of Dairy Milk.

However, back in the 1970s this *status quo* was seriously challenged by the arrival of a new and aggressive competitor. The scene had been set by a period of upheaval and external change in the conditions facing chocolate manufacturers. Following the oil crisis of 1973–74 there had been abrupt price rises in other commodities, including cocoa and sugar. This had led Cadbury's to reduce the thickness of Dairy Milk, which was then produced as a flat, rectangular bar. There was growing evidence that consumers found the thinner bars less satisfying, but Cadbury's was reluctant to increase price above 9p.

Meanwhile, Rowntree, then still an independent company, was developing a much thicker and chunkier bar in an effort to break out from their very small market share and seize some of Dairy Milk's sales. Initially to be called 'Rations' and then renamed 'Yorkie', the bar was launched in late 1976 with a costly and very carefully planned national marketing campaign. Yorkie was daringly priced at 11p, but weighed 62g against the 48.4g Dairy Milk bar. The market's response was immediate and highly favourable.

↑ Figure 4.2 Yorkie

Market shares by volume

1975		1980
79%	Cadbury's Dairy Milk	49%
0%	**Yorkie**	26%
21%	Galaxy	25%

Over the same period, total market volume increased by about 14 per cent.

In its first full year (1977), Yorkie achieved sales worth £18m. This spectacular market entry sent serious shock waves through Cadbury's management. Unless some recovery of market share was possible there would have to be a reduction in the capacity devoted to Dairy Milk, with resources reallocated to their next-best alternative use. Substantial advertising and sales promotion followed and it was exactly one year after the launch of Yorkie that Dairy Milk reappeared as a 'chunky-style' bar. Despite Cadbury's best efforts, it was still not possible to prevent Yorkie becoming a key national brand with annual sales reaching around £40m in the early 1980s.

Ironically, the tide eventually turned in the other direction. Nestlé bought Rowntree in 1988 and invested heavily in the brands acquired. But the real value of Yorkie sales began to flag and then seriously declined in the 1990s. By 2000 Dairy Milk was dominant once more.

5 Adding value

Overview

Adding value is the primary goal of all business activity. Put simply, this means that the value of the output from any productive process must exceed the corresponding costs of input. If the value of output falls short of its costs, then value is being destroyed. The ratio between costs and the corresponding increases in value is a key factor in making business decisions.

The concept of added value

Adding value is at once very simple and very complex.

Marketing lettuce

Lettuce was (and still is) sold as harvested in the greenhouse. Value is added from the time of planting the seedlings through to harvest and on via wholesaler to the retail outlet and eventual sale for consumption. At each stage market value increases, but the product finally sold remains an unbranded commodity.

How might value be *further* added to a lettuce? The answer came in 1990 with the launch of ready cut and washed lettuce in a sealed film bag. From zero sales at the end of the 1980s, the value of the US market in washed lettuce had reached $1.1bn by 1996.

The value of one lettuce is routinely multiplied four times through being washed and presented in a bag. What exactly adds this extra value? First, the customer is saved the labour of preparing and washing the lettuce. Second, its presentation in a film bag increases its attractiveness as a product and allows the retailer's brand to add further value.

Only by adding value can a firm remain in business. Put another way, the stream of costs that a business incurs must be matched by a greater stream of value expressed through sales in the market. At an obvious level, this means that the selling price of a product must exceed the cost of the labour, materials and overheads (rents, marketing, administration, etc.) involved in its production.

Less obviously, but critically, the threshold for that selling price to add value also includes the cost of capital (see Chapter 30). This includes interest payments on any debt and a return on the shareholders' funds that is sufficient to retain their investment. Firms that make a profit *before* their cost of capital (their operating profit) but cannot satisfy both their creditors and shareholders will, in the long run, lose control of their assets.

This is another application for the concept of opportunity cost. Firms only add true value when their returns are greater than the opportunity cost of capital. Indeed, even within the firm, the returns made by business units need to exceed the internal opportunity cost of capital. Clearly this will normally represent a higher threshold. Logically any activity failing to cover its opportunity cost within the firm should have its resources transferred to that better alternative use. Thus, the idea of added value is an important tool of strategy.

Added value in practice

Consider a bicycle manufacturer. Should a new model be fitted with a carrier? If the full cost of fitting an appropriate carrier is £7.50, then will the value of the bicycle be increased by £7.50 or more? If the answer is positive, then the carrier should become a source of added value in the business process of manufacturing bicycles.

It has already been noted (Chapter 1) that value is extrinsic and depends on the perception of buyers. So services are as likely as manufacturing to add value. The quality of after-sales service, for example, may be more effective in adding value than the tangible product to which it relates. Advertising a product or conferring on it a brand may greatly increase added value without any change or improvement to the product itself. Adding value means what the words suggest: making a product more valuable to its buyer.

The sales value 'turned over' by a firm is the product of sales and price. But it is a mistake to equate high or even growing turnover with success in adding value. Of course, expanding firms are often effective in adding value. Yet sales alone may disguise low or even negative rates of adding value. At a low enough price anything can be sold: the challenge is to secure sales at a value-adding price.

It is therefore essential for managers to recognise the difference between the *rate* of added value and the *total* added value achieved. Specialist firms in small markets can often generate high rates of added value but are not able to expand beyond a very limited sales base. Large firms usually have to accept moderate rates of added value in serving a mass market where competition is intense.

┌─ Monsoon ◄──────────────────────────────

Monsoon evolved from a market stall operation in the early 1970s. Today it is a fashion retailer aimed at ABC1 women in the 25 to 45 age range. Often working in professional and executive jobs, Monsoon customers are looking for fashion that is slightly more exotic and colourful than the styles offered by Next.

Sales at Monsoon were worth £204 million in 2002, up by 18.3% on the year before. The cost of the goods sold was £79 million, leaving a gross profit of £124 million and giving a gross margin of 61%. After subtracting administrative and marketing expenses, together with other adjustments, the company's operating profit was £31 million on an operating margin of 15.4%. Given share capital and long-term loans amounting to £344 million, Monsoon's return on capital was 53.8%.

The data shows that Monsoon managed to sell for £204 million, goods that had cost the company £79 million to purchase and a further £93 million to sell (taking all expenses into account). Put another way, every pound of product sales had only cost the business 39p to procure and 84.5p inclusive of all costs. What services did Monsoon perform to add this value?

First, the company had used its skill and experience to design or select the fashion ranges that would appeal to its target market. Then it had arranged the logistics of distribution and had provided merchandising services through its chain of shops. And finally it had overlaid the customer's shopping experience with the Monsoon brand. This had provided a signpost for the customer and a sense of identity and reassurance in buying and wearing the clothes.

Source: Monsoon Annual Report, 2002; interview with the company.

Analysing the value chain

It is not just the firm as a whole that must pass the test imposed by the ratio of cost to value. Many firms have a wide range of constituent business units within them. These may be subsidiaries, branches, divisions or stand-alone enterprises. In the long run, each strategic business unit must achieve an excess of added value over apportioned cost.

The same principle can be extended to disaggregating the activities that combine to make a business unit. At the broadest level this might involve distinguishing the key functional departments: marketing, operations, human resources and finance, for example. More narrowly, marketing might be broken down between sales, advertising and promotion, distribution and market research. And within the sales department there may be such activities as telephone enquiries, customer calling and database updating. Telephone enquiries could include incoming calls from potential customers and outgoing calls to arrange salesforce visits. More specifically still, those incoming calls may provide opportunities to take orders, send brochures or simply arouse customer interest.

There is no necessary end to this process of disaggregation. It can be taken as far as is useful for the purpose in hand. It is immediately clear that each activity contributes to one or more others.

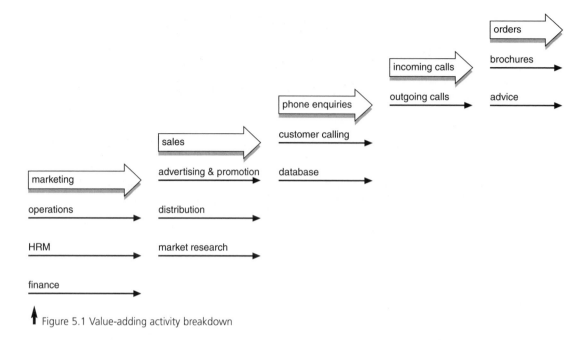

↑ Figure 5.1 Value-adding activity breakdown

For this reason any sequence of linked activities is called a value chain. This concept was clarified and explored by the Harvard academic, Michael Porter in *Competitive Advantage* (Free Press, 1985).

> **Every firm is a collection of activities that are performed to design, produce, market, deliver and support its product. All these activities can be represented using a value chain.**

The value chain is made up of value activities, the linkages between them and a margin or surplus at the end of the chain.

Value activities are 'strategically relevant activities' embracing every distinct process throughout the firm. Their exact specification will depend on the nature of the business. For example, a hotel restaurant's value activities would include menu design, food procurement, cooking, waiting, table reservations, cleaning and so on. Linkages connecting these activities can be internal (e.g. food procurement and reservations) or external (e.g. relationships with a local farmer or tourist information office). Finally, the margin represents value added by the productive process. Although it can be measured in different ways, this effectively has 'depth' in the percentage of profit relative to sales and 'breadth' in the volume of sales earning profit at this rate.

Porter distinguishes between primary and support activities. There are five generic primary activities:

- **inbound logistics** are all activities connected with obtaining, allocating and delivering inputs from supplier organisations
- **operations** are the activities that directly transform inputs into outputs for sale in the market
- **outbound logistics** include those activities required to distribute and deliver products to their buyers
- **marketing and sales** refers to the activities such as pricing, selling, advertising, promotion

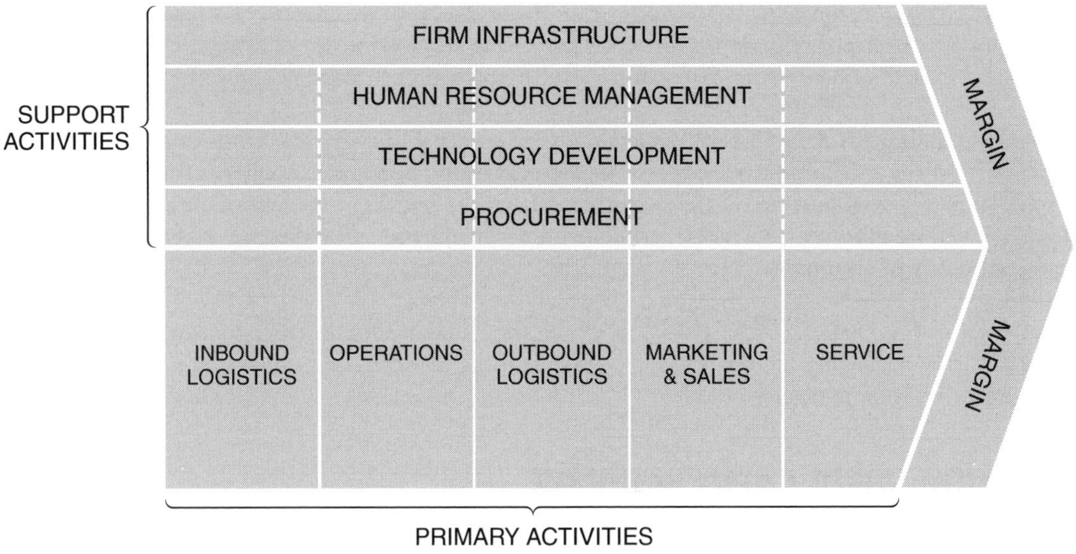

Figure 5.2 Porter's generic value chain

and channel management that draw products from operations to sale in the market
- **service** features the activities that sustain or increase the product's value to the customer – for example, installation, training, repair and troubleshooting services.

Support activities do not directly add value but contribute to the value-adding effectiveness of primary activities.

- **Procurement** involves buying the resource inputs required by the organisation.
- **Technology development** relates to any kind of innovation intended to improve the firm's products, processes and resources. The term 'technology' is used in a broad sense to include any kind of practical knowledge.
- **Human resource management** is a wide activity that embraces the recruitment, co-ordination, motivation and development of people in the business.
- Finally, **infrastructure** refers to all the systems and structures in the firm that sustain primary activities. The quality and character of the infrastructure have a vital influence on the effectiveness of the whole organisation.

Linkages

Disaggregation of the value chain works like a kind of X-ray in identifying value-adding activities, but it should also reveal the importance of co-ordination or linkages between the activities in adding value. A firm is far more than a catalogue of tasks and activities performed to a given specification. It is the design – or organisational architecture – through which those activities are arranged that determines their final market value. There are many different kinds of activity linkage. In a large hotel, for example, there are operational linkages such as booking rooms, scheduling meals and orchestrating conferences. Marketing linkages might include the relationship between the bar and the restaurant, or the promotion of the health club through the offer of all-inclusive weekends.

Organisationally, too, linkages are very powerful. In the hotel, a cancellation of a major conference would need a co-ordinated response between marketing surplus rooms, adjusting plans for catering and entertainment and ensuring that staffing levels remained both flexible and sufficient.

Often, as important as these internal linkages are the external linkages that connect the firm to other parts of the total productive process. In the case of the hotel, the suppliers of food to the restaurant have a vital bearing on the performance and reputation of the whole enterprise. To a lesser but still significant extent, relationships with taxi firms add value through meeting the transport needs of customers.

Thus, each firm is part of a value system in which total added value is dependent on a number of different firms. Managing the relationships between these firms is itself a source of added value and a key factor in competitiveness.

Applying value chain analysis

Since every activity has a cost (it uses resources with an opportunity cost), it can only be justified by adding equal or greater value. In practice this process of adding value can be difficult to evaluate — after all, most activities do not have an output that is sold directly in the market. However, best estimates can be made and sometimes a real or simulated internal market is effective. Many activities have a customer or next user in the chain. How much is the output of the 'supplier' worth to that 'customer' or next user? Such a question not only heightens awareness of costs and values, but also prompts consideration of opportunity cost: how much would an external supplier charge for the same added value?

Analysis of each value activity and each linkage often prompts ideas for reducing cost relative to value, or increasing value relative to cost. Sometimes a very small percentage improvement in cost or value translates into a large percentage increase in profit. In a firm with a high turnover of low-value products, the profit margin may be very small. In this situation, even minuscule improvements in cost or in price commanded become significant gains in terms of profit margin.

Equally, the relationship between cost and value can be volatile and subject to discontinuous surges. Peters (1994) draws attention to the potential, hidden in the value chain of many products, for modest increases in costs to yield dramatic increases in value. For example, an enhanced styling to the gear lever of a car might add £2 to costs but £50 to the customer perception of value. The same principle underpins such factors as the packaging of chocolates, the lighting in a restaurant or the rivets in a pair of jeans.

Recent years have generally seen much sharper tools of analysis being applied to the value chain. Increasingly, firms are applying more sophisticated audit techniques to every allocation and flow of resources. Performance levels in terms of added value may be benchmarked, tested and targeted. Progress can then be tracked and evaluated relative to the changing assessment of opportunity cost.

Such rigour in management thinking and process can be highly motivational in itself. Where resources once 'slept' within the fabric of the organisation, they may now be actively managed in their proper role of adding value.

Evaluation

The value chain is a powerful idea that can equip managers with a coherent model of how surplus is generated. By exposing the interactivity between cost and value, it is often possible to increase a product's value at less than proportional cost. In this way, resources are reconfigured to yield higher returns as the organisation achieves stronger competitiveness.

However, despite acknowledging the power of linkages between activities, Porter's value chain can prove too mechanistic. Firms are more than 'a collection of activities', being closer to a *configuration*, part designed and part organic. Within every firm there exists a number of interactive subsystems, while the firm itself is part of a larger system that carries the product from its origins to its final delivery. Checkland (1984, 1999) argues:

> **any actual social system observed in the world will be a mixture of a rational assembly of linked activities and a set of relationships such as occur in a community. In practical work in the real world it will be necessary to take both aspects into account. A purely behavioural approach based upon the idea of man as a gregarious animal will neglect the power and influence of rational design; but an approach which assumes human beings to be rational automata and ignores the cultural dimension will also pass the problems by.**

A systems approach suggests that a firm adds value through rationally designed linked activities *and* through complex cultural relationships or encoded feelings and beliefs. The latter are usually very difficult for rivals to imitate and can be a major determinant of success in the market.

Porter's idea of 'infrastructure' as a support activity recognises the importance of integrative systems within the organisation. As such, it may be adequate in describing a manufacturing process; but where style, culture and the innovative use of knowledge are at the heart of a business, then multiple social systems actually define the very nature, structure and interactivity of the value chain itself.

Finally, it important to remember the source of value in the market. This depends on the strength of demand relative to a product's availability or supply. For example, organic stoneground wholemeal bread might sell for £1.50 per loaf in a prosperous city, but for little more than a sliced white loaf in an area of high unemployment. As Porter argued later (*Harvard Business Review*, November–December 1996), positioning of a product in the market is a critical part of any strategy to add value.

PART B

STRATEGY
explained

6 The concept of competition

Overview

Competition is the extraordinary but critical force that makes a free market economy operate. To survive or expand in business every producer is obliged to offer not just what customers want but what they want more than the alternatives offered by competitors. This means that in every part of the economy where competition is able to reach, there is an upward pressure on quality and a downward pressure on price.

Competition and the market

It is only possible to supply any product without losses if its market value exceeds its cost. The fulfilment of this condition means that the resulting surplus value can be divided between the producer (profit) and the consumer (consumer surplus). However, we have seen (Chapter 4) that the existence of consumer surplus is not enough to ensure sales. The *level* of consumer surplus anticipated by the consumer must exceed the level of surplus offered by the consumer's next-best use of the necessary expenditure. In other words, every decision in favour of purchasing a product must stay ahead of its opportunity cost.

What is represented by the opportunity cost of most purchasing decisions? Usually, the answer is the chance to purchase a similar but not identical product offered by a competitor.

Buying a Ford Ka

Assume that a consumer wants to buy a small, economical car. She also wants a model that is stylish and enjoyable to drive. Her first choice is a Ford Ka, but possible alternatives include a VW Lupo, a Nissan Micra and a Vauxhall Aglia. The approximate prices of the cars (Summer 2003) are:

Ford Ka	£6 650
VW Lupo	£6 995
Nissan Micra	£7 495
Vauxhall Aglia	£5 995

On the basis of value for money (anticipated benefits relative to price) the customer selects a Ford Ka, but the VW Lupo is not far behind. Were Volkswagen to offer some more attractive colours or a better price, then the Ford's opportunity cost would be too high and the choice would be different.

Sales in any business depend. therefore, on beating the competition and offering a proposition to the target market that is selected as first choice.

Free markets

This competitive scenario for business is the basis of a free market economy. Under such a regime, every market is open to competition and no firm is allowed to gain an unfair advantage over others. Consumers enjoy the widest possible choice and can weigh up each purchasing decision to gain maximum advantage.

Where free market conditions prevail, no firm can afford to relax. Every sale achieved is vulnerable to competitors who strive to offer customers higher quality, lower prices or both. The result among all firms is a continuous upward pressure on the quality or performance of products and a relentless downward pressure on costs. This, in, turn drives a restless search for innovation. To defend or extend its market share, each firm needs to improve its capability in offering value for money (consumer surplus relative to price). This may require technical or managerial innovations that cut unit costs. It might imply better product design, enhanced service, improved marketing or any change that increases consumer value. Alternatively, the innovation may involve new products or product varieties and the entry into new market segments.

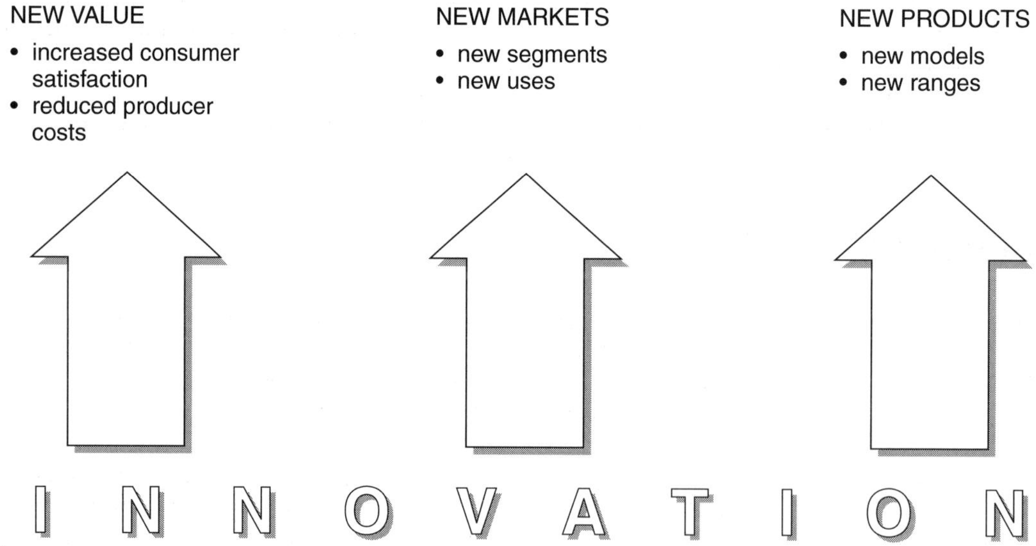

NEW VALUE
- increased consumer satisfaction
- reduced producer costs

NEW MARKETS
- new segments
- new uses

NEW PRODUCTS
- new models
- new ranges

I N N O V A T I O N

Figure 6.1 Directions for innovation

One of the best-known advocates for free markets is the Chicago economist, Milton Friedman. In his classic *Capitalism and Freedom* (University of Chicago Press, 1962), he argues that the power of markets to deliver higher quality and greater variety at lower cost depends on fair, vigorous competition and the relative absence of government interference with business decisions. In building support for his argument, Friedman (1980) later points to the success of Far Eastern economies, such as Hong Kong, where a free market environment has been associated with rapid economic growth. However, this view has many critics, whose arguments will be explored in Chapter 37.

Commodities

Bed & Breakfast

At a West Country seaside resort there are several streets where many of the town houses offer Bed & Breakfast. Almost all of these establishments provide TV, central heating and tea-making facilities. The ruling price or going rate is £18 per person per night.

The proprietor of the Victoria Guest House explains that she has experimented with charging £20 but found that too many of her rooms remained vacant. She sees no point in reducing her rate to, say, £16, since she is already fully booked and a lower price would reduce profits to a point where it was not worth remaining open. Interviews with other Bed & Breakfast proprietors confirm a similar view.

A commodity is any product that is widely traded, such as potatoes, flour, cotton or steel. In its business usage, the term can be applied to a widely traded product where the output of one producer is identical or very similar to the output of another. The market value of a commodity tends to be governed by a 'ruling price' or 'going rate'. This normally reflects the typical producer's costs plus a profit margin that is sufficient to remain in business. Any firm trying to charge above this going rate will be unlikely to receive orders, since a nearly identical substitute can be obtained from other producers at a lower price.

It is now important to explore more carefully the principles of commodity pricing since they contain a key to understanding *all* business strategy.

Perfect competition

In any market it is highly likely that firms enjoy *some* protection against the full force of competition. For example, a soft drink manufacturer's brand may hold customers' loyalty. A village shop may charge high prices but its geographical isolation ensures continuing custom. A radio station has a franchise agreement that prevents the entry of competitors.

In the most extreme situation a firm may have an outright monopoly, meaning that for a particular product or class of products it is the only producer. A firm enjoying a monopoly has substantial market power. It can dictate either the price charged or the quantity of the product released to the market. Usually it maximises profits by charging relatively high prices and accepting relatively smaller sales.

At the other end of the spectrum, it is possible to envisage a situation of total or 'perfect' competition. Under this market condition, firms have no protection whatever against the logic of competition. This will depend on the following conditions:

- **Homogenous products** – there is no reason for a customer to prefer the output of one firm in comparison to the output of another.

- **No barriers to entry or exit** – any firm can enter or leave the market without obstacles or additional cost at any time.
- **Many buyers and sellers** – no one buyer or seller is large enough to exert any power over price or output.
- **Complete market information** – everyone in the market knows exactly the prices being agreed by everyone else.

When all of these conditions are met, some inevitable consequences follow. All prices will be competed downwards to a single prevailing price or 'going rate'. This is because, until the going rate has been reached, the firm(s) with the lowest price will take 100 per cent share of the market. Competitors will immediately be forced to offer a lower price and then they, too, will be rewarded with 100 per cent of sales. In theory this process of downward bidding would continue until the single going rate was established. In practice, going rate prices emerge as more perfectly competitive conditions develop.

We now confront the vital questions. What is this 'going rate'? How is it reached? What does it mean?

Selling ice-cream

At the same West Country resort there are a number of firms selling ice-cream. Each kiosk has a board outside that prominently displays its prices. The mainstay of sales for all firms is a single vanilla cornet. The market is highly competitive since the ice-cream quality is very similar, it is cheap to enter the market, there are a substantial number of outlets and prices are easily compared.

The going rate for a single cornet is 80p. For a typical seller, such as The Promenade Cafe, this price breaks down into 40p direct cost, 20p overhead cost and 20p profit. It is clear that any price below 60p would incur losses. What about prices between 60p and 80p? Every firm needs to earn a basic minimum level of profit that is just sufficient to make the business viable. For the ice-cream sellers, this basic minimum is 20p or a 25 per cent margin. In effect, competition pushes down the going rate to a price that is exactly poised on the threshold of closing down. The profit that remains is just enough to induce the firm to stay in business, but any further reduction in price and profit would tip the balance in favour of leaving the market.

In the case study it follows that the profit zone that lies between a price of 60p and 80p is different from any profit that might have been made at prices above 80p. Economists call this minimum profit to stay in business (or to retain resources in their existing use) a normal profit, and all additional profit a supernormal profit ('super' meaning 'above'). These terms are precise in theoretical meaning but are not widely used in business and are easily misunderstood. It is, after all, 'normal' for firms to make more than a normal profit!

However, the idea is very powerful. Embedded in the accounting and decision-making process of any business is a 'normal' level of profit even if it is never formally identified. This is actually the long-term opportunity cost of the capital employed by the firm. A business investment only remains valid while it earns a rate of return that is ahead of the next-best alternative. Once returns fall below those offered by that next-best option, then resources are likely to be switched from one use to the other.

In this sense, a normal profit is only 'profit' in a nominal sense and is really part of the firm's underlying cost structure. This makes sense when remembering that any business must pay a rate of interest on its borrowed capital. By the same token it must achieve a minimum rate of return on its equity, this approximating to the opportunity cost of the capital involved.

Kay (1993) uses exactly this distinction in clarifying the idea of added value. Not until a firm has covered the opportunity cost of its share capital, he argues, as well as the interest on its loan capital, can it start to add true value. Indeed, a company could be making conventional *accounting* profits while failing to make a normal profit – or to earn the necessary returns that justify its use of equity. In the long run, the financial markets should find it out – a hostile bid from another firm whose potential activities represent the opportunity cost of that capital becomes increasingly likely.

Breaking the rules of perfect competition

In the real world of business activity, no firm is content to earn a normal profit. To do so would be to live precariously on the threshold of viability, with sale or closure a constant threat. Instead, the goal of every enterprise is to leave as far behind as possible the opportunity cost of its resources. Firms aim to maximise supernormal profitability or, put in more traditional business language, they aim for superior long-term performance.

We have seen that perfect competition allows only normal profits to be made. This is because the conditions for perfect competition allow no protection from the forces of competition. All profit in excess of the barest minimum ('normal' levels) will be competed away. It follows, therefore, that the central aim of all business management is to find ways of defending supernormal profit and breaking the rules of perfect competition. In Chapter 11 we shall investigate in more detail some of the strategies that firms use to achieve this end. For now it is essential to recognise the importance of blocking the action of competitors.

What might a firm wishing to break away from its competitors do? Perhaps it will improve product quality in some way. Perhaps it will manage to reduce costs and so charge less. Or maybe it will make its product different and less easily comparable with those of competitors. These are all valid approaches but are of no value unless they can be defended from imitation by other firms. The art of winning in a competitive environment involves finding ways of adding value for consumers that either cannot be copied by competitors or cannot be copied at the same price.

Blocking the competition ←

BED & BREAKFAST

The Victoria Guest House has decided to try once more to increase its price to £20 per person. Its marketing now stresses the warmth of welcome, traditional, home-cooked food and views across the bay. The proprietor is hoping that these qualities will be difficult for other Bed & Breakfast operators to match.

ICE-CREAM

The Promenade Cafe is intending to reduce the price of a single cone to 75p. Profit will be protected through a contract with a cheaper supplier whose quality standards are at least equal to key competitors. The proprietor is worried that this arrangement may prove possible for other firms to copy.

Most methods of 'blocking' competition are subject to erosion or attack over time. Firms that are successful in the long run are not complacent about their competitive strengths. This is why a continuous effort to improve and innovate is necessary in all markets.

In some circumstances, firms are able to achieve a total block against competitors. Examples include state monopolies (such as the Post Office in some markets), franchises (such as broadcasting or oil exploration rights) and patents (giving exclusive legal rights to exploit an invention). When other firms are actually barred from entry, a market is said to be non-contestable. In all other cases where competition is possible, then the market is contestable.

However, in an economy based on enterprise and competition, even non-contestable markets are a dangerous place to rest. Glaxo made handsome profits from its anti-ulcer drug Zantac, but these swiftly fell away once the patent expired and other firms entered the market. Rail operators who took profits without delivering adequate performance found that their franchises were not renewed. The Post Office's share of the parcels market has been declining as new legislation allows increased competition from firms such as TNT, Amtrak and Securicor.

In the long run, every successful product will be hunted by substitutes. The task of management is to keep ahead of the leading predator. The greater their success in this mission, the greater the reward in terms of superior profitability. But the greater the prize of profitability, the faster and fiercer will be the likely predators.

7 Competitive advantage

Overview

In a market economy, every firm (or organisation) must, in the long run, at least achieve a rate of return that covers all costs including those of capital. Most enterprises will also aim to expand their sales while adding net value, i.e. maintaining a superior level of profitability.

The ability to generate earnings in excess of all corresponding costs requires a competitive advantage. This will always be attractive to other firms who will attempt, using their competitive strength, to capture some or all of the surplus. Business strategy is therefore critically concerned with building, exploiting and defending a competitive advantage.

Superior performance

Every firm/organisation needs a clear answer to the questions:

• Where are we going?
• How are we going to get there?

This sense of direction or focused intentionality is usually captured in the firm's strategy. For most firms this reflects a range of aims designed to satisfy the owners and other stakeholders, i.e. groups with an interest in the firm's performance. Central to the pursuit of any set of aims, however, is the need to add value and to earn a sufficient return on the resources in use.

What, exactly, represents a sufficient return? Clearly there is no simple answer to this question. An organisation in the public sector may measure its return in qualitative (non-numerate) rather than in quantitative (numerate or accounting) terms. For instance, a probation service might focus on a reoffending rate as one of its key performance indicators. But for most firms, measurable success in the transformation of resources from an initial cost to a higher value remains the dominant goal.

The next step is to bring some precision to this idea. Notice that an adequate model should also show that even where output is not strictly measurable, the same underlying criteria for the formation of strategy remain equally valid.

A superior return (or supernormal profitability) is any rate of return that exceeds the minimum rate necessary to keep resources in their present use. This minimum 'sufficient' return will vary from industry to industry and from market segment to market segment. The variation is caused by differences in relative risk. A high-risk market will require a premium minimum rate of return, while for a low risk market, the minimum rate will be lower. In effect, the minimum rate is inflated or discounted by a risk factor. For example, the risk of losing resources is much greater in hi-tech pharmaceuticals than it is in, say, confectionery retailing.

All profit above this minimum rate is a kind of 'bonus' – earnings that were *not* necessary to remain in business. The real nature of superior returns is defined by this 'extra' profit. Such profit is 'extra' in the sense that it is net of all direct and indirect costs and all costs of capital. It is 'superior' in being greater than the threshold or minimum profit required as the reward for operating in the market concerned.

The gravity of profit

Unsurprisingly, superior returns are extremely attractive to competitor firms. Suppose, as a hypothetical situation, that perfect competition existed in a market where firms were earning superior returns. Being a perfectly competitive market there would be no barriers to entry or exit. The result would be an inflow of firms and resources, and a rapid competing away of all profit above the normal rate. Almost certainly, however, perfect competition will *not* exist. Instead, firms find shelter from competition behind barriers, explicit or tacit in character. These barriers provide an advantage over competitors and this is termed a competitive advantage in the relevant market.

Since obtaining and defending a competitive advantage is the central strategic goal of all firms, it is necessary to explore this model a little further. The scenario of perfect competition is largely theoretical, but it does represent a situation of equilibrium. Every firm is earning just enough profit to stay in the market. No firm can secure any advantage in the market that will permit any gain in profitability or market share. Each firm supplies the market on terms that exactly cover all costs, including those of capital. By contrast, the existence of competitive advantage and its associated superior (supernormal) profits represents a disequilibrium. Notice that this disequilibrium is highly dynamic. It impels firms with a competitive advantage to defend their barriers to entry against firms inside and outside the market. It also incites all other firms to attempt the seizure of the supernormal returns by copying or improving on the source of competitive advantage. In this sense, there is an action of 'gravity' on all returns above the normal or minimum rate. Such returns are, in effect, a 'honeypot' that attracts rivals. No matter how well defended, any source of competitive advantage will be subject to erosion by competition over time. The higher the rate of return, the more intense the likely contest for the source of advantage.

In reality, many firms make patterns of return that oscillate above and below the minimum (normal) rate. A short period of returns below the normal rate will not make a business unit withdraw from the market since investors and managers may expect performance to improve. Similarly, superior returns are often short-lived as performance fades or other firms copy the source of competitive advantage.

It important, therefore, to distinguish superior returns that are *sustainable*. What this means is that the source of competitive advantage is proving difficult to reproduce or surpass. Competitors are, to a greater or lesser extent, obstructed in their efforts to compete.

Value and cost revisited

The two key underlying variables in a wide range of business decisions are cost and value. This is because the problem confronting every enterprise is how, in relation to a given market, the 'jaws' of cost and value can be prised apart.

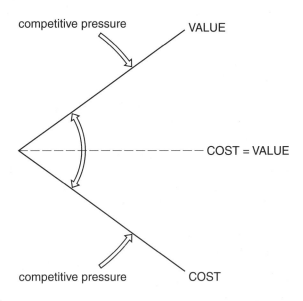

competitive pressure   VALUE

COST = VALUE

competitive pressure   COST

Figure 7.1 Strategic thrust

In Figure 7.1, the broken horizontal line represents minimum or normal profit in relation to cost and value (i.e. total costs equal total value). The firm's strategic thrust is to push apart the 'arms' of value and cost. This at once represents competitive advantage and carries a superior (supernormal) rate of return. The result in the market is a continuous competitive pressure, the tendency of which is to neutralise advantages in both value and cost.

Porter's generic strategies

What enables a firm to enjoy a competitive advantage? What types of business strategy give rise to the largest and most resilient positions of competitive advantage? How can competitive advantage be sustained? These were the kind of questions that Michael Porter addressed through his work in the 1980s. His analysis started with a simple but vital assertion: despite the almost infinite range of means by which firms seek to be competitive, he argued, competitive advantage ultimately rests on either *low cost* or *differentiation*. A low-cost advantage means that a firm is able to generate output of a quality comparable with competitors yet at a lower cost. This allows its profit margin to widen or market share to be gained, or some mix of both. By contrast, a differentiation advantage involves achieving a degree of uniqueness by adjusting the product to improve the fulfilment of consumer demand. This is rewarded by a premium price that represents a higher margin, or a greater level of customer satisfaction that increases market share, or again, some mix of both.

These basic types of competitive advantage are presented by Porter as the basis for three generic strategies.

STRATEGIC ADVANTAGE

	high customer value	low producer cost
mainstream market	DIFFERENTIATION	COST LEADERSHIP
niche market	FOCUS	

(left axis label, read vertically) STRATEGIC TARGET

Figure 7.2 Porter's generic strategies

1 Cost leadership

A cost advantage strategy is usually based on a standard product of average quality that will satisfy a broad target market. Costs are typically minimised through favourable supply contracts, use of new technology and a mix of managerial and motivational efficiencies. The whole strategy is frequently underpinned by economies of scale that grow with gains in market share. Wal-Mart, the US retailer, is a classic exponent of cost leadership with its reach extended into the UK via its acquisition of Asda in 1999.

The strategy is most likely to succeed when all aspects of the firm's operations are geared towards reducing or holding down cost. This resolve becomes embedded in the organisational culture (see Chapter 32) and represented by the brand (see Chapter 19).

2 Differentiation

A differentiation strategy for a broad or mass market must find some distinctive criteria that drive customer satisfaction and then fulfil these at reasonable cost better than any other competitor. Within any product there exists a range of dimensions that add market value. These depend on the product and the types of customers targeted. For example, in the consumer market for car tyres, exhausts and braking systems, key criteria for differentiation might be integrity of the staff (an honest verdict on the repairs needed) and the professionalism of the work. Cost still matters: mass-market differentiation is usually based on average prices, while offering distinctive qualities that customers value. These qualities may be tangible in the product (e.g. advanced diagnostic technology), the service (e.g. faster repairs) or intangible in the brand (e.g. reputation or image).

3 Focus

A focus strategy involves selecting one or more market segments and focusing the firm's resources on superior fulfilment of the corresponding customer demand. The essence of the approach lies in the idea that broad market strategies fail inevitably to meet the specific needs of market subgroups.

Cost focus provides a narrow market with a lower-cost product that still meets the defined need. A segment with cost-focus potential might be identified through the products of broad market competitors overperforming for certain customers. For example, a hotel chain might offer conference facilities yet overprovide gardens and lounges that are little used by this segment.

Differentiation focus is based on finding customer value criteria that only apply to narrower market segments. These can then be targeted for a distinctive product that better suits the needs of the relevant subgroups. For example, a hotel might specialise in meeting the needs of parents with babies and young children. This time it is identifying the respects in which broad sector providers are underperforming relative to the needs of specified subgroups.

The three generic strategies are each distinct. Cost leadership and differentiation are not merely different ends of a spectrum. Cost minimisation is a business philosophy that requires very exacting skills and cultural norms. Differentiation only succeeds where the differential criteria are significant, targeted and effectively delivered. Meanwhile, focus is not simply a narrower application of cost leadership and differentiation. The identification and servicing of smaller segmental markets demand a specialised management and distinctive resources. Too many focus strategies get overextended and lose their competitive advantage as they attempt to enter inappropriate markets.

'Stuck-in-the-middle'

Porter warns managers against becoming 'stuck-in-the-middle' *between* his generic strategies. Supported by research findings, he argues that firms attempting to occupy the middle spaces in his model (see Figure 7.2) will tend to become underperformers, earning relatively low rates of return. This is because superior performance is secured through the orientation of management and resources towards a generic source of competitive advantage. Middle-ground positions hope to win on all strategic dimensions, yet are likely to be made ineffectual by the contradictory forces that these dimensions imply. In a sense, Porter's view only reflects the principle of specialisation. To achieve a sale means being a customer's first choice. To be first choice means being special – either in terms of price or differentiated quality.

Criticism of Porter's theory

It has been argued that the competence- and resource-based approach to strategy has eclipsed the notion of generic strategies. However, the idea of core competencies (Prahalad and Hamel, 1990) seeks to identify the strengths on which competitive advantage is based (see Chapter 8). Instead, Porter offers an analysis and classification of competitive advantage itself. He does not (in his matrix) try to explain the organisational sources of competitive advantage.

Sainsbury's

In the early 1990s Sainsbury's was Britain's leading food retailer. Its slogan 'Sainsbury's: where good food costs less' was a variant on its long-established refrain 'Good food costs less at Sainsbury's'.

A few years earlier, in 1987, Thames TV featured a debate between David Sainsbury – then the company's Chief Executive – and Michael Porter. Was not Sainsbury's 'stuck in the middle' with its implicit claim to be offering both low prices and quality food? asked Porter. Put more directly, was the brand ultimately about quality or price?

Porter construed Sainsbury as offering low prices based on low costs with adequate quality as benchmarked against competitors. Sainsbury argued that his company did not pursue customers only interested in price or those only wanting quality, but targeted the much larger market that demands 'really good value for money' – a favourable balance of price and quality.

In the event, this was exactly the route of attack adopted by Tesco during the 1990s. Led by Ian McLaurin, the firm upgraded quality and drove down costs, seriously undermining Sainsbury's leadership in the process. When, in 1998, David Sainsbury was replaced by Dino Adriano, a new slogan was adopted: 'Sainsbury's: making life taste better'. This might have been thought to signal a new focus on quality, yet during 1999 the company's advertising stressed mainly its refusal to be beaten on price. In the face of competition from Tesco and an Asda now owned by Wal-Mart, this looked a questionable basis for competitive advantage.

Interestingly, after Adriano was replaced by John Davis, the emphasis in 2000 abruptly shifted, with a new sub-slogan in all stores: 'leading on quality'.

Many firms that are 'stuck-in-the-middle' on Porter's criteria still enjoy success with hybrid strategies based on a mix of cost/price and differentiation. This is certainly true and only illustrates that it is the combination of cost, price and value that underpins every business proposition. Adding value is the objective of *all* strategies. Meanwhile, Porter might argue that in terms of its strategic thrust, the great majority of firms have a *primary* orientation towards either cost or differentiation.

Mintzberg (1991) and others argue that firms can use all the elements of the marketing mix, including price, to differentiate. This is entirely valid and many successful firms use a co-ordinated suite of features, including price, to identify different product ranges or brands. However, it can still be maintained that every marketing mix contains a price and a differentiation dimension, and that one or other is ascendant in what is offered.

Porter uses the term differentiation to mean a product with distinctive features that add value in its market. It is important to recognise that the idea of 'distinctive features' embraces superior quality in the same product, as well as features that make the product explicitly different.

In using Porter's model there is a danger of strategy becoming one-dimensional in its emphasis on cost or differentiation. While one factor is typically dominant, both factors need outstanding management if competitive advantage is to be sustained (see also Chapter 11).

8 Competencies and capabilities

Overview

Lying behind every competitive advantage is some distinctive ability to perform better than competitors. To sustain a competitive advantage, this ability must be relatively difficult for other firms to imitate or surpass.

Such an ability is often termed a core competence. It involves a focused network of capabilities that gives the firm an outstanding ability to add value across a range of related applications. This is 'core' for the organisation because it supports their competitive advantage. The challenge is to analyse, sustain and apply core competencies in a dynamic marketplace.

Looking behind competitive advantage

Every purchased product – everywhere – is a winner. At least for the moment of purchase that product defeated all other competitors and became the first choice of a consumer. Some products, like Coca-Cola, triumph millions of times every day all over the world, and do so decade after decade. For others, victory in the market is fleeting and insecure. Launch leads only to withdrawal. But any market success that is not achieved on the back of losses must enjoy some degree of competitive advantage. What is the source and origin of competitive advantage?

By the very nature of competitive advantage, there can be no simple answer. If there were, then such an advantage would be swiftly copied or bettered and so neutralised or eliminated. The essence of competitive advantage is the existence of performance drivers, contestable or not, that block the effect of competition.

It is easy to forget that competitive advantage depends ultimately on the negative capacity to obstruct competitive pressure rather than the positive achievement of excellence in the business. It is tempting simply to equate competitive advantage with a 'good' business that sets high standards in cost control, product quality, customer service or whatever. The flaw in this thinking is its reliance on absolute or objective benchmarks when competitive advantage is actually a *relative* concept. An organisation does not necessarily have a competitive advantage because it is well managed or has an acclaimed product. It has a competitive advantage because it is able to achieve superior performance relative to its competitors. This relative superiority depends on the inability of those competitors to match or surpass its performance. Of course, that inability may well be due to the sheer excellence of the organisation's management, systems or resources; but it could equally derive from monopoly power, including various kinds of restrictive practice and unfair competition. There is nothing inherently 'commendable' or creditable about competitive advantage. It means an advantage over competitors – a neutral condition.

The terms for competitive advantage ←

During the 1970s the quality of mass-produced American and European cars was perceived to have been overtaken by standards being set in the fast-expanding Japanese industry. Sales performance flagged as Japanese manufacturers such as Nissan, Toyota and Honda made rapid inroads into Western markets.

The response in the early 1980s was a new interest in the principles of manufacturing quality. By the end of the decade the quality of most American and European cars was reaching a very high – but shared – international standard. Although the haemorrhaging of market share to the Japanese was largely halted, the earlier losses were not regained. By now the key criteria for success in the industry were shifting towards consumer-oriented design and customisation of manufacturing process for smaller niches in the market. Once again, some Western car makers were struggling to identify and catch up with the competition's leading edge.

We have seen (Chapter 7) that the origins of competitive advantage lie on a spectrum of contestability. At one extreme a firm may rely on a government monopoly that allows no contest at all. At the opposite extreme another firm may simply offer more colours in a given product range, a strength that could clearly be copied by competitors. In between, there are infinite patterns and permutations for competitive advantage that are contestable to a greater or lesser extent.

Take the example of superior customer service. On the face of it, this is a highly contestable source of advantage. Certainly, there are no explicit barriers to any firm setting its own standards at an equivalent or even higher level. Yet in practice this may not be so easy. At the very least, procedures have to be put in place, staff have to be recruited and trained and management has to monitor performance. Immediately costs will increase. Either this will put pressure on margins or prices will have to rise. Will the competitive benefits achieved outweigh these factors?

But the whole basis of outstanding customer service has deeper foundations within the enterprise. Real quality in customer service springs from a climate or embedded culture that places appropriate value on the way in which customers are treated. This needs to be consistent with commitment at all levels of management. No sudden decision to 'improve customer service' is likely to match this kind of organic capability.

Core competencies

It was the issue of the underlying capabilities or competencies within organisations that was analysed by Gary Hamel and CK Prahalad in their book *Competing for the Future* (Harvard Business School Press, 1994). The authors advocate that a firm should base strategy not on one or more business entities (or strategic business units) but on one or more *core competencies*. These then achieve the recognition they deserve as the driving force of competitive success.

A competency (as distinct from a *core* competency) may be regarded as any value-adding activity in which the organisation is proficient. A firm, for example, might have competencies in electronics manufacturing and in related research and development. Competencies of this kind are essential for any firm to compete in any market or industry. But even where they involve costly technologies or high levels of skill, these remain only entry-level requirements and are often termed 'threshold competencies'. A firm equipped with only these competencies can do no more than survive, since superior profitability depends on the exercise of some distinctive quality or resources. Such critical competencies that give rise to better performance than rivals, and thus support a competitive advantage, are called core competencies.

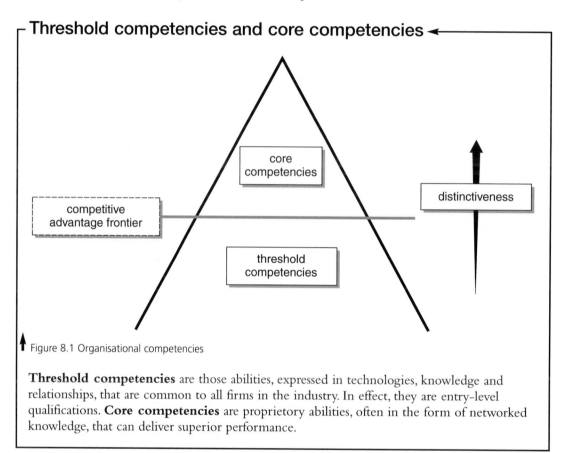

Threshold competencies and core competencies

core competencies

distinctiveness

competitive advantage frontier

threshold competencies

Figure 8.1 Organisational competencies

Threshold competencies are those abilities, expressed in technologies, knowledge and relationships, that are common to all firms in the industry. In effect, they are entry-level qualifications. **Core competencies** are proprietory abilities, often in the form of networked knowledge, that can deliver superior performance.

Hamel and Prahalad use this concept to explain the long-term, sustained success of certain companies in delivering superior returns. Core competencies are rarely based on a simple formula for advantage in the market. Usually, they represent a complex, linked and embedded body of expertise that competitors would find hard to unravel, let alone replicate. Competencies of this kind are robust and flexible. They tend constantly to give the firm's products outstanding quality and functionality. Usually they spawn new products that embody powerful forces of innovation.

In many of the cases quoted by Hamel and Prahalad, core competencies are based on cutting-edge technology. In fact, the same concept applies to expertise in human resource management, marketing, finance or any other business discipline that can yield a competitive advantage. Indeed, a core competence usually depends on elements of all business functions 'wired' together in patterns that are effective but difficult to copy.

However, the 'gravitational' quality of profit means that core competencies are under constant erosion and attack. As a source of competitive advantage and superior performance, a core competence will always attract the interest of competitors who may attempt to 'decode' its formula. Indeed, over time most core competencies that are not nurtured tend to decay and revert to the status of threshold competencies that carry no competitive advantage.

Some core competencies ◄

3M has core competencies in substrates, coatings and adhesives and has developed products ranging from coated abrasives to magnetic tape and Post-it notes. Honda has core competencies in engines and power trains, leading to success in such markets as cars, motorcycles, lawn mowers and generators. Canon has core competencies in optics, imaging and microprocessor controls, which have widened its frontiers beyond cameras to embrace copiers, laser printers and image scanners.

Adapted from Gary Hamel and CK Prahalad Competing for the Future *(Harvard, 1994)*

All this means that the terms for competitive advantage may be bidded upwards in a continuous race between players in the industry. What was outstanding performance in one year may represent only an entry level of competence in the next. This kind of pattern is a reality in most industries and the speed of its unfolding is tending to increase. To be a winner on these terms implies exceptional proficiency, or an exceptional ability to innovate, or some judicious combination of both.

The power of core competencies

If we analyse the power of core competencies we can see that they tend to be generic, with multiple applications that offer progressive access to a widening range of markets. Thus, they tend to offer high strategic growth potential. Core competencies add value. They capture value from the technological, logistical or cultural foundations of the product and breed quality through internal and external supply chains. Because products are derived from a dense configuration of corporate knowledge, they carry a natural authenticity and often make successful brands. The flexibility with which knowledge in the organisation can be combined often allows an ever-advancing repertoire of features to be added at competitive cost. The same strengths make possible a rapid response to new opportunities, with flexibility in the use of resources across organisational boundaries.

With the dimensions of strategic growth and value in place, core competencies also protect competitive advantage from predators. They can take many years to develop and are based on experience curves with fractal★ qualities as they dovetail on different scales, one inside the other. Although generic in applications, a core competence is unique in construction and even the business itself would have some difficulty in describing its exact operation.

★Fractals are generic patterns that repeat on many different scales. They were discovered in the 1970s and are now known to occur in many natural phenomena.

Core competencies are often well hidden. As Hamel and Prahalad warn: 'Remember Canon appeared to be in the camera business at the time it was preparing to become a world leader in copiers.' There is a tendency to conceive competitiveness in terms of high-profile products and brands with leading market shares. Advocates of core competencies argue that this is to 'miss the strength of trees by looking only at the leaves'. What are these competitive trees?

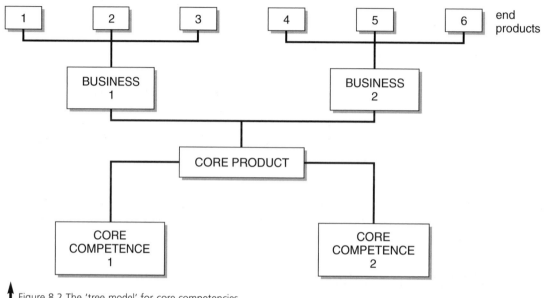

Figure 8.2 The 'tree model' for core competencies

Reprinted by permission of Harvard Business School Press.
From Competing for the Future *by G. Hamel and C. K. Prahalad. Boston, MA 1994, p. 254.*
Copyright © 1994 by the Harvard Business School Publishing Corporation; all rights reserved.

To highlight the idea of core competencies as a source of strength for the business activities that they support, the diagram in Figure 8.2 is effectively inverted. The starting point at the 'trunk' of the tree is core competencies. These are deeply rooted configurations of corporate expertise. They give rise to 'core products' that are the critical building blocks of end products further downstream. For example, Canon has a huge market share in the 'engines' that power laser printers. These core products are the unseen but definitive 'contents' of the many branded end products that crowd the marketplace of final consumption. They represent a significant part of the value added in the overall supply chain. Core products themselves can also become the components feeding downstream business units whose products compete in national or global consumer markets.

Hamel and Prahalad point out that core competencies are the collective learning in an organisation. This learning hones a market-led intelligence that can integrate multiple streams of technologies and co-ordinate diverse production skills lodged in different parts of the organisation. This matching, melding and generating process involves working across organisational boundaries with a widely shared understanding of how core competencies shape the way forward. It is a feature of successful transnational companies and is discussed further in Chapter 36.

It is also a focused, strategic energy that should guide the growth of a firm through diversification and market entry. Attractiveness of markets alone is not enough. A competence-based business is not just a rag-bag of success stories, but a mutually supportive network of selected opportunities. Hamel (1996, 2000) stresses the importance of 'strategic innovation', where the firm invests in emergent technologies or systems that may later be the basis of new products in a major market. The conjunction of computing and communications across the 1980s and 1990s is a classic example.

A strategic architecture

If top managers accept the argument for building core competencies, there is no blueprint to guide their strategy. Each firm must conceive its own architecture that links existing capabilities and identifies directions for development. This strategic architecture ultimately defines a firm's identity and specifies the market types within which it can profitably operate. Its form will be shaped by the expected value of competencies in terms of sustainable competitive advantage and potential market scope.

In larger firms, the making of strategic architecture increasingly suggests the formation of alliances and partnerships. These can be a faster route to filling gaps in evolving competencies and ensures that the goals of such agreements are clearly focused.

Kay's distinctive capabilities

We have seen that there is nothing tangible about competitive advantage. In itself, it is purely an ability to generate returns in excess of the opportunity cost of capital. John Kay, in his *Foundations of Corporate Success* (Oxford, 1993), aimed to uncover the essential bases on which sustainable competitive advantage rests. He identified three foundation factors.

1. The first is the firm's **reputation**. This may be invested in its brands, but may also exist more implicitly in the quality of its stakeholder relationships. Reputation adds value because it reduces risk. It keeps customers loyal and reduces price elasticity of demand. It gains entry to new markets.
2. The second factor is what Kay calls **'architecture'**. This is the network of relationships, both internal and external, that a company's trading activity requires. When well built and well managed, corporate architecture reduces costs and adds value – for example, supply chains are more likely to be more effective, while better employee relationships are likely to enhance customer service.
3. The third factor is **innovation**. This drives the terms of competition forward as each innovation builds a new 'platform' of competitive advantage. This may prove sustainable far into the long term – especially if protected by a non-contestable barriers such as patents. Equally, it may only be a contingent position and under attack. But if innovation builds on innovation, the process itself becomes a defensible strategy.

These factors remain, of course, largely contestable. They are key dimensions in the classic arena of competition. But Kay also recognises what he rather problematically calls 'strategic assets'. These are the 'blocking factors', the walls in that arena behind which firms enjoy non-contestable advantages. They vary from simple geographical location to the complex sources of monopolistic power wielded by some global corporations.

A less obvious strategic asset highlighted by Kay is the phenomenon of incumbency. This means that a business gains competitive advantage simply from being established in the market. The likely cost and risk of challenging the incumbent form a barrier to entry. Meanwhile, the incumbent's customers face switching costs and a degree of risk if they defect to the competitor. This incumbency factor works in favour of many firms ranging from a village shop to a world media agency such as Reuters.

In explaining competitive advantage, Kay's distinctive capabilities form a useful taxonomy. However, his analysis raises questions as well as answers. If reputation, architecture and innovation are the sources of competitive advantage, what makes them accessible to some firms and not to others? And what is the role of human factors such as leadership, culture and knowledge management in the making of distinctive capabilities? These are open questions that will be explored in Chapters 31 and 32.

Comparing concepts

Competencies and capabilities are essentially very similar ideas and both need to be 'distinctive' if they are to yield a competitive advantage. However, there is a difference between the two concepts that partly derives from the purpose and vantage point of their use.

Kay is really classifying the types of phenomena in business that give rise to a defensible competitive advantage and calling them distinctive capabilities. Hamel and Prahalad are explaining how networks of competencies in a firm can form core competencies that then have a range of applications in generating competitive advantage. Kay's is an analytical 'top, looking down' view, while Hamel and Prahalad's is a more formative 'bottom, looking up' view. Both are useful.

9 Introducing strategy

Overview

A strategy is a pathway of intentionality. It is the essential dynamic direction in which an organisation's resources are deployed. This articulated sense of direction must correspond with the aspirations of key stakeholders. It must also give rise to competitive advantage. This needs to be sustainable in a changing environment.

A strategy is often expressed in quite simple terms. For example, a firm might intend to 'build a 10% market share in segment X while developing brand loyalty strong enough to support above average margins'. But in reality the expression of a strategy through the structure and behaviour of a business is highly complex. In fact, in most cases it will be complex to such a degree that a rival firm would find it impossible to unravel. That is why firms are willing to state their strategies openly in the press and in their publicity. Senior management know that only they have the value chain 'codings' that may make the strategy work.

The idea of strategy

The dictionary says that strategy is 'a long-term plan for future success or development', but the meaning is not so straightforward in business. In fact, the whole nature of strategy is very complex and highly controversial. It is not a field in which a central model and some supporting techniques are all that need be considered. Instead, we have in strategy a multidimensional concept where even the effort to define its essential nature draws lines of deep disagreement between opposing schools of thought. This is not to say that little is known about strategy, or that any point of view is as good as any other. On the contrary, a great deal of useful theory has been assembled and the various perspectives offered all project light on to the knowledge and experience that exist. Yet strategy remains an emergent discipline where theories are necessarily provisional and the search for new insight continues.

The word *strategy* is derived from the ancient Greek words for an 'encamped army' and 'to lead'. The term *strategos* meant an elected member of the Athenian war council. An interesting early definition comes from the Roman leader Frontinus in the first century AD: 'everything achieved by a commander, be it characterised by foresight, advantage, enterprise or resolution'. In fact, historically, the word strategy has always been associated with the art or science of military decision making. Interestingly, the Oxford Dictionary, until around 1980, defined the word strategy exclusively in military terms. Although the word has taken on a new modern meaning, the military link remains appropriate in significant ways.

Given the importance attached to strategy by almost every major organisation in the world today, it seems odd that the subject was scarcely studied before the 1960s. This reflects the slow and uneven emergence of management as a recognisable discipline.

Two hundred years earlier, the onset of the Industrial Revolution had seen the origins of economics as an academic discipline. Despite the nature of economics as a study of resource allocation and deployment, very limited links were made with the process of managing business enterprise.

Similarly, although business enterprises clearly adopted *de facto* strategies, there was no systematised body of theory on the subject. On the whole, management remained a personal, often idiosyncratic process for most of the 19th century.

It was FW Taylor in the early 20th century who first gave management some quasi-scientific basis. In Taylor's words, 'science, not rule of thumb' was a view that began to prevail in some larger organisations. But it was Henri Fayol who identified the central importance of management and planning. His *General and Industrial Management* (1916) explained concisely the purpose of management: 'to manage is to forecast and to plan, to organise, to command, to co-ordinate and to control'. His themes were extended and enriched by Drucker (1954) in his highly influential *The Practice of Management*. This required managers to decide on the nature and scope of their business and to make strategic decisions towards the fulfilment of objectives.

Chandler (1962) provided the classic definition of strategy (see below) and focused on the strategic function of management with a logical and linear approach:

1 set objectives
2 decide on route to follow
3 allocate necessary resources.

What is strategy?

Drucker (1961)

The pattern of major objectives, purposes or goals and essential policies or plans for achieving these goals, stated in such a way as to define what business the company is in or is to be in and the kind of company it is or is to be.

Chandler (1962)

Strategy is the determination of the long-term basic goals and objectives of an enterprise, and the adoption of courses of action and the allocation of resources necessary for carrying out these goals.

Not long after came Ansoff's landmark book *Corporate Strategy* (1965), the first full-length academic book devoted to organisations and their strategy. This echoes Chandler in arguing that strategy involves recognising an existing position, selecting a desired position and clarifying the tasks that will close the 'gap'.

Ansoff was first to recognise the central place of competitive advantage in formulating strategy and stressed the role of opportunity cost in deploying scarce resources. In particular, he represented a firm's strategic options in terms of a growth matrix.

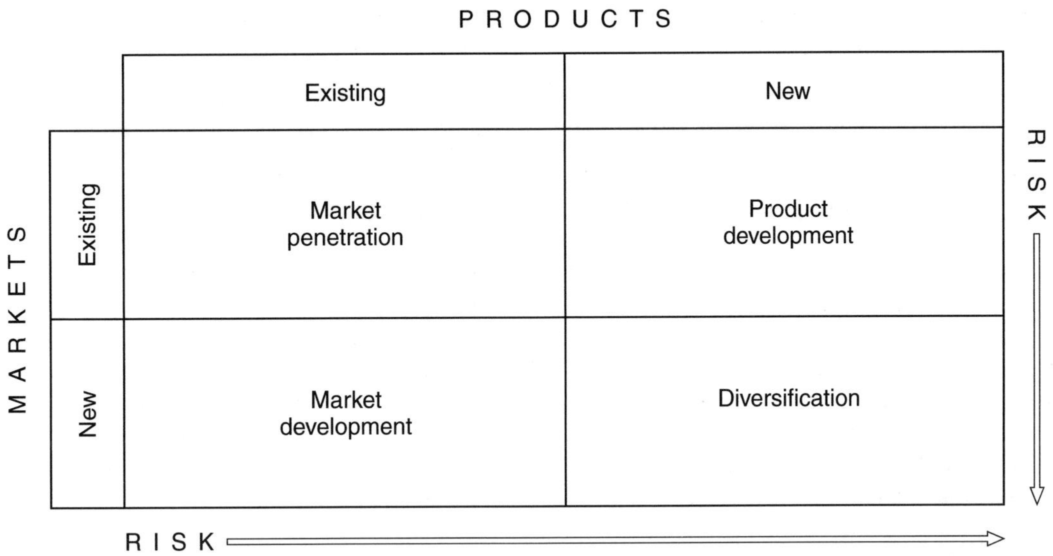

PRODUCTS

	Existing	New
Existing	Market penetration	Product development
New	Market development	Diversification

MARKETS (vertical label) — RISK (vertical, right side, arrow down)

RISK (horizontal, bottom, arrow right)

Figure 9.1 Ansoff's matrix

This has been used widely as a framework within which to build a product portfolio (see Chapter 15).

It was also during the 1960s and 1970s that the concepts of rational planning and scientific decision making became popular. The power and availability of mainframe computers were increasing rapidly and, following Herbert Simon's *The New Science of Management Decision* (1960), a range of quasi-scientific techniques such as the Capital Asset Pricing Model (CAPM), critical path analysis and decision trees came into general use. Large firms produced detailed corporate plans with tight systems for implementation and monitoring progress.

The challenge to this rationalist consensus gathered force slowly. The 1960s saw the zenith of faith in scientific problem solving, but the period also bred some radical counter-currents affirming the primacy of instinct, intuition and inspiration. As Apollo 11 landed on the moon, half a million hippies gathered for the Woodstock festival. This paradox echoed through the 1970s, a decade that saw the emergence of an environmental movement and a new interest in empowerment and culture at work.

The 1980s brought nothing less than a tidal wave of new thinking about competitiveness and business strategy. Two strands of research-based theory stand out. We have seen that one was incubated by the growth of import penetration in Western economies, and especially by the threat of high-quality yet low-cost Japanese goods. Both Richard Pascale's *The Art of Japanese Management* and Peters' and Waterman's *In Search of Excellence* stressed the importance of the 'soft Ss' in their jointly designed Seven-S framework (see Figure 2.1).

Peters argued later:

> **Search** was an out-and-out attack on the excesses of the *rational model* and the *business strategy paradigm* that had come to dominate Western management thinking.

Mintzberg (1989) forcibly made the same point:

> **In Vietnam they [hard data] supported the military goals; the humanitarian goals, supported only by soft data, were driven out of the analysis. We see the same thing in corporations when the hard data line up behind the economic goals – cost reduction, profit increase, growth in market share – leaving the social goals – product quality, employee satisfaction, protection of the environment – to fend for themselves.**

Meanwhile, Michael Porter in *Competitive Strategy* and *Competitive Advantage* used microeconomics to give strategy a conceptual underpinning and to develop some effective tools of analysis. His work supported the rise of the positioning approach to strategy (see Chapter 11), where stress is laid on a firm's competitive position in the market and its ability to defend a competitive advantage.

In the early 1990s Gary Hamel and CK Prahalad launched the core competencies movement, around which a very different resource-based view of strategy has been built. This sees competitive advantage arising from the embedded competencies of a firm, and the ability to use superior capabilities in entering or even creating new markets. Alongside this trend in thinking has been a growing interest in the knowledge and experience accumulated by firms that is a distinct source of added value and very difficult for competitors to replicate.

What is strategy *for*?

Friedman (1962) considers shareholder gain to be the only proper aim for a company. In practice most firms acknowledge some stakeholder interests and may also express their aims in terms of an overarching social or human purpose.

Aims set the broad direction in which the organisation intends to progress or the criteria for judging its actions. Strategy then articulates these aims in a pattern of specific intentions. At the apex of this process is the setting of strategic objectives. It is the function of objectives to crystallise aims into specific destinations or outcomes to be reached within a given timescale. When set for the firm as a whole, these will necessarily be totalised and all-inclusive; but objectives will still reflect the basic vectors of business performance. Which capabilities will the firm be retaining and building? Which markets will it be targeting? To what extent will it seek higher profit margins and to what extent larger market share?

This last question represents an important concept. Strategy aims to add value. This may be achieved by entering a market on a narrow front where an intense competitive advantage allows high levels of added value. Equally a firm may wish to exploit a broader competitive advantage that gives access to a mass market. The trade-off comes in the reduced rate of added value relative to the increased volume of sales.

This scenario is explored in Figure 9.2 where the firms illustrated face a downward-sloping added value frontier.

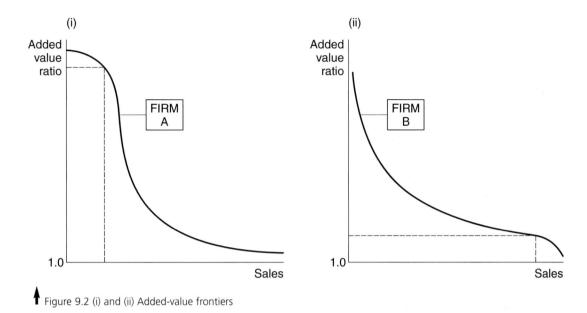

Figure 9.2 (i) and (ii) Added-value frontiers

The added value ratio is the value of the output divided by the corresponding cost of input. Firm A has chosen to exploit a limited market where it has a strong competitive advantage and can earn a high rate of added value. Firm B is exploiting its competitive advantage across a wider market but accepting a lower rate of added value. Both firms are confronted by competitive pressure that tends to reduce their ability to add value and foreshortens their strategic options. In reponse, each firm will have a strategy to defend added value and, if possible, push the frontier outwards.

To fulfil its various objectives, a firm's strategy maps interrelated pathways of activity judged most likely to be successful in a changing and uncertain environment. It will then specify the resource implications and how these can best be resolved. Below corporate level the strategy must be translated into the terms of operating divisions or strategic business units (SBUs) and then into operating plans across the business functions.

While senior management may feel that aims only represent very general guidance, objectives are hard targets that carry accountability for their fulfilment. Large firms may publicly state their corporate objectives but these will always break down into multiple interim and subsidiary goals inside the organisation. For example, to become the UK's leading retailer of sportswear might involve increasing market share by ten percentage points. This could then imply higher sales targets from each market segment or product line, increased production or purchasing requirements, improved brand recognition, new sponsorship deals and much more.

Prescriptive and emergent strategy

We have seen that in the early development of business strategy, a scientific style of model was adopted. There has remained an influential school of thought that expects strategy to be linear, sequential and demonstrably rational. A firm sets its objectives and then designs a strategy for the 'journey', clearly waymarked by measurable criteria. A strategy in this sense is rather like a complex plan. This prescriptive approach to strategy is often linked to analytical models designed to optimise a firm's position in the market and to maximise its competitive advantage.

In its favour, the prescriptive approach ensures a rigorous analysis of the firm's environment and evaluation of the available options. It also ties SBUs and managers to quantitative budgets against which their performance can be judged. However, the approach is based on some assumptions that are increasingly widely being questioned. A relatively rigid planning process is at odds with a turbulent and unpredictable business environment where opportunities and threats can materialise abruptly on the back of barely perceptible evidence. Strategy is not a mechanical process and needs a different paradigm if it is not to lose the flexibility and creativity that characterise competitive success.

The contrasting emergent strategy model moves away from fixed objectives with predetermined routes for their realisation. Instead, strategy *emerges*. It is shaped through orchestrated patterns of activity and behaviour. These are guided but not directed towards objectives that are themselves adaptable.

Mintzberg (1987) in his landmark article 'Crafting Strategy' likens the making of strategy to the working of clay on a potter's wheel. Fundamental principles underlie the craft, but the potter must feel the clay and realise the pot in an intuitive and contingent spirit.

By its nature, this approach is able to accommodate change and is difficult for competitors to imitate. Continuous use can be made of organisational knowledge and experience, with learning as an in-built reflex. As long as there is underlying coherence in the organisation's pattern of response, managers can exploit much greater discretion in their repertoire of strategic moves.

The dangers are apparent. Without the explicit discipline of the prescriptive approach there is a risk that focus and direction will be lost. The constituent parts of the organisation may become uncoordinated, while the sense of urgency and mission may be lost.

In many ways the two approaches to strategy-making represent somewhat polarised views of the process. In practice, firms that are prescriptive in setting strategy also allow for flexibility, adaptation and – when necessary – complete changes of direction. Similarly, firms with an emergent style of strategy formation also set broad planning vectors based on prior analysis.

Somerfield and Kwik-Save ◄──────────────────────

The Somerfield chain of mainly smaller high street supermarkets was formed from the Bristol-based Gateway foodstores in 1996. A new image and corporate identity spoke for an optimistic vision:

> **Our strategy since flotation has been to position Somerfield as a national chain of dependable, good quality, friendly local stores; extend its appeal to more ABC1s, family groups and younger shoppers; leverage the Somerfield brand ...**

By 1998 Somerfield's results were impressive: operating profit was up 11% on the previous year to £128 million on sales of £3.4 billion. Return on capital employed (ROCE) was around 13 per cent, while the share price had risen by 133 per cent in two years.

It was at this moment that Somerfield acquired Kwik-Save. The business purchased was a North Wales-based discounter of mainline branded goods trading on a 'no frills' strategy and concentrated in less prosperous areas. The deal nearly doubled the company's sales and more than doubled the number of outlets. During the early 1990s Kwik-Save had been the most profitable supermarket chain in Britain. Then competition from an aggressive Tesco, a recovering Asda and the entry of continental discounters began to tell. A sustained economic boom meant that consumers were trading up rather than down.

Somerfield's new strategy was the complete integration of the two (very different) chains with rebranding under the Somerfield name. The combined chain – billed as 'the right combination' – was to be:

> **The emergence of a single powerful brand in neighbourhood retailing... Our vision for the enlarged business is to build our stores into the fabric of Britain's local communities – a niche that we are uniquely positioned to fill.**

The speed and scale of the disaster that followed was unexpected. During 1999 sales and operating profit collapsed as the conversion of Kwik-Save stores to the Somerfield format, in the Chairman's words, 'proved unworkable'. The effort disrupted supply chains and alienated staff and customers alike. The company made an £80 million loss with long-term damage to the customer base. The CEO David Simons and other senior directors resigned.

Meanwhile, the deteriorating situation brought a change in strategy. In late 1999 it was decided that half the Kwik-Save stores would be converted to the Somerfield format while the rest would be sold. This plan also proved to be untenable. Kwik-Save was thrown into further disarray and as morale fell, so did sales. A few months later, in April 2000, a strategic U-turn brought the Kwik-Save stores off the market with the restoration of a twin-fascia approach. Kwik-Save would benefit from shared services and supply chains but retain its identity and a distinctive discounting strategy.

By 2002 the group had returned to profit, albeit on a slender ROCE of 3.6 per cent. The two fascias were now being developed with separate management teams, but continuing losses at Kwik-Save remained an outstanding problem. Improvements in efficiency had been helpful but could not compensate for the loss in market share.

10 Strategic fit

Overview

The only meaningful starting point for strategy is purpose. A strategy is a pathway from an existing position towards a preferred position. Before a strategy can be conceived, a preferred position or objective must be identified. This in turn depends on the aims of the organisation. Ultimately, what is the enterprise about?

While the competing claims of stakeholders exert a complex set of forces on any firm, the search for growth and superior performance is almost always at the heart of strategy formation. Success in this search depends on an effective conjunction between distinctive capabilities at the disposal of the firm and targeted demand in the market. This matching or strategic fit has to be achieved in a changing, turbulent and uncertain market.

Despite the solid theoretical foundations for the concept of strategic fit, there is nothing predictably formulaic about setting strategy. Within the conceptual framework an important role can be played by chance events, creative surprise and the emergence of unforeseen patterns.

Strategy and the SWOT model

Almost all writers agree that business strategy is concerned with the fit between the capabilities of an organisation and its external environment. This statement indicates the wide-ranging scope of the subject but does not in itself provide any framework for the formation of strategy. A useful starting point is the simple model for SWOT analysis.

This involves relating an organisation's internal strengths and weaknesses to its external opportunities and threats. Senior management carry out an in-depth audit that should avoid any prior conditions or conclusions. It will involve open-ended and critical thinking about the organisation and its theatres of interaction with the external environment. The criterion that gives the process form and discriminatory meaning is, of course, added value. Thus, the cutting edge of SWOT analysis lies along the axis of actual and potential matches between the firm's capabilities and the competitive marketplace around.

In its simplest form, SWOT can become little more than a scoreboard of bullet points, but when these are grouped and related vertically across the internal/external axis, then some guide to strategy formation may emerge (see Figure 10.1). Often, though, some interesting and unexpected features or patterns emerge from the analysis, all triggering new streams of thought or the discovery of emergent possibilities. In these ways strategy begins to form.

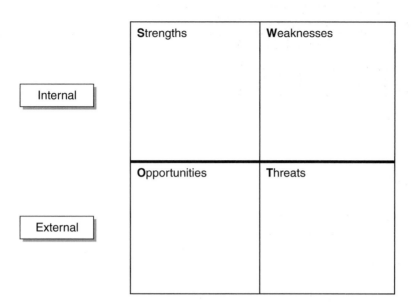

Figure 10.1 Basic SWOT model

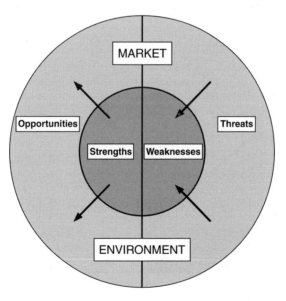

Figure 10.2 SWOT and the market

It should be noticed that there is danger in using SWOT analysis as a static model or a kind of cross-section through the organisation's internal and external realities at a given moment in time. Two key problems arise. First, the capabilities and external environment of a firm are in a state of constant change (see Figure 10.2). The nature of this change may be incremental, but it can – usually unexpectedly – become discontinuous (see Chapter 32). In particular, a business often has potential access to strengths and opportunities (with their attendant risks) outside its own boundaries. Mergers, acquisitions and divestments can abruptly transform the picture, while alliances and partnerships alter and widen its characteristics.

The second factor relates to the apparent separation of the firm's internal and external reality. In fact, the dividing line is often indistinct and highly permeable. Movement in human resources provides an obvious example. A firm might headhunt and win the creative talent of a rival. A key threat now becomes a key asset. Similarly, the strength invested in a critical team may become a threat if the staff involved decide to leave and set up in competition. The whole model is alive with interactivity, and the complex family of strengths, weaknesses, opportunities and threats can change places at any time.

Added value

In 1980 Michael Porter published his *Competitive Strategy* followed in 1985 by *Competitive Advantage*. If Peters' and Waterman's *In Search of Excellence* is the best-selling business book of all time, then Michael Porter's books must be the most influential. They represent a thoroughgoing attempt to explain the origins of superior performance and the rational bases for strategy formation. Although much criticised by some writers, they continue to enjoy high academic status and offer a range of analytical tools used all over the world. The school of thought that is characterised by Porter's work is known generally as positioning.

To understand fully the positioning approach, we must return to the fundamental mechanism of business in a market economy (see also Chapters 4 and 19). Firms are transformers of scarce resources into saleable products. Necessarily they must identify and target markets with customers who prefer the product to its substitutes at prices higher than cost. Put another way, some part of the demand function must be above the corresponding cost function. This gives the firm a range of sales levels that yield surplus to the consumer and a profit to the firm (see Figure 10.3).

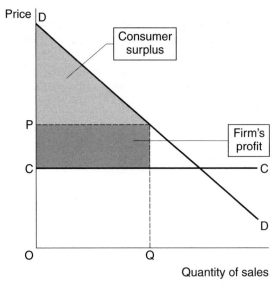

Figure 10.3 Demand and cost functions

What is the essence of this process? The firm must seek to achieve the closest possible match between its own internal capabilities and the external demands of the target market. This will maximise the potential for added value. The process is two-way in its implications. The firm surveys potential markets for evidence of demand that makes a close 'fit' with its own capabilities. Equally, its capabilities should be critically and imaginatively assessed in the search for the same 'fit' with characteristics of market demand.

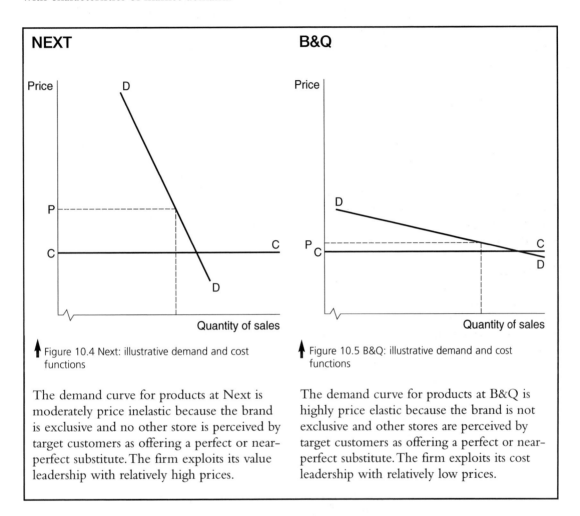

Figure 10.4 Next: illustrative demand and cost functions

Figure 10.5 B&Q: illustrative demand and cost functions

The demand curve for products at Next is moderately price inelastic because the brand is exclusive and no other store is perceived by target customers as offering a perfect or near-perfect substitute. The firm exploits its value leadership with relatively high prices.

The demand curve for products at B&Q is highly price elastic because the brand is not exclusive and other stores are perceived by target customers as offering a perfect or near-perfect substitute. The firm exploits its cost leadership with relatively low prices.

Competitive advantage and added value

Because the concept is often defined in terms of superior performance, it is widely believed that all firms wish to increase their competitive advantage. This is often not the case. Consider The Gondola, an independent pizza and pasta restaurant that has an outstanding competitive advantage in a small town. The restaurant has obtained a perfect position in the market square. It is well known locally for the excellence of its food and service. There are no other Italian-type restaurants in the town. Profitability is outstanding, with returns far above the opportunity cost of capital. However, the proprietor sees little prospect of opening a second branch. Nearby towns already have established Italian restaurants.

Now consider Pizza Express. Founded in 1965, the company has a strong reputation for quality and style, with many prime locations. It, too, enjoys a competitive advantage but its percentage returns run at only half the level of The Gondola. And there is another, rather important difference. Pizza Express now (2003) has 311 restaurants, while The Gondola has only one. Pizza Express turned over £214m last year, against the Gondola's £500 000. Pizza Express generates £38m in operating profit. The Gondola makes £200 000. The owner of The Gondola wishes he had invented Pizza Express.

A very small business occupying an exclusive and well-fortified niche market might secure an extremely high level of competitive advantage, but the potential scale of profit is limited by the nature of the niche. The critical extra dimension of added value is reach into the market. Given the inevitably downward-sloping profile of the demand curve, most firms sacrifice the rate of profitability (reflecting competitive advantage) in the pursuit of market penetration. It is the actions of competitive advantage and market penetration together that create added value.

The Body Shop

Financial performance at The Body Shop 1987–97

	1987	**1992**	**1997**
Sales	£28m	£147m	£271m
Profit margin*	21.1%	18.9%	14.2%
Return on capital**	87.4%	35.0%	26.8%

* Based on operating profit before interest, tax or exceptionals.
** Operating profit
Shareholders' funds + long-term liabilities.

Logically, a firm will continue to expand while it is adding value (net of capital costs). Put another way, it will always make sense to invest an extra pound while its return is greater than the cost of its being available to invest. Once again, this is an application of the principle that resources must keep their returns ahead of their opportunity cost.

Strategically, however, there is a rising risk profile attached to expansion as the related returns erode towards zero. Quite a small deterioration in the business environment may push a causeway of investment decisions into negative returns. This may have serious implications for the company's overall performance and cash flow – and even endanger its independence. Highly geared firms (heavily dependent on borrowed capital) are especially vulnerable.

In the case of a focus-based strategy, the achievable rates of added value are likely to fall away steeply beyond the boundaries of the market niche. This is because such a firm may have a strong competitive advantage within the niche, but no special capabilities that would enable it to compete outside the protective territory of its specialist market. Its goal will be to sustain a high level of competitive advantage while accepting that the scale and scope of added value are necessarily limited.

Strategic fit

Miles and Snow (1984) were early advocates of strategic fit. In attempting to add value, a firm faces a market environment. Defining the meaning of fit and originating the energy in that market is the demand of target customers. Also influential in this frame are the nature and extent of competition and the norms of the industry that it represents. So, for a hydraulics engineering firm, the market environment might feature:

• a few key players
• a premium on technical expertise and understanding of customers' needs
• pressure on operational efficiency
• importance of flexibility and quick reactions to market change.

Miles and Snow stress the dynamic nature of fit. Strategy, they argue, is the means to achieve and maintain *alignment* between the organisation and the market environment. This is supported by the internal structure and management processes that must necessarily be adaptable to change.

The mechanism of market fit can be extremely sensitive. Think of tuning a radio, manually. You start with hiss and crackle. As the correct frequency is approached the station begins to emerge, all distortion at first and then increasingly clearly. When tuned, the reception is often still slightly less than perfect and a final adjustment silences the last vestiges of interference. Suddenly, the station is loud and clear and pleasingly resonant in the quality of reception. Of course, if the 'needle' is turned further forward, then the whole corrective sequence unravels until there is only 'noise' once more.

'Tuning' a business can be comparable. A firm mobilises its capabilities to track the signals from a market environment and attempts to 'lock' on to the 'frequency'. In practice, the 'tuning' or fit is almost always suboptimal. However, a reasonable approximation to the ideal fit might yield some modest level of competitive advantage and consequent profitability. For most firms this is as good as it gets.

What prevents firms from achieving that last stage of fidelity in fit? Partly the problem is a deficit in skills and knowledge. The firm lacks the necessary receptivity to the market signal for that critical fine tuning to take place. Its resources may not include some of the smaller and more delicate capabilities and connections required for that precision of fit. Equally likely, the continuous and sometimes discontinuous shifts and lurches in the active environment may result in a chronic shortfall of fit between capabilities slightly uncertain at their endings, and a market signal that surges and fades.

The problems of achieving very high levels of fit are in evidence throughout the business world. So often a firm achieves 80 per cent or 90 per cent of true customer satisfaction, but finds the last 10 per cent or 20 per cent elusive. Customer service is a good example. As attentiveness to customer needs improves, so satisfaction rises. A peak of satisfaction that exceeds all reasonable expectation may flare up if a customer's personal needs are anticipated correctly and aptly fulfilled. But all too easily the level of service slips past the optimum. Perhaps it is now experienced by the customer as overfamiliar or intrusive. Problematically, the nuances of fit are complex and cultural. For example, perfect, formal service on the one hand and down-to-earth familiarity on the other, will please different customers in different locations and different settings.

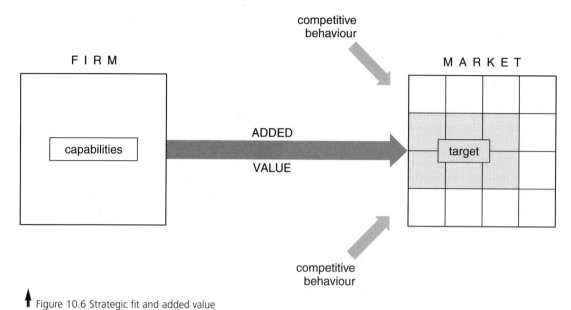

Figure 10.6 Strategic fit and added value

Similarly, the task of maintaining fit in an unpredictable and fast-changing environment is highly exacting. The very achievement of fit is often the makings of its loss. Customer satisfaction is high and competitive advantage is secured – or so it seems. Without any tracking device, a car radio may lose its signal as location changes. Slowly but significantly receptor and signal drift apart.

A comparable strategic drift occurs in business. This is not normally because the management team have lost interest or even lack competence. As Sull (2000) observes, success breeds failure as firms get framed by a winning formula that mesmerises its makers. Systems get programmed to a single repertoire of delivery where all innovation can seem like compromising principles. By the time the drift is showing seriously, in falling market share or increasing competition, it may be too late to kick-start the learning process and loosen the bolted structure of capabilities.

Yet fit remains a touchstone of strategy. Achieving fit is not only a key source of competitive advantage, but it is also a powerful engine of competitive exclusion. Once a firm has successfully locked on to a target market, it becomes increasingly difficult to dislodge. Capabilities are honed, linkages get snapped into place. Relationships develop with customers while experience and reputation build. In these ways fit can fortify competitive advantage and make it sustainable.

Once again we meet the distinction between the firm as a mechanistic set of linked devices and the idea of a business resembling a living entity that can be vigilant while learning, thinking and adapting. This second type of enterprise can maximise the value of its incumbency in a market and still be ready for abrupt and, in some cases, total reinvention.

This need may occur when the forces for change have worked through all adaptive responses possible and the argument for a discontinuous remaking of the enterprise reaches a critical mass. A breakpoint of this kind is far more fruitful if it is enacted at the front end of strategic necessity. This wrong-foots competitors and keeps the initiative in the strategic unfolding that follows. As a run of success with a given identity comes towards a close, it is reassuring to see a field of cash cows still dignifying the firm's portfolio. But the relative absence of new stars may be the signal that is needed to risk closing one frame and opening another.

'Stretch'

Such a shift is often possible using what is widely called a process of 'stretch'. Every organisation has within its grasp a set of competencies and linked capabilities. These are deployed within the scope of its activities, searching, as we have seen, for value-adding fit. But because a vibrant business depends on continuous renewal, there should be a constant tendency to 'stretch' competencies and capabilities to activate hidden or emergent opportunity. In practice this could mean finding new applications for fixed assets such as specialised machinery. It might involve using some accumulation of expertise to enter a new market. Perhaps a modification to a product line would generate sales in some small but growing high-margin niche.

The essence of the stretch concept is a restless and creative search for new ways in which assets can add value. Sometimes this will be by aligning selected assets with an opportunity and sometimes it will be by using assets to create an opportunity. In all strategies of stretch, fit has undiminished importance. A weak fit may survive the early stages of exploiting an opportunity, but must rapidly tighten if the bridgehead or position is to be sustained and competitors prevented from seizing the market or destroying its profitability.

In configuring a portfolio of business activity (strategic business units or specific products), a balance of risks and returns is usually required. A firm will typically operate mainly in markets where demand is well established and understood. Unless significant barriers to entry exist, these are likely to be competitive, with steady if unexceptional returns and a moderate to low level of risk. In portfolio terms, stretch implies entering newly identified markets where demand is more speculative but competition much less intense. High returns are possible but with higher attendant risks.

11 Strategic positioning

Overview

Every strategy aims to add value. This is achieved through making sales in the market on the basis of a competitive advantage. Those sales that earn profit above the cost of capital will attract competition. Thus, the maintenance of the firm's competitive advantage depends on its ability to defend its price and sales levels against the threat of substitute products offered by competitors.

This chapter will explain how a firm can use both its positioning and its resources in the making of a competitive strategy. It will analyse the generic forces that threaten to erode competitive advantage and explore the means available to lock out competitors.

Positioning and strategy

A firm's position means the key characteristics of its proposition to customers relative to competitors in the market. For example, EasyJet is positioned as a low-cost, no-frills airline, competing with Ryanair but differentiated from British Airways by its direct ticketing system, no meals on flights and use of secondary airports.

The positioning approach to strategy starts with the external environment in general and the market in particular. It involves detailed analysis to uncover market opportunity where potential customers have needs that could be better served by the firm's distinctive capabilities. A relationship can then be built with customers that is clearly distinguished from the propositions offered by competitors. This reflects every firm's dependence on winning among customers the status of 'first choice' for value. A business whose proposition is 'nothing special' in terms of either price or differential quality is unlikely to win ground on either margins or sales. This is the 'stuck-in-the-middle' position against which Porter warns (see Chapter 7).

In later writing, Porter (1996) argues more fundamentally that strategic positioning requires sharp definition. Firms, he argues, should avoid the temptation to net more and more customers through a broadening of their strategic position. The effort will only end in the loss of exactly that distinctiveness on which competitive advantage depends. A strong position requires clarity about customers who will and *will not* be served.

Competitive positioning

No business can supply or sell anything without demand. As the ultimate generative power in every business, demand forms and moves like the isobars on a weather chart, following patterns

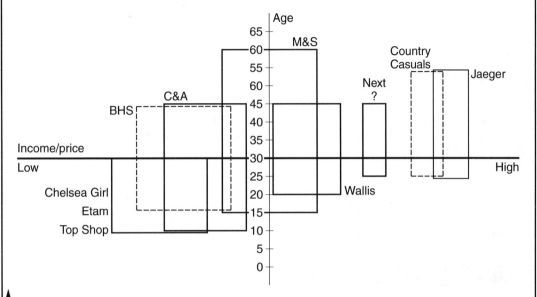

Next

When Next was launched in 1982, it was carefully positioned in terms of customer age group, price range and key competitors.

Figure 11.1 Positioning: the original concept for Next

In the retailing of ladieswear for the 25–40 age group, there appeared to be a gap in the market between the mainstream offering of Marks & Spencer and the much more expensive chains such as Country Casuals and Jaeger. In practice, the Next hypothesis was quickly confirmed as correct. The company gained a dominant position in what turned out to be a rapidly expanding segment. The same formula worked equally well for menswear.

but always changing, always unique, always defying linear predictability. Every business is attracted by demand and drawn to its field of transactional opportunity. Finding and holding a position in that field is the challenge.

Competition hits demand. It invades a firm's relationship with its customers and pushes that firm below the line of first choice. Every first choice converted to second choice is a sale converted to no sale.

When competition is head-on and a rival moves in to occupy the same position, or virtually the same position, then the original position-holder's differentiation is significantly annulled. Because the products of one firm are now a close substitute for the products of the other, price inelasticity is lost and the ensuing competitive battle drives down market price. Except to the extent that the first firm can re-differentiate, the basis of competitive advantage swings towards cost and its drivers in terms of operational effectiveness.

Tesco

During the 1990s, Tesco gently converted Sainsbury's from first choice to second choice in the judgement of more and more customers. By stages, it neutralised a crucial zone of Sainsbury's added value and used the appropriated sales and cash flow in building the stronghold that is Tesco.

The first step – in the early 1990s – was to 'catch up' with Sainsbury's in the quality of its products and shopping environment. As Tesco pushed down its cost base and accelerated the speed of innovation, so Sainsbury's was out-manoeuvred and driven into the formula of price cutting that damaged its famous margins.

Quickly Tesco was building market share and strengthening its brand. Having matched or eclipsed its rival's sources of differentiation, it could develop its own differential features even as it accepted the crown of 'Britain's favourite grocer'. Sainsbury's only started to recover when it searched back to find its roots as a 'real grocer' and to offer a new interpretation of its old slogan 'Good food costs less at Sainsbury's'.

This is an important concept. As Porter's term 'cost leadership' implies, competition based on cost only allows one winner. In the total absence of differentiation, a firm that comes second on cost can have no competitive advantage without permission from the cost leader who can, at any time, give competitors the simple choice of zero sales or sales at a loss. It is no wonder that differentiation is the first resort of most firms.

Differentiated positions are based either on a set of activities that are different from those of competitors, or on similar activities that are performed in a different way. For example, a self-service coffee shop might decide to install a bar and play club-type music, or it could simply focus staff selection and training on exceptional customer service. Instead of fighting for one winning condition, differentiation offers no limit to the conditions for success. There is an inevitable trade-off against potential market size, but this is a small price for the competitive shelter that differentiation provides.

What is the power of differentiation, the significance of being different? In an important sense the firm that differentiates is granted a 'monopoly' – to the extent that the features of the differentiated position have no adequate substitute. This 'monopoly power' depends on the strength of differentiation in the perception of consumers and on the positional proximity of competitors. The key concept is substitution: the extent to which available alternatives can become the customers' preferred choice. This, in turn, determines the options for premium pricing. The differentiated firm can achieve wider profit margins but only at the expense of constrained sales. The severity of this trade-off depends on the effectiveness of the differentiation and the pressure from competitors.

Focus-based strategies offer the same choice between cost leadership and differentiation, but in the context of a single market segment or market niche. Sometimes the goal is to harvest profit in a small market, but other times the hope is rapid market growth as a life cycle begins.

In terms of generics, it follows that strategy is either about differentiating and obstructing competitors so that differential 'monopoly' can be exploited or about facing up to the competitors and defeating them on cost – or about judicious combinations of both. We have discussed (Chapter 7) Porter's view that strategies 'stuck-in-the-middle' between cost leadership and differentiation yield relatively inferior returns. Cost-based strategy only rewards those firms that are real cost leaders while a differentiation strategy requires acute positioning to build a secure plateau of added value.

But critics of Porter's view argue that a hybrid strategy based on elements of cost focus and elements of differentiation can give rise to a sustained competitive advantage. This apparent paradox may be explained by the idea of market fit. A pure cost leadership or differentiation strategy usually has a clear target market even if it is widely defined. A hybrid strategy often depends for its success on cost leadership in some parts of the value chain and differentiation in others. If such a strategy becomes confused, blurred or compromised, then Porter's view of 'stuck-in-the-middle' is likely to be justified.

Positioning for demand

The remaining key factor is the pattern of demand. Usually, centres of heavy demand are heavily positioned, while areas of lighter demand are more lightly positioned. Isolated concentrations of demand are classic niches, especially attractive if they may later (or sooner) expand. A feature of a niche market is that one firm may gain strong incumbency advantages (explained in Chapter 8).

Choosing zones of demand to form target markets is a critical part of strategy. It is often observed that there is a strategic trade-off between attractiveness of demand pattern and the relative intensity of competition. This is true, but the effect can be counteracted. Returns flow from attractive segments when the firm's capabilities achieve a high degree of relative strategic fit in the chosen market. Fit simultaneously allows the alchemy of added value and its protection through unique codings of capability linkage. We see here the importance of both the positional and resources approaches in gaining competitive advantage.

When a firm identifies and occupies a position that is uncrowded (or vacant), and when a high degree of fit can be achieved, then an exceptional competitive advantage may be secured. Its sustainability will depend on the extent to which the firm's capabilities in occupying that position are distinctive and non-replicable. Of course, if the position is obviously attractive and draws competitors who all adopt similar strategies and display similar sets of capabilities, then supernormal profits will be competed away and the value all released to the consumer. However, this does not in any way contradict the potential value of a strong fit between internal capabilities and a well-judged position.

Porter's 'five forces model'

A position only has strategic value if it can be successfully defended against erosion by competitive forces. We saw earlier how the possession of any significant competitive advantage that is remotely contestable will always attract predators. Porter (1980) offers his 'five forces model' to explain the generic means by which competitive advantage – and added value – can be eroded.

The threat of new entrants to the industry depends on the height of entry barriers relative to the levels of competitive advantage enjoyed by existing players. These realities of market entry form a

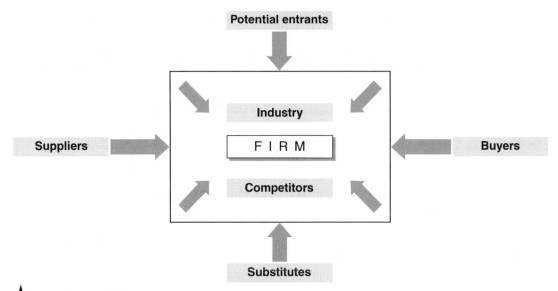

Figure 11.2 Porter's five forces model

kind of threshold wall over which new entrants must climb. Entry to some industries involves heavy capital costs which, once incurred, are 'sunk' or difficult ever to retrieve. Economies of scale (see Chapter 20) may also mean that a substantial market share must be achieved before a competitive average cost base can be reached.

There are also many ways in which the systems and relationships of incumbent firms set up resistances to new entrants. Brand and customer loyalty may be strong, switching costs (customer costs of changing supplier) may be high, distribution channels may be entrenched. Finally, there is the risk of retaliation. Incumbents may attack new entrants with their marketing power, including predatory pricing in some form.

The bargaining power of buyers and suppliers depends on the potential for substitution. Where buyers or sellers have good access to reasonably close substitutes, then they will tend to enjoy greater power in the market. If the options for substitution are limited or problematic, then their power is correspondingly reduced.

The threat of substitutes extends the substitution principle from sellers and buyers to the product itself. Every product is, to some degree, a substitute for every other. It follows that products representing the closest substitutes – even if they are outside the industry's perceived boundaries – pose a competitive threat. What restrains the force of substitution is only the lesser price–value performance offered by other products. The danger from substitutes comes when these relative ratios change. This can occur slowly, as consumers gradually reassess their balance of price and value between products or technologies. It can also happen very suddenly, as a tipping point is reached and demand 'pours' from one industry or product to another.

Rivalry among existing firms varies between industries and over time. The firms within an industry are necessarily in a state of dynamic opposition as they seek strategies to gain advantage in terms of profit margin or market share. The intensity of competition changes as opportunities for gaining advantage open and close. The competitive arena is also highly interactive. As the strategy

Le Train Grande Vitesse (TGV)

Back in the late 1970s, French railways (SNCF) embarked on a massive capital project: to build a completely new direct line between Paris and Lyons with trains running at 250 kph.

The new service – complete with computerised reservations – was launched in 1981, cutting the journey time to around two hours. It was an immediate success, reducing car journeys and taking over 30% of the corresponding air travel market. The TGV network has been expanding ever since.

of one firm cuts into the market share of rivals, so they are likely to launch counter-strategies in retaliation or self-defence.

The overall effect of competition depends on the weapons used and the competitive structure of the industry. Where competition involves releasing cost–value surplus to the customer, then relative profitability is likely to fall among all firms in the industry. Competition through cutting price is particularly unstable and can quickly escalate into price warfare. Offering improvements in the quality or quantity of a product without a corresponding increase in price can also drive down profits. Competition through increasing cost–value surplus, however, can benefit the industry. Advertising campaigns, more efficient distribution and advances in design and technology may reduce costs, expand overall sales and open new routes to differentiation.

The intensity of competition in an industry runs along a spectrum on which relative stability may exist for long periods. Yet sudden outbreaks of competitive activity can intensify and then subside or may escalate into successive waves of attack and counter-attack. These patterns have complex origins, but there are some important underlying drivers.

First, it must be recognised that it is in the nature of a market economy that firms are in competition. Unless a monopoly exists, every firm faces the reality of consumer choice and the threat of substitution. There is therefore competitive pressure on every firm, which is always liable to erupt into open warfare. The extent of opportunity and the degree of need for competitive gains are critical factors. Opportunity is created by changes in the balance of strengths and weaknesses between competitors, so that the possibility of gain at acceptable risk emerges. The perceived gains from active competition are the driver from behind. A firm may want access to new markets; it may seek economies of scale; it may have excess capacity and need contributions to fixed overheads. Some firms also become committed to staying in a market and fighting as a result of prior strategic decisions or heavy costs of exit.

Yet competitive interaction has its own dynamics. Firms whose power is evenly balanced, with weak differential boundaries between them in terms of products and markets, are more prone to intensify competition when provoked. When a firm does decide to increase competitive pressure on its rivals, it does not know how they will react. A degree of gamesmanship is involved as events unfold through the power of feedback. An aggressive move may be met with an amplified response, which is then amplified yet again in the spiral of competitive intensity that follows. Equally, an initiative may meet a muted response where the spiral works downwards to stability.

These patterns are extremely difficult to predict and represent part of the risk built in to competitive activity. Once again we can see the difference between perceiving the firm as a machine that may be complicated but is ultimately knowable, and perceiving the firm as a living entity where outcomes lie beyond calculation.

In a sense, Porter's five forces model is a classification scheme for the threat of substitution that faces every firm in a competitive market. But business strategy is the art of being first choice: switching every customer preference upwards and tipping seconds into first. In this battle to tilt substitution in favour of the product and not away, Porter's model systematises the analysis and prompts both the defence of weaknesses and the exploitation of strengths.

In a five forces analysis, the firm's strong and weak flanks are usually exposed. Often it is only one or two of the five forces that are found to be critical, thus helping to focus the thrust of competitive strategy. A weakness of the model is its emphasis on the industry as a whole as opposed to the specific firms within the industry. Profitability and competitive resilience do vary by industry, but depend more intimately on individual firms with their different histories and capabilities.

How are competitors locked out?

If a firm was able to prevent any competitor from entering its market, then even low-quality output inefficiently produced could still enjoy high margins and high sales together. Given the reality of contestable markets and the consequent pressure of competition, a firm must drive up value and protect its extension into sales.

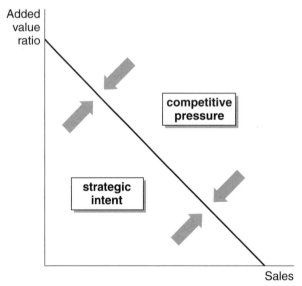

Figure 11.3 Added value and competition

There is ultimately no secure way in which competitors can be locked out of any market, but the threat of substitution can be obstructed in a number of ways. Incumbency or prior occupation of a position appears rudimentary as a defence, yet can be surprisingly robust. Even if the incumbent firm lacks any legally non-contestable assets, such as copyrights or patents, it may still benefit from other minor 'monopolies', for instance, a hotel with a sea view. Over time incumbent firms build increasingly complex networks of links with creditors, suppliers and customers that are difficult for challengers to match or dislodge. These links are further strengthened by the 'soft' defence of reputation which is not easily reproduced, especially in the short run. Finally, the incumbent has usually moved to the upper plateau of the relevant experience curves, which represent a steeply graded defence against would-be competitors.

Connected with experience curves is one of the toughest locks on the competitive door: the accumulation of proprietary knowledge, skills and capabilities. These become interrelated and mutually reinforcing in a pattern of what Porter (1996) calls internal fit. Often, these capabilities develop a high strategic value as they combine to form a core competence that can establish competitive advantage across a range of applications (see Chapter 8). Profitability becomes a source of positive feedback as retained profits are reinvested in the business and help raise the threshold of acquired defence.

Rapid movement can also be an effective way to escape from predators. Firms with the necessary agility and flexibility can make a high-speed strategic 'getaway' just as one or more competitors believe they are gaining ground. This may involve exiting or entering a market, stretching capabilities in unexpected directions and announcing alliances or acquisitions. Fast strategic driving disorientates competitors and may even throw them off the road.

Finally, softer qualities can also form effective blocks to predatory competition. As Deal and Kennedy (1982) suggest, a firm develops a culture to support its chosen means for adding value. Organisational cultures are notoriously difficult to change, let alone copy, and finding an alternative culture that works as well or better may involve challenging all the ground rules in a given market. Even more intangible, but no less important, may be the sense of mission or organisational purpose that runs like a pulse of energy through a particular firm. Such defences cannot be unpacked or replicated: they are often not understood by competitors, and not fully understood even by the firm itself.

12 Macroeconomic uncertainty

The circular flow model

The economy embraces all sources of demand and supply and any devices for their regulation. It forms a system of interdependent dynamics driven by consumers, firms and the government sector. In effect, the economy is a vast network of market-embedded transactions, each of which helps direct resources towards their most efficient allocation. The UK economy is a system within a system: it functions in terms of itself, as a member of the European Union and as part of the global economy.

In order to appreciate how it works, it is important to expose the basic dynamic cycle on which its operation depends.

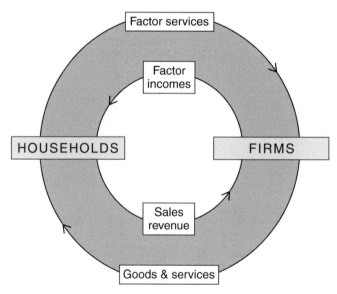

Figure 12.1 Circular flow pattern: simple model

Consider a simple economy without government or trade. Firms and households are in a mutually dependent relationship. Households demand goods and services. That demand is made 'effective' by the incomes earned from the output of those products. A basic circular flow exists in terms of money and goods or services.

In practice, households will save some part of their income while firms will invest some part of their revenue. Once government is introduced, households will lose part of their income in taxation but firms will experience additional demand from government expenditure (e.g. provision of healthcare). Finally, with the introduction of trade, households will spend a part of their income on imports, while firms will receive revenue from their exports.

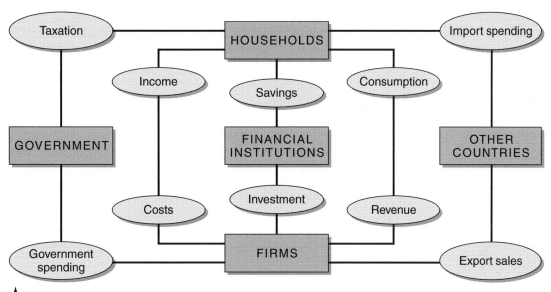

Figure 12.2 Circular flow pattern: full model

The business cycle

This system is the fundamental circulatory mechanism for the transmission of demand and supply. It is clear at once that unlike the simple model, this real-life system is unstable. In the simple model, all money paid for factor services (using the factors of production) is returned by purchasing the output of those same factors. In other words, what is produced generates the income that ensures its own purchase. In the full model there is no such guarantee. Aggregate demand (AD) (i.e. the sum total of buying decisions) now depends on a series of variables:

AD = Consumption (C) *plus* investment (I) *less* saving (S)
　　　　　plus government spending (G) *less* taxation (T)
　　　　　plus exports (X) *less* imports (M)

Suppose that demand and supply in the economy are in balance: what is being produced is also being sold. Then households increase their savings, or the government increases taxes, or demand shifts in favour of foreign products and there is a rise in imports. Perhaps even two or three of these events happen together. Supply is now greater than demand. Stocks are likely to build and output will be cut back. Some firms may cut prices and see profits fall. Given excess capacity and falling profitability, investment will be cut back and staffing reduced. As households and supplier firms find their incomes reduced, so they too will spend less. Demand falls again in a negative feedback loop. Pessimism among business decision takers grows. A downward spiral has begun. The economy is likely to contract.

Equally, of course, the whole process may work in reverse. A rise in investment or government spending or exports will stimulate increased business activity and the expansion of capacity. The result will be positive feedback and the beginning of an upward spiral. The economy is likely to expand.

It follows that aggregate demand is the essential 'current' that animates the economy and that changes in its level can have very favourable and unfavourable consequences. The aggregate for measuring changes in the size of an economy is *Gross Domestic Product* (GDP), meaning the value of all the goods and services produced in an economy over one year. GDP is equivalent to the *national income*, since production must generate factor incomes equal to its value.

Economic performance in Poland and Ireland, 1990–2000

GDP in 1990 = 100*	1990	1992	1994	1996	1998	2000
Poland	100.0	95.5	104.2	118.2	132.5	143.3
Ireland	100.0	105.3	114.4	135.6	163.2	201.6

*Data adjusted for constant purchasing power

Source: UN Economic Survey of Europe

In practice, aggregate demand tends to move in a cyclical pattern where boom conditions tip into a downswing, which leads to a slump, which in turn tips into an upswing, which leads to a boom.

However, in most modern economies these cycles are strung along an upward trend that in the long run represents cumulative economic growth. The UK economy, for example, grew over most of the 20th century at a compound rate of about 1.5 per cent. This was enough to increase GDP and associated living standards by around four and a half times. Of course, it should also be recognised that the underlying trend in GDP can be stagnant or downwards over quite long periods.

Income elasticity

It is inevitable that the effect of macroeconomic patterns on individual firms will vary widely. Some firms will be very subject to the operation of specific variables within the system. Road construction firms are likely to be sharply affected by changes in the level of government expenditure. Car exporters are heavily dependent on the strength of the American and continental European economies.

Almost all firms are significantly affected by movements in aggregate demand and national income. The measurement of sensitivity to changes in household incomes is income elasticity of demand:

$$\text{Income elasticity of demand} = \frac{\%\ \text{change in sales}}{\%\ \text{change in incomes}}$$

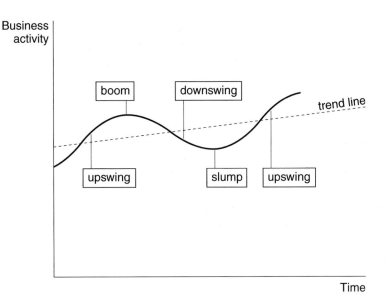

Figure 12.3 The business cycle

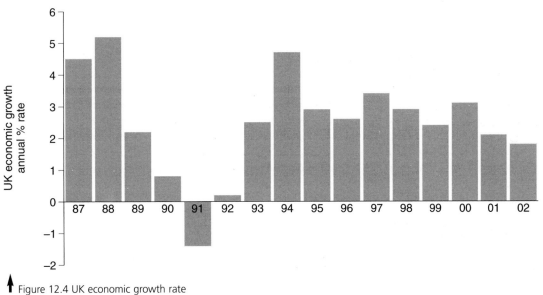

Figure 12.4 UK economic growth rate

Products for which this relationship is in the range zero to one are said to be 'normal goods'. In other words, an increase in demand of, say, 5 per cent would bring about an increase in sales of between 0 per cent and 5 per cent. Products where the change in demand is more than proportional – in this example where the increase in sales is greater than 5 per cent – are called 'luxuries'. There are also some cases of 'inferior goods' where the income elasticity is negative, meaning that as incomes increase, so demand falls. Paraffin for heaters would be an example.

Having some approximation for income elasticity attached to product types and even specific brands can greatly assist the formation of strategy against the backdrop of the business cycle. Rover

Group, for example, have used data of this type to assist production planning and to inform their marketing strategy. However, many other factors will also affect sales, including the interrelated decisions of competitors.

Meanwhile, the surging motion of every boom produces a degree of business 'froth' – business start-ups that are only viable in conditions at the top of the cycle. For example, a Thai restaurant in a country town might prosper during a boom, yet fail to survive a sustained downturn. Income elasticity can be very high for luxuries with reasonably close substitutes. The phenomenon is amplified by the high gearing of most households in relation to non-discretionary and discretionary spending. For example, a typical household may find that 90 per cent of its income is required to meet essential outgoings such as mortgage payments, routine bills and spending on basic foods. This leaves 10 per cent of income for all desirable but inessential items. Say the household income now increases by 5 per cent. The cost of essential outgoings does not change, but discretionary spending can increase by 50 per cent. This simple principle also works in reverse and is a major source of instability in the action of the business cycle.

The importance of the 'feel good' factor should not be underestimated. Keynes (1936) famously referred to the effect of 'animal spirits' on business decisions. The spending of firms and households is determined partly by present income and wealth, but also by expectations of future income and wealth. While the business cycle is in a steepening or sustained upturn, optimism often runs ahead of reality and there is high confidence in spending decisions by both households and firms. But even a slowing of the growth rate with its suggestion of a downturn to follow is enough to reverse that confidence and trigger a mood of caution and growing pessimism. Luxury products then suffer from an 'expectations elasticity' augmenting the simple income elasticity effect.

Next

Next was nearly destroyed by overexpansion, high gearing and the effect of the early 1990s' recession. Under the charismatic leadership of George Davies, the up-market fashion retailer had expanded furiously. In just four years from the launch in 1982, the number of outlets increased from seven at launch to a startling 1362, while the company entered new markets in fashion accessories, childrenswear, jewellery, household goods, gardening and catalogue sales. Turnover soared in the same period from under £50m to £1210m.

Until 1988 profits also increased rapidly. Then the long house price boom abruptly ended. In London and the South East, with the highest concentration of Next outlets, prices went into free fall. The Next lifestyle concept suffered from high income elasticity as sales and margins fell.

By 1990 the UK was in its longest and deepest recession since the Second World War. The interest rate nearly doubled from 8 per cent to 15 per cent, punishing Next with its high gearing. It was clear that the company had bought or rented far too much sales space, yet the value of its property portfolio was now seriously reduced.

After a dramatic change of chief executive, losses still reached £41m in 1990 while the share price touched bottom at 16p. Surprisingly, the company retained its independence and after severe retrenchment and major redundancies, Next began a long – and now famous – recovery.

Conversely, firms producing normal or necessity products are much less at risk from the business cycle. The supermarket operators, for example, are relatively 'recession proof'. Indeed, firms whose products have very low income elasticity may enjoy counter-cyclical effects. The food discounter Kwik-Save (now merged with Somerfield) achieved extremely good results during the deep recession of the early 1990s.

Regional and micro spirals

Just as national economies can follow cycles that are different from any broader global cycle, so regions and localities can experience their own cycles independently of the national trend. The more distinctive and self-referential the economic base, the more this phenomenon is likely. For example, the opening or closing of any business unit that is a large employer in the local economy sets off strong upward or downward spiral effects in terms of the circular flow. The more the unit uses local suppliers and outsources services in the area, the stronger the likely effect.

Once again, the issue is aggregate demand. The faster the incomes grow in an area, the faster the growth in net spending and the higher the likely investment in capital that should generate still higher incomes in future. Better transport and social infrastructure, such as schools and hospitals, tend to follow business investment, making a region or locality more attractive to incoming firms. Unfortunately, the same logic can work equally strongly in reverse, leading to the decline of certain regions, cities, inner-city zones and even small towns. In the language of the business cycle, it can be very difficult to shift a depressed locality into a sustained upturn despite pump-priming efforts by public agencies.

Cycle dynamics

Rather like weather systems, the dynamics of the business cycle are volatile and sensitive to changes in initial conditions. Economic forecasting carries very high potential value, but is subject to wide margins of error. No mathematical model has ever managed effectively to capture the complexities involved, and beyond the short term it is doubtful if forecasting has more value than merely offering some possible scenarios. Some commentators (e.g. Ormerod, 1996) consider that even reasonable accuracy is inherently impossible to achieve since the economy represents a non-linear chaotic system.

The role of government

The Great Crash of 1929 triggered a worldwide collapse in demand and by far the longest and most serious slump in modern history. By 1932–33 unemployment had reached over 16 per cent of the UK's registered workforce and GDP had fallen by 30 per cent in the USA and 4 per cent in the UK. Although interest rates and prices fell, consumer spending did not recover. Although disregarded at the time, JM Keynes argued that governments were not helpless in the face of a slump and their discretionary spending could kickstart the upward spiral of recovery.

In the event, for nearly 30 years after the war – a period of generally sustained underlying growth – various techniques of Keynsian demand management were applied with moderately favourable outcomes. However, the associated movement for social and industrial planning was much less successful.

This period ended in the 1970s with the quadrupling of oil prices, surging inflation and a new phase of high unemployment. The result was a fundamental change of policy in Britain and many other countries. From the 1980s the government distanced itself from demand management and concentrated instead on 'supply side policies' that stress the need for free factor markets and a favourable social, legal and physical framework for business enterprise. The hope was that downswings would be milder in such conditions, as governments become the facilitators rather than the planners of economic growth.

13 The total environment

Overview

The macroenvironment includes all the external forces that act on a firm. Taken together, these determine the underlying pattern of demand, the available means of production and the constraints within which the firm must make decisions. This total environment unfolds as a continuously changing landscape sculpted by people, institutions and events in the world. It is the same forces that shape the essential contours of demand and supply and so make and remake the marketplace in which firms compete. Because the complexity of these forces is beyond any calculable model, firms can only make sketches of what is likely to happen based on best information and a significant degree of intuition.

Indeed, the macroenvironment often fails to conform even to such academic principles as attempt to explain its action. In practice, it is a highly unstable background against which every business has to judge each move with an element of dead reckoning.

STEP analysis

STEP analysis explores the **s**ocial, **t**echnological, **e**conomic and **p**olitical domains of the external environment. It is also called PEST analysis, but STEP arguably provides a more effective ordering of the evidence. An effective STEP analysis involves a thorough scan of the external environment, capturing all changes that could present an opportunity or threat to the firm. The STEP domains are summarised in Figure 13.1 and explained more fully below.

The social domain

Social forces in the external environment include all the drivers of demand arising from the way people think, feel and live. An important dimension of that universe is formed by demography and social structure. The population size, its location, density and age structure help to define the patterns of demand. Equally significant are socioeconomic and ethnic groups, neighbourhood types and structures of work. These and other social forces continuously make and remake the contours of demand and how they shape outcomes in the market.

Even more fundamental are the cultural forces that interact with the population and social structure. Cultures contain the complex assumptions, beliefs, values and constructs of reality that characterise certain groups and types of people. In interacting with the population and social structure, these forces form the landscape of demand with its mass and niche markets that are positioned against by firms.

Social	**T**echnological
Economic	**P**olitical

 Figure 13.1 The STEP domains

The technological domain

The technological environment or the state of applied knowledge is a kind of marketplace of opportunity. Technology is about interaction with the tangible world around: finding better ways of doing things. It has many points of impact on the competitive performance of a business. Many costs depend on the effective choice and use of technology. Both the design and functionality of products depend on technological applications. Consider the production of all-terrain bicycles. Cost minimisation depends vitally on the use of new technologies in production. Meanwhile, design and functionality have been revolutionised by the creative application of technology.

Technological breakthroughs create whole new classes of products that drive the products of the superseded technology into niche markets or extinction. The effect of compact disks on vinyl records is an obvious example.

Technology has a huge impact on business processes of all kinds. Communications were revolutionised in the late 20th century and the same technologies have opened whole new vistas of marketing opportunity. Indeed, the internet and e-commerce have actually made certain types of physical transport unnecessary – which itself has undergone technology-driven improvements in efficiency and availability.

Lastly, technology is a major force shaping the nature and pattern of demand. Not only does technology define the range and form of products demanded, but arguably it also has an agenda of its own, generating new horizons of want that previously did not exist.

The economic domain

We have already explored the importance and complexity of the macroeconomy in shaping the landscape of demand. In terms of the circular flow that drives business activity, it is the level of aggregate demand that is critical. This is represented by consumption plus the net value of savings and investment, taxation and government spending and foreign trade.

Consumption itself depends largely on the level of incomes. An interdependent factor is the savings ratio (proportion of income saved), which is influenced by the rate of interest. This rate in turn affects the level of investment by firms (see Chapter XX). It also sets the cost of consumer credit which is an important element in aggregate demand. In Britain, the benchmark rate of interest is set by the Bank of England's Monetary Policy Committee, taking into account a variety of factors including the need to keep within targeted limits for inflation.

Taxation rates affect demand not only in their magnitude, but also through their incidence. Direct taxes that are charges on income are progressive or redistributive, falling proportionally more heavily on the higher income groups. Indirect taxes on spending, such as VAT, are regressive and work in the opposite direction since those on low incomes save less and spend a high proportion of their incomes on goods and services. Government spending affects the incomes of public sector employees and is also a key source of demand in capital goods industries. Significant government spending is directed to transfer payments (government revenues returned to households), such as social security benefits that are redistributive in effect from high to low income groups

Britain runs a deficit on visible trade in goods (£34bn or 3.3 per cent GDP in 2002) but a surplus on 'invisible trade' in services (£15.5bn or 1.5 per cent GDP in 2002). Export performance is partly a function of aggregate demand in overseas markets, just as imports grow in periods of rising home demand. Much also depends on Britain's relative competitiveness. This is obviously dependent on the outcomes of business strategy, but is also greatly affected by the rate of exchange, particularly against the dollar, euro and yen. For as long as Britain is outside the eurozone, this last factor will remain a major source of uncertainty. It is probably a reason why the majority of large firms as represented by the Confederation of British industry (CBI) is in favour of adopting the euro.

It should be remembered that the economic environment is increasingly interdependent between different countries. It used to be said that 'when America sneezes, Europe catches cold'. Contagious relationships of this kind now have wider implications than ever. With capital able to move freely in the world, there is a convergent pressure on rates of interest, taxation systems and regulatory regimes.

The political domain

Likely changes in government or changes in government policy are key factors in the political domain. Typical areas of concern for firms might be competition policy, minimum pay legislation or changes in the trading relationship between the UK and other countries. Any possible extensions or changes in European Union law may also be relevant.

Prospective government policy is set out in political party manifestos before elections, and actual policy is developed in reports and White Papers over the term of office. Unpredictable changes in policy may also occur following political crises or unforeseeable events, such as the terrorist attacks on the USA in September 2001.

STEP dynamics

Although the STEP classification is useful, it should be recognised that the shaping forces of the business environment are without clear boundaries and are highly interactive. For example, the technological development of mobile phones has spawned new patterns of social and business life. The technological development of effective search engines in the mid-1990s popularised the internet and allowed the emergence of home shopping. Such changes affect the structure and behaviour of the economy and require new regulatory laws.

STEP analysis is a way of placing labels and 'handles' on the systemic complexity of human society and its organisational linkages. The active variables are beyond calculation in number and most of them have unpredictable impacts on the behaviour of one another. This explains why macroenvironmental change is so difficult to forecast.

The macroenvironment and business opportunity

Because the forces of external change form such complex systems, it is not surprising that their tracking, interpretation and forecasting are difficult and prone to error. Some firms focus on the shorter-term surface patterns of fashion and style. These support short product life cycles where innovation is continuous, although they often reflect deeper underlying trends. Other firms, such as house builders, electrical appliance manufacturers or package holiday operators, aim to tap into the longer-term patterns of social change that will help guide product development over an extended timescale.

Other firms again seek the slowest-moving generics of demand and, in some cases, make these their own through the establishment of 'classic' products with low price elasticity and perennial popularity. Finally, there are always niche market specialists who develop acute understanding for the behaviour of a subculture or a highly specialised customer profile.

Seeing the whole picture

Is the macroenvironment an external reality that can be viewed as operating independently of the firm? In the case of small and medium-sized enterprises this is sometimes a fair assumption. However, when analysing larger organisations, the micro- and macroenvironments are strongly interactive. Examples abound. Fashion designers identify the start of a new social trend. Quickly they launch products to express the trend, and run advertising campaigns to intensify and spread its currency. The trend mutates and more products, more advertising and more media coverage shape and amplify its progress. Cause and effect blur. The fashion industry, the media industry, youth culture and even the technologies that transmit opinion are all tightly intermeshed.

Often, firms themselves define the external environment of other firms. Microsoft's operating system is the key external condition for thousands of firms. Television companies, mobile phone networks, airlines and supermarket chains are just examples of business worlds where individual firms routinely and even unknowingly set the terms of existence for many other firms. Business is intensely parasitic. Firms and industries continuously adopt one another as host environments and survive on an interactive basis.

Even agencies of change with a more obviously independent and external status reveal significant mutual dependency on closer analysis. For example, a change in interest rates may be announced by the independent Bank of England, but the change may reflect trends in the borrowing and spending decisions of households and the investment plans of firms. Investment levels themselves

Farewell to the village shop ◄─────

It is estimated that by 2000 78 per cent of all villages in England and Wales had no general store selling food. This occurred in spite of vigorous marketing initiatives and help from branded wholesalers such as Spar and Happy Shopper.

The external environment has become increasingly hostile to small-scale rural retailing. More and more families opt for the choice, value and convenience of the major supermarket chains. Among women, the increasing extent of employment combined with rising car ownership points away from use of the village shop. The associated social trend towards shopping in the evenings and on Sundays is also very difficult for rural shops to accommodate.

Some village shops have attempted to introduce more up-market lines such as cooked meats, cheeses and local produce where there is more opportunity to add value. Unfortunately the most affluent members of the community are least likely to be shopping locally on weekdays. Even retired people are increasingly mobile and likely to shop away from where they live.

Technology has not been helpful either. The supermarkets have gained further advantage from their lean inventory and electronic re-ordering systems. The appeal in rural areas of internet shopping with campaigns such as Tesco's 'Mouse-to-house' has further eroded the customer base of a typical village shop.

Sources: Council for the Protection of Rural England (CPRE)

depend on the underlying level of demand and the apparent prospects for sales in future. Demand depends on consumers' incomes and expectations of income in future, itself a variable with multiple dependencies across all its many links. And this only begins to unravel the tangle of cause and effect. What now stands independent of what? We have a complex, dynamic system in which forces can be identified but where outcomes are only ever a matter of probability. The unexpected will always be happening. This, of course, includes those truly unconnected events, the wild cards that are beyond extrapolation: accidents, natural disasters, or political discontinuities such as wars or revolutions.

Firms are, after all, the collective endeavour of human beings. As such, they are sizeable chunks of socially networked reality. The STEP factors are not independent forces acting from a closed system. They are actually connected dynamic systems where 'environment' is only a relative term. From the epicentre of any one system, all other systems become 'external'.

PART **C**

MARKETING

explained

14 Targeting the market

What is marketing?

Marketing was once considered to be mainly about selling. The firm had a product and that product needed to be sold – at a profit. Today's interpretation of the events leading up to a sale – and a repeating stream of sales – is more complicated and more interesting. Indeed, marketing has become one of the most popular dimensions of business, and record numbers of students are choosing it as a centrepiece to their studies. The word has entered our everyday language and, more significantly, it permeates our consciousness. What exactly does it mean?

The briefest definition is offered by Philip Kotler: 'meeting needs profitably'. The concept is more fully described by the Institute of Marketing:

> **Marketing is the management process involved in identifying, anticipating and satisfying consumer requirements profitably.**

This definition explains effectively what marketing aims to achieve, but does not crystallise a distinctive conceptual role for the marketing function. What, specifically, does marketing expect to achieve in the total business process of adding value? In this sense, marketing involves *translating capabilities into sales that add net value.* In other words, marketing is a connecting function. It links the firm's transformative potential with the forces of customer demand. It aims to do this in such a way that the value of outputs exceeds the cost of all corresponding inputs. It is not enough to find a market opportunity that *could* be fulfilled profitably. The need is to build the best possible relationship between such an opportunity and the firm's special capabilities.

Market orientation

In 1960 Theodore Levitt published an article in the *Harvard Business Review* called 'Marketing Myopia'. It has since been reprinted over 500 000 times and inaugurated a revolution in thinking about marketing. Levitt argued that too many companies were product orientated: their corporate energy was focused on their product and the need to find customers. Instead, they should be market orientated and begin not with a product but with the market. The wants and potential wants in the marketplace can then define a product that will sell from the outset. The US railroads, said Levitt, were suffering from a focus on railroads when they should be orientated to transportation. Similarly, the movie industry was preoccupied with film making when it should be orientated to entertainment. The key shift was to put the market, not the product, at the centre of the corporation. Products were expendable: the demand of customers was not.

As Levitt concedes, his basic ideas had been prefigured by Drucker (1954) and others. But Levitt showed how market orientation could drive a business and underpin its strategic success. In practice, Western firms were slow to become truly market orientated. In Japan, by contrast, the principle was well established. Indeed, it was Japanese penetration of Western markets that prompted a new status for marketing departments in the 1980s.

But being market orientated is not just a matter of carrying out market research and upgrading the marketing department. It involves a basic change of mindset and culture. Drucker remarked: 'There is only one valid definition of business purpose – to create a customer.' This goal is remote from the product-orientated organisation. In the UK today, banks, many professional services, and government agencies such as the NHS, are still in a process of transition.

However, market orientation needs thoughtful expression. The wants of a market may not chime with the capabilities of a firm. Sometimes these capabilities can be modified or extended, but there is no guarantee of success. Uncritical market orientation could lead a business to launch products that are uncompetitive in terms of cost or quality or both. The need, therefore, is to match the demands of the market with the capabilities of the firm. Then the catalyst of strategic fit can work.

Demand

No product can be sold – and therefore no value added – without the existence of demand. Crude demand is simply a want, but effective demand is the desire for a product in preference to something else – usually money in the form of a price.

However, for an exchange or sale to take place, the product must outperform its nearest rival. In other words, its perceived value must exceed the opportunity cost of its price. This relationship is made explicit in a simple demand function. In Figure 14.1 quantity of a product sold is now plotted against price. Unsurprisingly, as price is reduced, so more product is purchased. Price OP is relatively high and only OQ units are sold. When price is reduced to OP1, sales rise to OQ1. The original price, OP, carries a heavy opportunity cost for consumers (substitutes look attractive) and

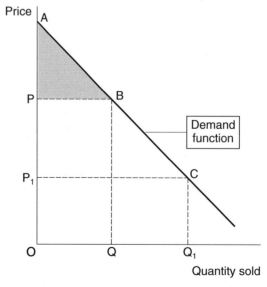

Figure 14.1 Demand and opportunity cost

only those expecting high levels of consumer value are willing to trade.

This is a common situation when a new technology or a new fashion is first introduced. A premium price deters most consumers from any purchase, but a determined few accept the loss of the other purchases they *could* have made and try the new product. For them the sacrifice (opportunity cost) is worthwhile.

At lower prices, this opportunity cost threshold is progressively overcome. Existing consumers buy more units of the product, while new consumers are drawn into the market and begin to buy. For each new purchase, the value offered by the product must still exceed the next-best alternative.

Notice that the demand function is a *frontier*. At a given price – say, OP in Figure 14.1 – each unit of the product purchased is worth more to the customer than they are paying. The extent of this surplus value is indicated by the path of the demand function above point B. The difference between consumer value and price paid (OP) is called consumer surplus. This is real consumer value above price conceded by the producer. It is represented by the shaded area in the diagram. Notice that at price P, the consumer surplus 'wedge' ends decisively at unit Q. The next unit *beyond* Q will not be purchased because its value to the consumer is *less than* the price. The demand function is actually an *opportunity cost frontier*.

This model is a key underpinning to marketing because it is opportunity cost frontiers that managers must detect and manipulate. Consumer surplus is the driver of all demand and the motive force behind any and every sale. As transactions in the market leave accumulations of consumer surplus, they create a reservoir of customer loyalty. The expectation of high value for money can become embedded in a brand and represent a formidable source of competitive advantage.

It is also clear that it is the goal in marketing a product to 'push' the demand function from left to right representing an increase in demand for a product right across a range of prices. As we shall see (in Chapters 16 and 17), the position and shape of the demand function have a key strategic significance.

Segmentation and targeting

Every business must begin by identifying or creating an effective demand. Finding this demand for some products is easy: Heinz can recognise the demand for canned soup, Cadbury's know there is a demand for milk chocolate. No market is completely universal, but these mass-market products are in very widespread demand. Most markets are more like a mosaic. Many different types of buyer exist, each with a different combination of preferences. At a simple level this can be seen with car manufacturers such as Ford: the Ka, Fiesta, Focus and Mondeo each appeal to a different group of customers. The common factor is the demand for a car, but the preferred combination of price and product benefits varies from group to group. Among those likely to buy a Focus, for example, the Ka has little appeal.

A market segment is any definable group of consumers who form part of a larger market. For example, professional and executive women who are single and under 30 might form a distinctive segment in the market for new cars. Some typical segmentation criteria are shown in the table overleaf.

Segmentation criteria

Criterion	Segmentation types
Demographic	gender, age group, family size, income, education
Geographic	country, city, region, neighbourhood
Psychographic	personality type, lifestyle
Behavioural	usage, loyalty, purchase occasion

This breakdown is far from exhaustive: there are almost limitless ways in which markets can be segmented. Most methods have some value but many segments would be too costly to target. However, there is a clear trend towards *niche marketing*.

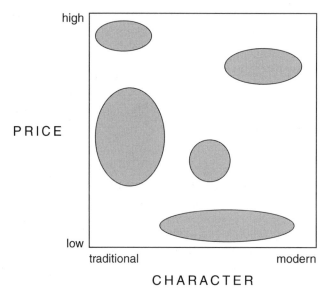

Figure 14.2 Furniture market segmentation

In Figure 14.2, a possible segmentation of the home furnishing market is based on price and character. The largest market appears to be for mid-price, mildly traditional furniture. A smaller but significant market exists for upper to mid-price modern furniture – occupied, perhaps, by Habitat. Constructing the segments is a matter of judgement. Essentially, a segment is a concentration of demand with common characteristics. Any segmentation criterion (e.g. age group) is really a convenient rationalisation for a 'want cluster'. There is also nothing final about the choice of segmentation criteria. Any market could be segmented in many ways. Normally the segmentation process is based on price and one or two key benefits that drive demand.

Mass and niche marketing

Henry Ford is reputed to have said that 'history is bunk', but when he broke with the craft tradition of car making and told his designers to create a car the average American could afford, he made history. From 1913 the Model T Ford was mass produced and opened a mass market. It pointed to the awesome power of specialisation and economies of scale to make affordable products by the million that almost everyone wants. Between 1908 and 1928 over 15 million Model T Fords left the giant factory at Highland Park, Michigan.

Yet, as General Motors demonstrated very soon after, people have different wants, and often the value added by meeting these preferences is greater than the cost. There are two main reasons. First, the better fit between product and preference adds value. Second, the seller is able to capture some of the consumer surplus necessarily conceded in a mass market. Put another way, many customers paying a low price would willingly have paid more. Segmentation allows some of this 'extra' value to be collected by the firm in the form of a premium price.

Strategically, the attraction of segmentation is its potential for competitive advantage through differentiation. By its nature, the process of meeting highly specific needs in the market is more complex and distinctive than producing for a mass market. A firm can develop special competence in meeting such needs. Furthermore, competition is often less intense within a segmented market.

Successful segmentation depends on the identification of different characteristics that allow superior match with both customer demand and with the firm's capabilities. It is strategically important that the match carries a degree of exclusivity. A strategic competitive advantage depends on excluding competitors or decisively outperforming them if they are already active in the segment or break through its boundaries.

The selection of market segments to target is a critical strategic decision. The deciding factors are market attractiveness and capability 'fit'. Every niche or segmented market has in itself different characteristics that affect its attractiveness. These change continuously. The size of a segment can be understood in terms of its breadth – the area of a market described – and depth – the number of people in that market area. For example, if the market for pop music is segmented by age group, then the over-60s segment has substantial breadth but lacks depth – relatively little demand is distributed over a wide market area. By contrast, a segmented market for reggae may be more concentrated within an ethnic group.

Much also depends on segmental dynamics. Segments can expand and contract quickly. The prospects for a segment's size are difficult to assess but critical to attractiveness. An ideal scenario occurs when a firm enters a niche market early, establishes pre-eminence and then experiences rapid growth in the segment's breadth and depth. The Body Shop in the 1980s came close to this model.

The other criterion is the level of competitive intensity within the segment. Generally, segments with significant potential will attract competing firms. This splits market share and reduces returns. The need, therefore, is to identify hidden segments or niche markets with hidden potential. These will still need defending from subsequent entrants. The only alternative is to claim and defend a segment with non-contestable barriers to entry such as a legal franchise.

Market intelligence

The process of segmentation and determining segmental strategy clearly depends on knowledge of markets. This is obtained through the process of market research and the operation of market information systems.

At the heart of all market information gathering is the customer. When a product sells it is because it represents the best available choice to satisfy a want. Customer choice is the stuff of demand. It follows that a firm needs information about every factor that drives demand and every factor that decides whether, for that demand, the firm is the best provider. There are three potential flows of marketing information as indicated in Figure 14.3.

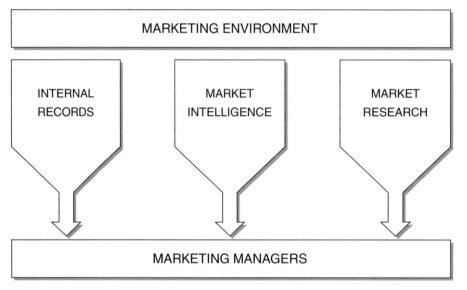

Figure 14.3 Marketing information system

Internal data is the cheapest and most readily accessible. Every business accumulates huge amounts of data relating to costs, sales and customer response as well as any earlier research studies. External data or marketing intelligence concerns the firm's marketing environment. Again, it is gathered automatically inside the firm but may be difficult to retrieve. The firm's staff should be a major source of knowledge and useful perceptions. In practice, it is often necessary to train staff in the collection and communication of intelligence and to build a supporting culture (see Chapter 31).

External parties, including suppliers, key customers and even competitors, can all be a rich source of information. In addition, data can be obtained from many published and on-line sources without charge. Surveying change in the external environment is vital to shaping and guiding products to their target markets. It is also a prime route to the identification of emerging or hidden segments.

Varsity Hotels ◄

This group of smaller, upmarket hotels situated in university towns needs a continuous flow of marketing information. The target market is affluent, older people who seek traditional surroundings and discreet luxury for short stay leisure and business. How are customer preferences changing? How could facilities be further enhanced? What will be the impact of increased competition from modern luxury hotels? How can the chain guard against a recession?

Market research

Marketing information from both internal and external sources should be feeding continuously into a firm's decision-making process. However, questions and problems arise that need the specific project-based methods of market research. Since this is a skilled and specialised process, most firms commission external agencies.

The starting point must be a clear formulation of the problem to be researched. This should prompt a costed research plan that will address the agreed objectives. It is likely that this will involve the collection and collation of both secondary (existing) data and primary (original research) sources. Putting secondary data into the context of distinctive research objectives can yield original insight. Primary research is more costly and time-consuming, but is focused on a unique data search that may be difficult for competitors to access or copy.

McCarthy & Stone ◄

Towards the end of the 1970s, the building firm McCarthy & Stone began to offer housing developments exclusively designed to meet the needs of retired people. These gave the buyers the independence of their own home, with the proximity of other elderly people and the reassurance of a resident warden. The firm had identified an expanding segment in the housing market. The numbers of elderly people were growing. The retired were remaining able-bodied and living longer. More people were enjoying company pensions and had the prior benefit of owning a home that had risen substantially in value.

Information and competitive advantage

Perhaps even more important in competitive terms is the market knowledge *already* inside the organisation. Information and research systems make knowledge appear to be disembodied, held in files or databases like a discrete commodity. In reality, much of the most distinctive knowledge is held in the minds and memories of key personnel and within their interaction as teams. Indeed, the key knowledge factors may lie beyond information, being more related to the organisation and interactivity of evidence. Pattern recognition, for example, can be very subtle but crucial in decision making. This kind of 'soft data' is mostly impossible for competitors to reproduce but may be a core success factor in project after project.

Scaled-down versions of all these approaches are also possible for small business where proprietors or employees can generate informal and cheaper flows of data. Marketing information systems always carry the problem of conveying the right information in the right form to the right people at the right time. The widespread use of information technology had greatly increased the availability of data and has often reduced its cost. The challenge is to achieve intelligent communication of data and its effective use by marketing managers. It is in these distinctive lines of transmission and exploitation that competitive advantage is likely to lie.

15 Marketing strategy

Overview

Marketing strategy is the plan for matching the firm's capabilities with demand. This means building, exploiting and defending competitive advantage generated through the strategic fit achieved.

Strategy may involve responding to change in the target market. It may mean extending or switching target markets and it may imply the development and launch of new products. The goal is the same: to align the firm's capabilities with the best available opportunities in the marketplace.

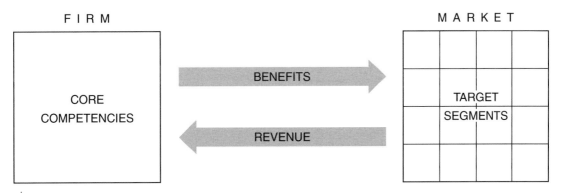

Figure 15.1 Foundations of marketing strategy

In turn, this requires investigation and analysis of target markets. The intelligence yielded forms and shapes the marketing mix. The process is dynamic: as the reality and understanding of the segments change, so the firm's capabilities can be developed and extended. In this way the mix is reconfigured to keep the value-adding fit at its most effective.

The strategic model

The essence of marketing strategy is finding a fit between the firm's core capabilities and the characteristics of demand in the market. The extent of competitive advantage depends on the quality and applicability of this fit relative to the offerings of competitors.

There is a simple logic to this scenario. We have seen that in any market a firm must find ways to combine inputs such that the resulting output has a value to consumers greater than its cost. It is the gap between cost and value that can be split by price into surplus for the consumer and profits for the firm. The dimensions of the total gap are inherently unstable and always liable to be squeezed or undermined by competitors.

The firm must therefore project its distinctive capabilities in a sharp focus on to the target market. The matching of capabilities with the market adds value. The distinctive and exclusive nature of the alignment protects that value and represents the competitive advantage.

Figure 15.2 Model for marketing strategy

In Figure 15.2 the firm contains a range of distinctive core competencies. These are directed at chosen segments in the target market. The added value generated is protected by a competitive advantage that resists the pressure of competition. Meanwhile, the whole process is continuously buffeted and realigned by the forces of external change. Insight and flexibility are therefore at a premium.

Industry analysis

We have seen (Chapter 14) that markets are segmented using a range of criteria. The segments identified are necessarily artificial. The same consumer may be included in a range of different segment constructions, each of which captures different common wants or sources of value. The boundaries to segments are also arbitrary. They are lines of convenience that help locate 'pools' of demand.

In exploring segmental 'maps', the firm aims to discover markets where the 'fit' between internal capabilities and market demand is greatest. One approach to this process was developed by General Electric in the 1970s. The *GE Grid* plots the attractiveness of the industry against the firm's relative business strengths.

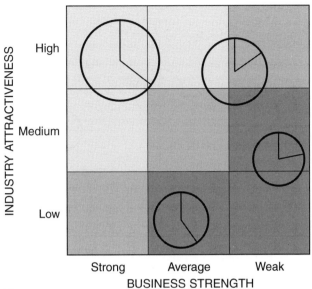

Figure 15.3 The GE Grid

Some key component factors

Industry attractiveness	Business strengths
market size	market share
market growth rate	product competitiveness
average profit margins	cost/price competitiveness
competitive intensity	market knowledge

The ideal position is clearly high industry attractiveness and high business strength. The grid's classification of strategic opportunity emphasises the importance of *fit* between the attractions of the market and the capabilities of the firm. If the firm lacks business strength, then even a highly attractive industry scores a medium rating. Strategic business units (SBUs) are represented on the grid by circles, each with diameter proportional to market size. The firm's market share is indicated by the relevant segment size. Use of the grid also involves a forward-looking perspective. How are the elements of industry attractiveness and business strength changing? Are market shares expanding or declining? How far could SBU positioning be improved through strategic action? The resulting analysis and evaluation assist the formation of marketing strategy.

The Boston matrix

During the 1970s, Bruce Henderson and the Boston Consultancy Group designed their model for the strategic analysis of a business portfolio. This was based on the assumption that profitability flows from a combination of market share and market growth. The resulting matrix has four

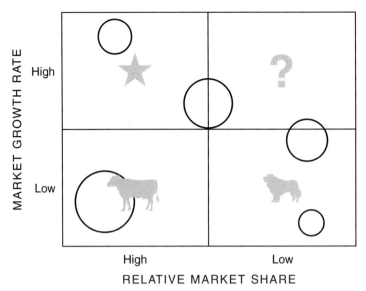

Figure 15.4 The Boston matrix

quadrants (see Figure 15.4), on which SBUs are represented by circles, the diameter of which corresponds to existing sales.

Stars have high market share in a high growth market. Sustaining their success often requires heavy cash outflows.

Cash cows are established success stories with a high share of a slower growing market. They usually generate strong cash inflows.

Question marks have a low share of a fast-growing market. Given the right support they may turn into stars but this is not assured.

Dogs have a low share of a low growth market. With minimal marketing costs, profitability may be maintained, but otherwise such business units are usually sold or closed.

The model is analysed in a dynamic context with each SBU presenting a range of strategic options. A *build* strategy means injecting resources to gain market share while a *hold* strategy limits commitment only to sustaining share at the current level. A *harvest* strategy suggests exploiting the positive cashflow of an SBU without further investment and a *divest* strategy implies withdrawal from the market.

In an archetypal dynamic pattern, question marks turn into stars which fade into cash cows and may end their lives as dogs. In practice, all kinds of patterns are possible but firms do need to achieve balance in their overall portfolio. For example, cash cows are usually needed to meet the expense of supporting stars and selected question marks.

The product life cycle

The sales profile of a product can usefully be represented as its life cycle with five identifiable stages:

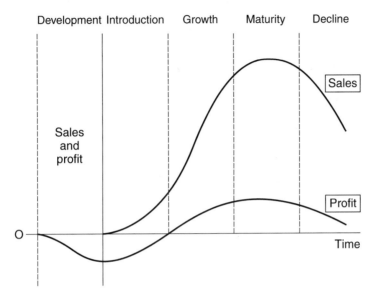

⬆ Figure 15.5 The product life cycle

During the development phase, sales are zero against increasing levels of investment. The introduction stage sees a selected product reach the market. Sales increase only slowly but promotion costs are typically heavy. However, the growth stage sees take-off in the market and a steep rise in profitability. Eventually the maturity stage is reached where sales plateau and profit begins a down-grade as competition intensifies. The decline stage sees both sales and profits falling until the product is eventually deleted.

However, marketing management often intervenes during the maturity stage with an extension strategy to re-launch the product. This may involve technical upgrading, remodelling or repackaging. The hope is a new growth stage and extended life cycle.

In practice, the product life cycle varies widely in its timescale and shape. The more broadly a product is defined, the longer its typical life cycle. At the other end of the spectrum, novelty products and narrowly defined brand variants are prone to brief and volatile lives.

The model is valuable as an archetype and emergence of its characteristic features can provide a useful prompt for marketing strategy. Unfortunately it is often difficult to identify the onset of life cycle stages with any certainty. Meanwhile it is often the case that little is known about the effectiveness of the levers available to influence a life cycle profile. As Kotler (1996) points out, in the relationship between marketing strategy and the life cycle, it is easy to confuse cause and effect.

Segmental dynamics

One critical effect of external change is its dynamic effect on segmental scale and structure. Segments expand and contract at widely differing speeds. Segmental boundaries form and dissolve while segmentation criteria rise and decline in significance.

This all implies an emerging stream of opportunities and traps. We saw in Chapter 14 that pioneering occupancy of a segment may lead to dominance of a profitable niche market or first mover advantage in a developing mass market. Alternatively, a smaller pioneer may attract a favourable bid from a slower moving but larger competitor.

The relative attractiveness of a segment also depends on the current and prospective intensity of competition. But initially attractive segments can see their profit potential largely eroded away by waves of competitors who offer differential advantages that eventually converge on commodity status. Ultimately, only the lowest-cost operators are likely to survive.

There is also the risk of marketing strategy carrying the firm into markets beyond the scope of its core capabilities. There is no reason why capabilities cannot evolve or be grafted on to an existing repertoire, but the risks are real. A learning curve is likely to be involved, rates of return often fall and hungry competitors are ready to attack those who struggle. Forging new capabilities can also be a distraction, weakening performance in the more familiar markets already served.

Segmental strategy

The same principles can be applied to the selection of segments within an industry. The ideal segment is therefore highly attractive in terms of demand levels, growth and the relative absence of competition. It also has characteristics that make it a close fit with the firm's actual or potential capabilities. The result would be a very high rate of return. In reality, the most attractive segments will always tend to host a high level of competition. There is, however, always the possibility of finding an overlooked segment or gap in the market that is rich with potential demand. Thus, the most promising segments are those that:

- offer intense demand where strong competition can be countered with outstanding capabilities.
- are innovative in character, relatively undiscovered and a focus of expanding or latent demand.

As always, a sustainable competitive advantage is crucial. In the long run, superior returns within any segment depend on the ability to exclude or outmanoeuvre competitors.

Since a segmental pattern exists in almost all markets, a firm must set a segmental strategy. This will depend on the size of the firm, the size of the market and the quality of fit between demand and capabilities. A mass-marketing approach requires a product with wide-ranging appeal able to deliver consistent and competitive benefits to all but minor segments in the total market.

By contrast, a multi-segment strategy involves targeting segments or segment clusters with a differentiated product. These are designed, through their marketing mix, to maximise advantage in their chosen segments. Finally, a single-segment focus on a niche market allows competitive advantage through specialisation. The business is able to develop advanced expertise in satisfying customer demand within the segment.

Mass marketing is an attractive strategy where the market is fairly homogenous and the firm can gain competitive advantage, either through cost leadership or through a strong brand. For smaller firms without these strengths, attempts to reach a mass market are usually dangerous.

A niche market may allow the small or medium-sized enterprise to develop in its own domain. This process is often based on highly specialised knowledge of the market. A high level of added value may be achieved with relatively little competitive pressure. Niche marketing can also act as a strategic bridgehead to neighbouring segments or even a mass market. Many key product types and allied patterns of consumption start as niche markets pioneered by smaller firms. Sometimes, the niche expands dramatically to form a large-scale market in itself. In other cases, the niche experience provides the firm with the necessary leverage to enter related segments with snowballing gains in scale and brand strength.

Mass and niche markets offer sharply contrasting demand profiles. In mass markets, a relatively generic product and intense competition are expressed in high price sensitivity (high price elasticity of demand). A 'going rate' tends to prevail and improving margins above this level is only possible with a strong brand or exceptional cost advantages. Niche markets, on the other hand, invite differentiated products with barriers to substitution. The market size may be fairly small, but demand is relatively price insensitive (low price elasticity of demand). Even a high margin may leave product enthusiasts with an ample consumer surplus and corresponding brand loyalty.

Despite the sometimes contrary impression given by models, market segmentation patterns are never static. They evolve continuously – and discontinuously. Segments expand and contract, intensifying and weakening in competitive pressure. New segmentation criteria become more relevant as markets are redefined with corresponding advantages to those who reorientate first. A close embrace between the business and its customers is important for its potential to add value, but is also critical in reading the signposts of segmental change.

Positioning

Why does a product sell? What are the attributes of a product that its customers most value? Exploring the value of a product through the eyes of its customers builds on the concept of market orientation (see Chapter 14) and creates a powerful strategic tool. The idea of market positioning was first described by Al Ries and Jack Trout in 1981. Essentially, it 'maps' the firm and its brands in terms of customer perception. A wide range of criteria can be used in the process, including the product's attributes, usage, associations and comparisons with other brands. A simple example might be a hotel mapping itself and competitors relative to perceived cost and character.

In effect, product positioning is the customer view of targeting. A product or brand is aimed at chosen target. Positioning is getting a 'fix' on where the product has 'landed'. To be meaningful, this must be reported by the customer: hence the customer-led criteria for positioning.

When firms segment the market, they group customers together through defined characteristics. The question then arises: how do customers perceive the product? Customers do not generally segment markets, but they do position each brand on a kind of mapping system in their minds.

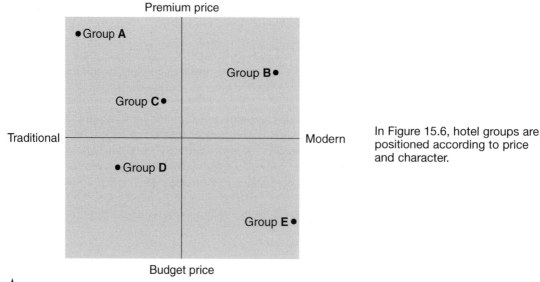

In Figure 15.6, hotel groups are positioned according to price and character.

Figure 15.6 Bi-polar positioning map

What is a good positioning? This should be closely related to the target zone of segmental strategy. It is based on strength of demand, intensity of competition and the matching of core capabilities. In practice, an active positioning strategy is needed since brands do not always 'land' in the market where firms intend, and are then prone to drift and displacement as events in the market unfold.

Often, a firm wants to strengthen the position currently occupied. This may mean rooting the brand's core identity more deeply in customers' minds through advertising and sales promotion. Shifting a brand's position – repositioning – may thus be a matter of relatively fine adjustment, but it can involve radical reinvention. For example, MFI was positioned as a mass-market retailer of low-cost flat-packed furniture. During the late 1990s the brand was repositioned to concentrate on the supply of fitted kitchens and bathrooms. Occasionally, a firm may try to 'de-position' a competitor. This involves an active plan to discredit a competitor's place in the perception of customers. The risk is obviously retaliation.

Dream

Cadbury's launched Dream (2001) into the female indulgence sector of the chocolate countline market. For the customer, Dream was positioned away from Milky Bar as a more sophisticated brand closer to Galaxy, yet more indulgent and more exotic.

Margin/share trade-off

A more basic strategic question confronting every business is the level of profit margin targeted relative to the market share or level of sales. Given a downward-sloping demand function, the trade-off is unavoidable. But its optimisation depends on marketing objectives and the expected development of the market itself.

In very general terms, a firm prioritises margin in a niche market and often at the introductory stage of the product life cycle. By contrast, it aims for sales and market share in a mass market or at the maturity stage of the life cycle. Plenty of variations in this pattern are possible. For example, a firm might enter the market with low prices and margins in order to build share, and then develop a brand presence in order to boost margins.

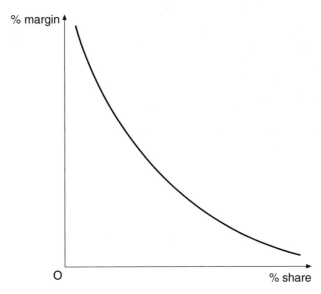

Figure 15.7 Typical margin/share trade-off

Thorntons ←

'A chocolate heaven since 1911' ran the strapline, but by the turn of the century Thorntons was in trouble. After rapid expansion in the 1990s, margins were falling steeply while ROCE had slipped to 11 per cent. In 2000, the new CEO, Peter Burdon, was facing a turnaround challenge.

Strategically, he considered that Thorntons had expanded too far and too fast, incurring heavy fixed costs that sales and margins could not support. His immediate priority was to restore profitability and in marketing terms, he now set a new strategy. Thorntons had not invested enough in its marketing mix, which in turn was poorly focused. The business operated in four distinct market segments: gifts; personal treat; family-share and children's. The new priority was to tailor the mix to each segment's different needs yet retain co-ordination and complementary benefits. There was also a need to smooth seasonal troughs in demand and ensure year-round sales in each segment. A particular aim was to re-merchandise the stores for stronger appeal to the core Thorntons customer: the family woman over 30. The goals of the new marketing mix were to increase footfall in the stores and raise the average spend on a year-round basis.

A year later, in 2001, performance had stabilised but not recovered. It was clear that Thorntons was under pressure from the widening availability of confectionery and growing competition from other gift sectors. On the other hand, UK spending on premium foods was increasing and the opportunity existed to 'stretch' the Thorntons brand across a wider range of 'sweet, special foods'.

The marketing strategy now focused on improving like-for-like sales with a simplified product range and accelerated new product development. The Thorntons brand was to be exploited further through a growing Café Thorntons chain and the production under licence of non-confectionery products such as cakes, trifles and puddings.

As margins began to improve, the share price bucked the market trend and moved strongly upwards.

16 Competitor analysis

The competitive arena

The competitive arena is often termed the 'industry' and experiences over time changing patterns of competition. A 'young industry' has its core product at early stages in the life cycle, with pioneering firms working out of niche markets. By contrast, a 'mature industry' has typically reached the stage of intense brand competition, merger activity and pressure on prices.

In developing a competitive strategy a business must be committed to understanding competitors with the same energy that is devoted to knowing customers. Sales are not achieved by the product, but by the customers' preference for the product *relative to the products of competitors*. Delivering value that is ahead of opportunity cost is the task of every marketing manager.

The first priority is to identify rivals and understand the nature of their competitive threat. Direct competitors – providing a comparable product in the same market – are normally well known. Beyond the immediate boundaries of the market lie firms offering different but related products. These indirect competitors offer bundles of benefits that are different yet still a potential substitute for the benefits of the industry product. A broader market view of competition embraces all indirect alternatives to the product. For example, a coach operator knows other firms in the charter and scheduled market, but the firm also faces indirect competition from railways, airlines and even car-hire companies. And the principle extends further: to some extent, all forms of transport offer some coincident benefits relative to coach travel. Indeed, even e-mail or video phones might affect sales if the firm defines its product in terms of communication rather than transport.

Competitor analysis

The marketing strategy of one firm cannot be set in isolation from other firms. The behaviour of competitors will hugely influence the viability of strategic options. In making an offering to potential customers, the key issue is the extent to which the offerings of the nearest competitor act as an effective substitute. This relative capability to act as a substitute is the opportunity cost experienced by every customer in buying a firm's product. In terms of marketing strategy, it is therefore essential to understand the existing and potential sources of substitution. These represent the energy 'force field' of competition.

Thus, the intensity of competition is a function of the potential for substitution. Where products are close substitutes, there is likely to be fierce competition between them. By the same principle, strategies that are similar are also likely to clash competitively. Where a competitive advantage is well protected, however, a competitive response is more likely to be defensive. It is a firm's relative *absence* of defence other than incumbent market share that tends to provoke an aggressive response towards new competitors.

In creating a competitive strategy, it is valuable to understand the basis for other firms' competitive advantage. Where the bias is towards differentiation, the competitive stress tends to be on protecting margins. If low cost is the goal, then the contest is more likely to be for market share. Where sustained or head-on competition with one or more competitors is likely, it becomes more important to maximise the market intelligence available. Rival products can be deconstructed and analysed to expose sources of added value open to attack. Weaknesses can be identified as targets for possible exploitation.

Gaining some understanding of competitor strategy is also very useful. This allows the firm to be more proactive in its strategic planning. For example, a sufficiently clear picture may indicate the best front and timing for a major market attack. Equally, it could illuminate strategic pathways to avoid or even suggest a route of retreat.

In practice, because strategy is often more emergent than prescriptive (see Chapter 9), intimation of a given plan may be less useful than an understanding of the 'springs' or mindset of competitor strategy. This implies reaching beyond the core competencies on which strategy is built and gaining some insight into the organisational culture within which these competencies are embedded. Needless to say, there is plenty of scope for error in interpretation. However, effective anticipation of competitor reactions can itself be a source of competitive advantage.

Strategies for the market

These are usefully analysed by identifying characteristic roles for firms in a marketplace. The main options are discussed below.

1 Market leader

This usually means holding the largest market share and making the pace-setting decisions about product and market development. Market leaders emerge in many industries, sometimes by being a first mover and other times by mounting a successful later challenge for first place. Some leaders are massively dominant (e.g. Coca-Cola), but others must fight to hold their lead in a more complex contest (e.g. Tesco).

The market leader usually enjoys a substantial competitive advantage, with a reputation or brand strength that allows a price premium and economies of scale that keep costs down. Nevertheless, constant vigilance is necessary to fight off market challenges.

2 Market challenger

A firm that is a significant player but not Number One in an industry may aim to challenge other firms and gain market share. A challenger needs some relatively strong competitive advantage to support its strategy which may range from attempting to topple the leader through to overwhelming minor competitors or simply taking market share. Much will depend on an evaluation of strength between challenger and challenged: this allows the probable risk to be matched with the expected gain. Challengers develop a strategic culture that is aggressive, ambitious, watchful and fast. This may become an asset in itself as the firm seizes market opportunity.

3 Market follower

A market challenge is usually based on a competitive advantage, but the very contesting of the market often reduces profitability for all involved. An alternative is to be a market follower, where the aim is to copy or adapt the market leader's product while avoiding confrontation. This is common in fast-growing markets such as that for PCs in the 1990s. The follower is likely to tread warily around the leader's core segments, while keeping down costs by piggy-backing on the leader's innovations. The risk, as in any parasitic strategy, is that the 'host' will become aggressive. In other cases, however, the follower may turn challenger.

4 Market nichers

Subsegments or niches in the markets are often ignored or underserved by the major players. This opens the possibility of a strategic focus on the relatively specialised needs of small-category customers. Usually, the market size is modest and corresponding costs are higher, but the much lower level of competitive intensity allows premium pricing. As expertise in serving niche markets grows, so added value increases and the competitive advantage becomes better defended.

As we saw in Chapter 14, niches can shrink or dissolve in larger and more open, competitive markets. But niches can also expand, yielding high rewards for the original and dominant brand.

Nutshell ◄─

Back in the mid-1990s the idea of sugar sticks – sugar for tea and coffee in paper tubes rather than flat sachets – was new in the UK. As a small player in the catering industry, Nutshell took the concept and added bright modern graphic designs that would appeal to coffee shop owners with a younger and professional clientele.

The strategy was a great success. Nutshell had differentiated an apparently unimportant product in the right way at the right time. However, as a unique selling point (USP), graphic design was clearly open to replication by larger competitors. Nutshell knew these companies well and lived in constant expectation of attack. The idea was to be innovative and daring but ready to move on quickly in unexpected directions. One senior manager likened it to a car chase: 'When they zig, we zag,' he said.

Marketing and the demand function

How, then, is marketing strategy illustrated by the demand function that underpins every transaction? The diagrams in economics textbooks are blunt instruments for this purpose. Generally, the demand function does slope downwards from left to right, but its shape and its position are constantly changing. These changes are driven partly by external forces and partly by the strategic intent of the firm.

Broadly speaking, every firm wishes to see the demand function for its product shift to the right.

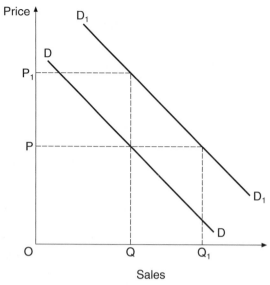

Figure 16.1 Shift in the demand function

In Figure 16.1, the demand curve has moved from DD to D_1D_1. On demand curve DD, price P was charged and quantity Q was sold. The new demand function allows a range of more favourable options from no change in sales and a higher price at P_1, to no change in price but a higher level of sales at Q_1. This is the generally intended outcome of product improvements, promotional activity and distribution development.

Firms are also interested in the variation of price elasticity along the demand curve. If the firm is thinking of price and cost cutting via economies of scale, then high price elasticity at the lower end of the demand curve may be the strategic target. This would mean that strategic price reductions would be met with a more than proportional increase in demand. This could make movement from a niche into a mass market feasible and could be the key to gaining distribution through outlets such as chain stores or supermarkets.

By contrast, a long-term niche marketer might aim for stronger price inelasticity in the upper reaches of the demand curve. This would allow a profit-maximising strategy of premium or super-premium pricing with relatively small sacrifice in sales.

When firms do find a more stable place in a market, they become loosely 'anchored' into their position. The product builds a certain reputation and achieves a degree of customer loyalty. Relative price and quality become familiar. Output gets adjusted to market share and fits available capacity, but in the process the interplay of competition often makes price elasticities unfavourable. A rise in price leaves the product very exposed to substitutes and high price elasticity. Yet a reduction in price may only provoke comparable cuts from competitors and little gain in sales. Price elasticity becomes very low. In this way strategic options can become severely constrained.

YORKIE

Introduced in 1976, Yorkie pioneered the 'chunky' chocolate bar and by 1980 had taken 35 per cent of the market, slashing the share of Cadbury's Dairy Milk from 74 per cent to 51 per cent. But despite marketing support, the brand gradually lost ground during the 1990s.

Despite some brand loyalty, a price increase would leave Yorkie very exposed to substitution in favour of competitors. Yet a price reduction would not only damage margins but also invite matching cuts from competitors.

SAFEWAY

Safeway was brought to Britain by its original US parent in 1962. Bought by the Argyll Group in 1988, the chain found itself a victim of Tesco's increasing success. What was the distinctive proposition of Safeway? As Sainsbury's rediscovered its roots in quality, Safeway faced further competition from a revitalised Asda.

In a frantically price-sensitive market, raising prices would be devastating to market share, but the alternative – a price war – would gain little and ruin profitability. Safeway opted for selective price cuts, a strategy that did not prevent takeover bids by 2003.

Sometimes a firm with an innovative or very competitive product can reverse this logic. Customers who have 'discovered' the product become increasingly loyal and a growing core market hardens. In the absence of convincing substitutes, upward price elasticity falls. At the same time growing mass market interest (often kindled by media coverage) only needs the trigger of a price reduction to translate into sales. Dyson vacuum cleaners might be an example of a firm and a product that have enjoyed this position.

Such a firm then has attractive strategic freedom. Higher prices will boost margins but do little damage to sales, while reduced prices are likely to access a much larger market with major gains in sales. Whichever option is pursued, a sufficiently competitive product may sustain this favourable pattern.

Both of these contrasting pictures are possible outcomes on the strategic battlefield: which applies depends on relative market power. Unstoppably powerful products create ideal strategic conditions. Beleaguered products for which easy substitutes are available face the default scenario.

17 Product and promotion

Overview

The value of all marketing activity depends on its consummation in the decision of purchase and sale. This moment of exchange is a calculation of mutual advantage. In effect, the customer is deciding that the offering of the producer or seller is worth more than the price agreed – and critically, more than the opportunity cost represented by that price. In this sense, every product offering on the market must cross a hurdle of consumer approval and evaluation. It follows, then, that the marketing function in business is concerned with the design of that total market offering.

What exactly is this total offering? How can it be analysed? The product of any business is best understood not its nominal form – an 'ice-cream', a 'Mars bar' – but as a bundle of *benefits* that are perceived and accessed by the customer. For example, cars are in demand because they offer convenient transport, but 'buying a car' and 'buying a new VW Beetle' are very different ideas. The first speaks generically of convenience and transport, while the second *includes* those functional benefits but adds a complex network of personal feelings and statements about the individual. Strategically, any firm with adequate access to capital and known technologies can make a car. Not anyone can produce a VW Beetle.

What is a product?

Kotler (1987) defines a product as 'anything that is offered to a market for attention, acquisition, use or consumption and might satisfy a want or a need'. His model analysis (Figure 17.1) starts with the 'core product' and its core benefits sought by the customer.

These may be functional (What does the product do?) or emotional (How does the product make one feel?). In the second ring, the 'actual product' is the form in the market taken by these benefits when they are expressed as a saleable product. The third ring, or 'augmented product', includes all the supportive extras that the producer wraps round the core product. This might feature credit facilities, delivery and after-sales services, and the terms of a guarantee.

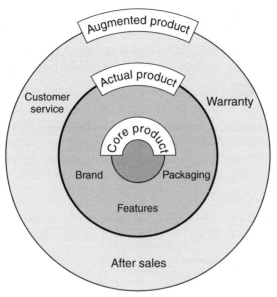

↑ Figure 17.1 Kotler's product levels

From MARKETING: AN INTRODUCTION, 1st edition, by Kotler, ©. Reprinted by permission of Pearson Education, Inc., Upper Saddle River, NJ.

To sell a Bell?

Computers for You recognise that many customers for PCs want word processing, games facilities and the internet above all else. Bell is renowned as an excellent manufacturer, while as a retailer the company prides itself on matching the customer with the right machine. After a sale, the firm offers its own helpline for installation and running problems, while a no-quibble refund policy allows second thoughts well beyond the statutory time allowed.

Another view stresses the generic distinction between cognitive and affective benefits. Cognitive or functional benefits relate to the product's objective qualities and its performance in action. These tend to be highlighted both in the design and manufacturing functions and in the marketing communications. This is predictable since a product's functional performance forms part of a legal contract with the consumer and is an essential underpinning to market value. Yet in many cases it is affective or emotional qualities that add critical value. Consider the appeal of Swatch watches or Haagen Daz ice cream. Here there is strong functional value *plus* an immensely powerful overlay of emotional value. As Charles Revlon at *Revlon* famously remarked: 'In the factory we make cosmetics, in the store we sell hope.'

This emotional value has a corresponding cost (e.g. advertising expenses), but the cost–value ratio may be very favourable when built on a platform of adequate function. Emotional value is also much more difficult to imitate. Its operation often depends on complex expressions of inner need and 'codings' of personal value. These may be identified through marketing information systems (see Chapter 14), but in practice some of the most powerful value drivers emerge from embedded organisational knowledge or from the insight or intuition of the entrepreneur.

It is clear that a total product offering has many dimensions. These combine in a bundle of benefits to which the consumer attaches value. This perception of value then forms a demand function or opportunity cost frontier relative to other purchasing options.

The marketing mix

What are the levers at the disposal of marketing managers to achieve this effect? The answer is the marketing mix – a range of tactical elements in marketing that are combined to implement strategy towards the target market. McCarthy (1960) introduced the simple 4Ps model – product, promotion, price and place – to categorise the ingredients of the mix. This classification has gained widespread currency and is now explored in more detail.

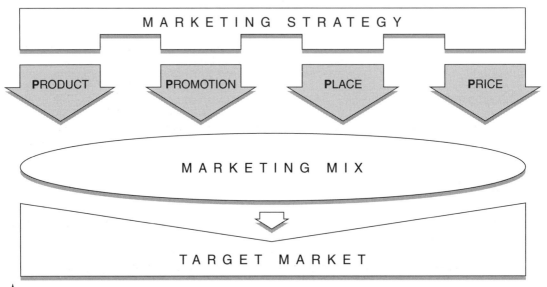

Figure 17.2 The marketing mix

Product

Product refers to all features of what is sold to the customer, both tangible and intangible. Products may take the form of goods or services and are sold in producer and consumer markets. It is clear from the outset that the product has a special status in the marketing mix. The product is, after all, the source of value and what the customer buys. A starting point is the generic product or basic bundle of core benefits offered by that product. This product is a concept that can exist independently of design, features, quality or brand (e.g. a car that is lawful and transports people from A to B).

Over and above the generic, design adds value. Good design combines outstanding functional performance with a quality of appearance and usage that has strong emotional appeal. Design is a major source of sustainable competitive advantage. Some firms have built a long-term reputation on the strength of their design expertise. In the 1990s, BMW described its product as 'the ultimate driving machine'. This strapline captures the customer experience of controlling a piece of very high-quality technology that is also a form of transport. Sony for hi-fi, Pentax for cameras, Apple for computers and Victorinox for penknives are all examples of firms that have found competitive advantage in design.

When Ford produced its Model T from 1908 to 1928, the features were standardised to reduce cost. It is said that Henry Ford actually wrecked a variant Model T, so great was his faith in the economies of standardisation. History was not on his side. The features offered by a producer can effectively target different segments in the market. Today variant features can be produced at ever lower costs and so hug more tightly the contours of a disparate market. Adding features to a basic product concept also builds differentiation. This tends to make competing products less perfect substitutes and builds barriers against the forces of competition. For this reason, features need to be innovative and distinctive. Easily copied additions to the product quickly become 'standard' and lose their competitive value. Patents and copyrights may be useful devices for less contestable protection of product development.

Quality is a basic ingredient of the product mix (see also Chapter 21). Often defined as 'fitness for purpose' (Deming, 1982), quality is determined in the specification for a product. Generally, standards of quality have been rising, often driven by global competitive pressures. But the cost–value ratio forms a natural frontier to quality improvement. It is only worth improving quality where net added value can be achieved. The nature of the segment is the determining factor. In certain segments a huge build-up of quality may form a competitive defence (e.g. at a famous luxury hotel). In other segments, basic quality is still a great seller (e.g. at PoundStretcher).

Branding

Beyond the design and specification of a product lies its identity. The idea of a brand dates back to the Middle Ages as a symbol of quality or origin. Modern branding developed in the 19th century and has come to represent a complex 'aura' of intangible qualities linked to a product and greatly enhancing its value. Consider trainers and *Nikes*, jeans and *Levi's*, a cola drink and a *Coke*. In each case the brand is adding an important – even the greater part – of the value. Brands still perform their traditional functions, especially in assuring the customer of quality. This can be highly effective, as in the case of car manufacturers ranging from VW to Rolls Royce. Yet there is a difference between the brands of BMW and Mercedes. Both represent quality, but aside from price, one brand is not a substitute for the other. The identities of BMW and Mercedes are subtly different and that difference enables them to sell profitably in different segments of the car market.

The extent to which a brand is recognised and valued is termed the brand equity. Successful brands with high equity are powerful springs of competitive advantage and can be used to boost both profit margins and market share. As prime sources of differentiation, brands can be rivalled but not directly copied. Despite taste tests showing that consumers marginally prefer Pepsi Cola, Coke outsells Pepsi 9 to 1. Why? Coca-Cola carries a mighty brand equity that expresses customers' deepest values and extends far beyond a soft drink.

Brands naturally carry financial equity. Some companies give them an explicit valuation on the balance sheet (see Chapter XX) as intangible assets. In any case, brand values can represent a major part of a company's capitalisation (market value) and some firms now express their whole business strategy in terms of acquiring and exploiting a brand portfolio.

New Coke ◄─────────────────────────────────────

Back in 1985 Coca-Cola was concerned by evidence of customers being attracted to Pepsi by its slightly sweeter taste. A costly development project led to the launch of 'New Coke', proved statistically in taste tests to be preferred by customers to the original formula. Briefly, sales took off. Then the complaints began, and growing numbers of consumers demanded the return of 'old Coke'. Soon, the company's Atlanta headquarters was inundated by protests and the original product returned, now called 'Classic Coke'. Within months Classic outsold New Coke on a ratio that could reach 9 to 1. Pepsi was delighted. The New Coke disaster was complete.

What went wrong? Not the taste tests. Consumers really did prefer the *taste* of New Coke. But they also wanted Coke's brand heritage. Drinking Coke is not just about cola. It is also about the American dream – the frontier, freeways, flying the star-spangled banner. Coke captures the essence of America. New Coke lost it.

Product presentation

Products also gain value through their presentation. Sometimes this is an extension of the brand: think Kodak, see a yellow box. In other cases, as with Perrier, the packaging actually defines the brand. Clearly packaging also has a physical function in protecting and sometimes dispensing the product. But increasingly in consumer markets it is a projection of the brand and, combined with liveries (colour schemes) and graphics, is a key element in the total mix.

Finally, the firm must decide how to specify the augmented product in terms of after-sales service, delivery options, credit facilities and guarantees. These peripherals are not details. They may add value significantly to the actual product and may express or enhance the brand. Some firms contract out these functions but need to monitor quality with care.

Promotion

Promoting a product means persuading customers that it represents better value for money than any available alternative. This means that the demand function must be 'pushed' to the right as customers decide to buy more of the product at any given price.

Advertising works in this way. If successful, an advertising campaign should increase the quantity of the product bought by existing customers and draw non-customers into making a purchase. It will also sharpen the intensity of demand and reinforce customer loyalty.

Expressed analytically, advertising should push the demand function to the right so that a greater quantity of the product is purchased at any given price. It may also affect the price elasticity of demand. For example, a campaign to differentiate the product and enhance brand value should reduce price elasticity above the existing price level. Potentially this would enable the firm to increase price – and profit margin – with a relatively low loss of sales. Alternatively, advertising to increase awareness of product benefits or availability may increase price elasticity below existing price levels. This might mean that a price reduction which allowed the product to enter a mass market with an increase in sales would more than compensate for the loss of margin.

Clearly, most advertising is not just informative. It aims to do more than merely increase awareness of products and their specifications or benefits. Persuasive advertising tilts and moulds perceptions of a product and its marketing mix. It blends reason with emotions in constructing a value proposition that can become increasingly of its own making. In a real sense the advertising adds content and value to the product. When consumers buy the product, they are wanting to buy with it the images and associations carried by the advertising. These are often key sources of differentiation in what might otherwise be a near-commodity product.

Airwalk

An 'airwalk' is a classic skateboard jump. After take-off, the skater takes a step or two in mid-air while holding the board and then lands back on it once more. A small San Diego company of that name started out in the 1980s as a specialist producer of skateboarding shoes appealing mainly to the surf and skate culture of teenagers. The shoes developed a cult status and by the early 1990s the firm's turnover was fairly stable at around $15 million a year.

Then Airwalk hired a new advertising agency, Lambesis. The product range was now widened to include footware for a range of individualistic outdoor sports. Building on a niche identity, the target market was young, innovative and experimental. This was decisive in 'tipping' the brand over into national success. The poster and alternative press ads were zany but cool. In each image, young Airwalk owners were using their shoes for some bizarre purpose, wacky and memorable. As in the TV ads that followed, the brand developed an irreverent, anti-hero image that was grainy, ironic and subtly sophisticated.

The desirability of Airwalk shoes became highly contagious. Sales exploded from just $16 million in 1993 to $175 million by 1996. For a short time Airwalk trailed only Nike and Adidas.

Adapted from M Gladwell The Tipping Point *(Little, Brown & Co. 2000)*

Sales promotion is more specifically tactical with its focus on special offers and merchandising. Special offers can have a dramatic impact on demand, but their effect is usually short-lived. They are most effective when working alongside the essential brand proposition, such as Tesco's 'unbeatable value'. Merchandising and point-of-sales displays help to create interest while creating an environment conducive to sales. Again, the image created must mesh with the values of the brand.

Personal selling is used where the value of direct communication with the customer exceeds the cost. This is likely for higher-priced items and especially in gaining orders for producer goods. The sales person represents the company and must act favourably on the demand function like any other ingredient in the mix. Larger firms may also use the more generalised tool of public relations to build demand and reputation. The role of public relations efforts ranges from merely backlighting the firm's overall image to deputising for advertisements in raising the demand profile (e.g. Body Shop's successful associations with environmental and human rights causes).

Promotional mix

The best mix of promotional methods will vary widely according to the industry and the firm. Like the marketing mix as a whole, the promotional mix should be mutually reinforcing and needs linking to the maturity of the product and the market (see Chapter 13). Sales promotion efforts may be focused on a 'push' strategy where the goal is to achieve take-up of the product by intermediaries (e.g. wholesalers and retailers) who use their expertise in selling to final consumers. In 'pull' strategies, promotion reaches consumers direct, who will 'pull' the product from the company through the distribution chain. The balance is shifting from pull to push as selling emerges as a separate pool of competitive capabilities, particularly in the retail trade.

18 Distribution and pricing

Distribution

Introduction

Distribution is the physical and commercial process of conveying goods and services from their point of production to their point of sale. Some producers perform the distribution function themselves (e.g. farm shops and factory shops), but most firms use some mix of agents, wholesalers and retailers. The underlying economic reason for this is that producers offer a relatively narrow selection of goods and services in large quantities, while consumers want a relatively wide selection in small quantities. Distributors or middlemen achieve this outcome for consumers with a gain in economic efficiency. Consider the wasteful transport and transactions involved if every producer had to distribute to every chosen outlet in the market. However, this classic economic argument may weaken with the potential of e-commerce. Conventional distribution chains may lose ground as virtual warehouses and customised just-in-time production become more widespread. Much will depend on the cost of technologies and their match with customer demand.

The principles of business management provide a further explanation. We have seen that to achieve superior returns, a firm must focus on the use of its distinctive capabilities. If a firm persists in performing these functions at a rate of added value below that which dedicated distributors could achieve, then it is placing a burden on its rate of return, and at least part of its resources could be better deployed elsewhere. There are, however, costs in relinquishing the distribution function. The producer often loses control over the product's journey to the market and the scenario of its sale to the consumer. This may blunt or distort the producer's intentions for the quality of customer experience. It may also weaken or divert the flow of feedback from the market that should stimulate an apt and rapid response.

Channel design

In theory, there is a strong coincidence of interests between the producer and the distribution channel operator. Both profit from a flow of sales and both depend on the product's success in the marketplace. In practice, channel conflict is common. This may be between distributors fighting for the same customers, or successive links in the chain disputing each other's role. Proper leadership and co-ordination are needed and are most likely when one organisation in the chain has decisively greater market power. This is increasingly expressed in vertical marketing systems where the entire distribution process is fully co-ordinated and operates as a single system. These are achieved through one firm owning the other players, through contractual relationships or by one dominant partner being able to set conditions.

Building strategy

Essentially, the business wants the most effective route for its products to reach their intended market. 'Effective', as in other business contexts, refers to optimising the combination of outcome and cost.

Building the optimum channel design for a product or product range is an important strategic challenge. The producer wants to maximise the extent and effectiveness of contact with the target market, but cost is the key constraint. The distribution chain must sustain and exploit the firm's competitive advantage, transmitting effectively the product's bundle of benefits to its potential end-users. This requires decisions about channel *length* – the number of intermediaries through which the product passes – and channel *breadth* – the numbers of distributors at any level in the chain. Relative market power will affect manoeuvring room in making these decisions, but the strategic aim is unchanged.

Distribution poses a challenge to almost any business enterprise. In most firms there is a necessary gap between the point of production and the point of sale. Sometimes this is bridgeable electronically through the internet or other automated systems. Even then there are usually problems of physical logistics to resolve.

Peterborough Plastics ◄

A small household goods manufacturer might ideally wish to reach a mass market by having the relevant product range in every retail outlet from chain stores to village shops. But the cost of achieving such widespread distribution may be unacceptably high. It could be more effective to negotiate distribution deals with the key retail groups who control, say, 80 per cent of the market.

Clearly, the distribution strategy chosen will depend on the wider marketing strategy of which it is part. If the firm wishes to take higher margins in a target segment with lower price elasticity, then its distribution effort will be closely targeted and perhaps quite narrowly specified. But if the strategic thrust is towards building market share, then distribution plans will ensure sufficient breadth in the channel with an accent on market coverage.

Overall, distribution will only be sought where the net benefits outweigh net cost. It may be desirable for a product to be stocked in remote retail outlets, but it may not be worth the associated cost. The producer will also aim to strike the best bargains possible with its distributors. If they make normal profits, then the channel is performing at minimum cost. All supernormal profit or competitive advantage in the distribution chain adds to final price and acts as a drag on sales. In practice, the best distributors are likely to enjoy a degree of competitive advantage – much depends on market power in the supply chain and competitive forces in the distribution industry.

Price

Introduction

Price determines the unit revenue to be achieved by a firm in return for its product. But price also represents the expenditure – or sacrifice – necessary by a customer to secure the corresponding purchase. Price is at the heart of the market mechanism and is a key element in both corporate and marketing strategy.

In the pricing of every product, there has to be a strategic choice. This will be framed by a superordinate corporate strategy that establishes the firm as seeking cost leadership or

Sainsbury's

Staff training at Sainsbury's stresses the importance of customer morale at the checkout. Managers recognise that this is a moment of 'loss' for the customer. Until this point they have often enjoyed fulfilling wants and placing goods in the trolley. Now, with their choices packed away into plastic bags, they face the moment of reckoning. Whether parting with cash or signing a debit transaction, they confront the realities of price. Staff are trained to welcome each customer and to offer a smile where possible. Light but distracting conversation is also encouraged. In these ways the perception of price is massaged downwards with positive effects on customer satisfaction and the likelihood of future purchases.

differentiation in a mass or segmented market. Within this conceptual matrix, the marketing manager must decide on the optimal trade-off between margin and share. In making this decision, the demand function provides an important model.

Price elasticity

In Figure 18.1(a), the demand function D_eD_e is gently sloping and initially sales level Q is achieved at price P. Then a reduction in price to P_1 yields a greater than proportional expansion of sales to Q_1. Suppose that the initial price was £1.00 and that 100 items were sold. Then say the new price is set at 80p and sales increase to 200 items. Revenue has clearly risen from £100 to £160.

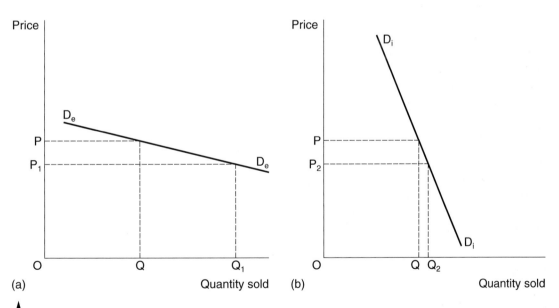

Figure 18.1 Implications of relative price elasticity

Now consider a parallel scenario in Figure 18.1(b). The demand function D_iD_i is steeply sloping, and initially sales level Q is achieved at price P. A reduction in price to P_2 now yields a smaller than proportional expansion of sales to Q_2. If the new price is again 80p and sales increase to 110 items, then revenue has decreased to £88.

It is clear that the responsiveness of sales to changes in price or the *price elasticity of demand* is crucial in all pricing decisions. Essentially, it indicates the rate of trade-off between price and sales. Its calculation simply involves a ratio of percentage changes:

$$\text{Price elasticity of demand (PED)} = \frac{\%\ \text{change in quantity demanded}}{\%\ \text{change in price}}$$

For Figure 18.1(a) the value is $\frac{100\%}{20\%} = 5$, and in Figure 18.1(b) the equivalent value is $\frac{10\%}{20\%} = 0.5$. Where the PED value is greater than 1.0, demand is said to be 'elastic' since its 'stretch' factor is greater than the causal change in price. Where the PED value is less than 1.0, demand is said to be 'inelastic' since its 'stretch' factor is less than the causal change in price. Where price elasticity is exactly 1.0, it is said to be unitary and a change in price will cause no change in revenue.

However, the ultimate objective of marketing is not to achieve revenue but to generate profit. Suppose that items in the example above were costing 50p each. In the initial position – with a price elastic demand function – profit was £50 on turnover of £100. After the change in price, profit was up to £60 on £200 turnover. For the price inelastic demand function, the outcome is reversed. Profit is down to £33 on a reduced turnover at £88.

Elasticity and pricing strategy

What determines price elasticity and can managers influence its value? It is often said that luxury goods are fairly price elastic and that necessities are price inelastic. This view might help to explain why there are often price reductions available for leisure travel at off-peak times, while those making business journeys at peak times face full rates and often special supplements. The rationale is that because luxuries are inessential, customers can more easily forego their consumption. Necessities, on the other hand, have by their nature to be purchased and customers will not readily be deterred by price.

However, in analysing marketing management, this is a simplistic view. The real issue is substitution. Any product that has a close substitute available at comparable price will exhibit high price elasticity. Equally, a product for which there is no satisfactory substitute or where the nearest reasonable substitute is far more highly priced will exhibit low price elasticity. Purchases of products with close substitutes carry a high opportunity cost, with most units sold on slim margins of consumer preference. Predictably, a rise in price will cause proportionately high losses of sales, while a price reduction will bring disproportionate increases as narrow preferences for competing products convert into sales. Where there is no close substitute for a product, opportunity cost is low and changes in price make relatively little impact on sales.

Accordingly, it is not whether a product is a luxury or necessity that determines price elasticity, but the availability of substitutes. Strictly, substitutes should be understood not in the literal sense but as competing value propositions. A customer attempting to decide between the purchase of a Mars bar and a Kit-Kat also has the option of purchasing Walker's crisps. The customer's goal is to identify the best value proposition available. The closer the contest, the higher the price elasticity of demand.

This explains why competition is so vital in determining price elasticity and thus the shape of the demand function. Petrol, for most people, is a necessity and, as a *commodity,* it does indeed carry a low price elasticity. But with a Shell and BP station close by, the demand for Esso petrol will be highly price elastic. Petrol lacks a good substitute; Esso does not.

As firms differentiate their products, so they build price inelasticity. This, then, allows the possibility of premium pricing without undue loss of market share. A cost leadership strategy can exploit the reverse logic. Here, the products of competitors are very close substitutes and a small decrease in price can be rewarded by a large gain in market share.

Pricing policy in action

In the light of price elasticity theory, how can a resolution be found for the trade-off between profit margin and market share? A producer is faced by a range of possible prices, extending upwards from the cost of the product (zero margin, maximum sales) to the level at which the product has no customers (maximum margin, zero sales).

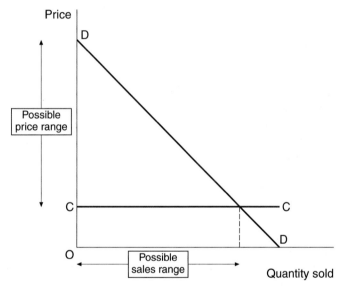

DD is the demand curve and CC is the relevant cost function.

Figure 18.2 Possible prices along the demand function

In practice, the use of the demand function for setting prices is often very difficult. Most firms have very limited data on which to base such a model. They may have historic information on sales at two or more prices. This would suggest an outline tracking for a demand function but would certainly offer nothing that was definitive. The result is that pricing can become like shooting in the dark, and firms tend to look at some serviceable benchmarks.

One such approach is called cost pricing. This is a traditional and simple method that involves adding a standard mark-up to the cost of the product. The approach is easy to operate and ensures some degree of profitability; but it has serious defects. First, it is indiscriminate (i.e. usually applied on a standard basis) and generally makes no allowance for relative price elasticities. Second, it takes no account of market conditions. The selected profit margin may be too high or unnecessarily low.

Third, it ignores the trade-off between margin and share, and fails to make any strategic choice between these two dimensions of profitability.

An alternative approach works from the opposite direction. Value-based pricing starts with the customer's perception of value, sets price as an appropriate discount to ensure sales, and then designs the product to fit cost constraints that permit an adequate profit. This is an approach typically used when shifting a product from a niche to a mass market. What the typical target customer will pay becomes the starting point for design and costings. Value-based pricing has the great advantage that it is derived from the perceptions of the customer, and is therefore embedded in market reality. Unfortunately, the customer's perception of value is often very difficult to assess especially if competitors enter the market with products that are close substitutes.

Since competing products determine the opportunity cost of purchase, some firms benchmark their prices against competitors. This may mean charging a 'going rate' on the grounds that it represents a concensus view on what the market will bear. It may also avoid downward price competition if all firms in the market adhere fairly closely to the going rate price. Often, one large firm emerges as a price leader whose decisions on price are followed by smaller competitors. Some firms announce their intention always to offer the lowest price or to match any competitor's offer. 'Never knowingly undersold' is the slogan of the John Lewis Partnership, while Esso maintain their 'Price Watch', guaranteeing the lowest prices within a given locality. Competition-based pricing is most used where competing products are very similar and therefore close substitutes. Such firms are vulnerable to competitive price-cutting, and benchmarking competitors can provide some protection. Firms with differentiated products can *distance* their prices from competitors to the extent that their product lacks a substitute.

Target return pricing takes a more global view of price and aims to ensure that profits after all costs represent a desired rate of return. This means that price must be set against some knowledge of the demand function so that revenue, and hence profit, can be evaluated across a range of price options (see break-even analysis, Chapter 20).

It should be noticed that there can be no certainty of any price option yielding a required rate of return. The approach is also disconnected from the strategic trade-offs that managers will often engineer. For example, with the introduction of a new product, a firm may wish to maximise short-term profit by charging a relatively high price ('skimming' the market) and exploiting price inelasticity among committed customers. But managers *may* aim to pursue a policy of market penetration in the hope of building long-term market share. This is likely to imply a much lower price and some sacrifice of early profitability for the sake of longer-term objectives.

19 The architecture of value

Overview

Value in business is a subjective phenomenon: products are worth what people are willing to pay. Often, it is small changes in products that provide differentiation and sharp increases in market value.

The difference between cost to the firm and value to the customer is, in effect, a dicretionary space. By setting or agreeing price, the firm divides this surplus between itself and the customer.

Every firm is interested in enlarging the total surplus available. This may be achieved through adjustments to the product and its cost structure, or by creating new market space through redesigning product benefits or redrawing segment boundaries.

Value and demand

Value is often counter-intuitive. What one person values highly another person may value hardly at all. The question of whether any scale of intrinsic value exists is a philosophical problem, but in business value is always extrinsic and determined in the marketplace. Thus, adding value is not based on objective standards but is subject to the desires and preferences of a target market. For example, it is not rational that 30 minutes' work in cleaning and polishing a second-hand car can add £200 to its value. It remains, after all, the same car with 30 minutes' unskilled labour attached. Yet the increase in value can be real.

The same kind of paradox surrounds the effects of branding. A product that would otherwise be a budget-priced commodity leaps in value with the simple imprint of a brand. Sometimes all that has changed is the lettering on a label, yet the price and profit margin are transformed. This, again, is real value and derived from the interaction of demand and supply. On the one hand, customers gain a sense of well-being from the brand (increasing demand) while on the other, the brand owners are able to control its use (restricting supply).

It is important to distinguish between value in the form of market price, and consumer valuation in terms of the maximum price consumers will pay.

In Figure 19.1, the demand function marks the outer limit of consumer valuation. We have seen in Chapter 14 that the demand function is also an opportunity cost frontier. At all points inside the curve, the product is judged more valuable than its opportunity cost, but outside the curve the opportunity cost is too high and no purchase will be made. It therefore follows that at price P, the quantity Q will be demanded and the area of value PBA will be enjoyed by customers as

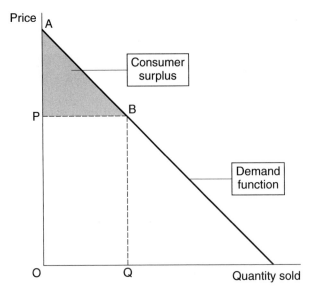

Figure 19.1 Demand and consumer surplus

consumer surplus. Notice that every unit purchased, except the final or marginal unit, will carry consumer surplus but at a diminishing rate.

In the same way that profit as a surplus signals firms to produce more, so consumer surplus signals the likelihood that customers will repeat their purchase. Economists tend only to observe consumer surplus as a phenomenon, but devote little attention to exploring its nature. For business managers the extent and origins of consumer surplus should be of great interest. The reputation of firms and their products is built on consumer surplus.

A Mars bar ◄

You buy a Mars Bar for 35p. It yields satisfaction with a value in excess of 35p, in excess of the opportunity cost of spending 35p. It performs this feat again and again. Mars consistently delivers superior value for money. It is a huge brand and a long-term winner.

The expectation of consumer surplus ahead of its corresponding opportunity cost is the fundamental source of all consumer demand. It is therefore a priority to understand and support its drivers and to monitor their performance at all times. This principle lies behind the evaluation forms so often given to customers by firms who wish to know more about their customers' behaviour and preferences, and to assess how well their product has performed.

It is also clear in Figure 19.1 that the extent of consumer surplus is determined by the setting of price. In Figure 19.2, assuming no change in costs, an increase in price from P to P_1 will improve the firm's profit margin. But it will also reduce sales from Q to Q_1 and cut the amount of consumer surplus enjoyed by those customers still purchasing the product. Conversely in Figure 19.2, a decrease in price from P to P_2 will squeeze the firm's profit margin. At the same time, it will increase sales from Q to Q_2 and give existing customers a boost in their consumer surplus.

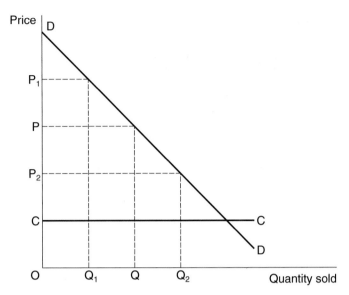

Figures 19.2 Price changes and consumer surplus

This relationship explores the crucial strategic problem affecting every business product: how – on a given cost base – to reconcile the trade-off between profit margin and market share. Much depends on relative price elasticities and the dynamics of the business environment. Meanwhile it is important to remember that in practice firms must make decisions based on incomplete information.

Managing cost and value

Driving up value and pushing down costs are the tasks of managers in confronting their target market. This is the alchemy that every business performs with varying degrees of success. There are two main difficulties. First is the tendency for cost and value to rise and fall together, and second is the problem of identifying the most favourable target markets and keeping the strategic aim steady.

It is not difficult to see why cost and value tend to move in tandem. Any rise in value is prone to triggering a comparable increase in costs, while any cut in costs is liable to have a similarly depressing effect on value. The trick is partially to break this relationship and to exploit every favourable differential.

Costs are incurred to add value. When a cost is reduced (i.e. some part of that cost is removed), there should be a reduction in value. A key task of management is to search for reductions in cost that carry no loss (or very little loss) in value. This is a basic element in the philosophy of lean production (see Chapter 18). The whole issue becomes more complex when a cost can only be cut with a significant but less than proportional effect on value. What exactly does this mean?

At the simplest level, a chocolate assortment with an unit cost of £2.00 might be valued by a sample customer at £4.00. A cost-cutting exercise that reduced the specification of the packaging might save 10 per cent on unit cost, while only reducing the customer's valuation by 5 per cent. This should leave more value to be divided between producer and customer. However, the change

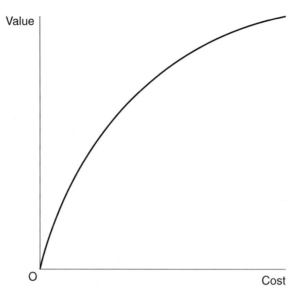

Figure 19.3 Typical cost–value function

does not just affect one customer but all customers – and some non-customers. A reduction in value will pull the demand curve to the left. This movement occurs relative to two dimensions – the *y* and *x* axes, or value and sales (quantity demanded). The new demand curve is likely to change its gradient as well as its position. Thus, a cost reduction is likely to affect some combination of consumer valuation and potential sales.

This mix is strategically important, impacting directly on available margins and scope for market penetration.

All the same principles apply to driving up value. A firm will search for increases in value at zero or minimal cost. This searching process is also an aspect of lean production. Even a significant increase in costs may be acceptable if the boost to value is proportionally greater. In other words, the prospective cost–value ratio is favourable. This is the reasoning that actually led Cadbury's to use thicker card in their Milk Tray boxes. Indeed, upgrading specifications has been a trend across a wide range of markets. Increasingly demanding customers are often willing to pay more for a better specified and better made product. All other things being equal, a rise in a product's valuation by consumers shifts the demand curve away from the origin. This may allow a simultaneous increase in the potential price and level of sales. The balance of this change in potential again has strategic importance.

The second dimension to the management of value is connection with the target market. A product that is highly prized in one market may be hardly valued at all in another. Even a small error in the marketing mix can transmit the product's benefits into a zone of demand where their valuation is not high enough to sustain profitability. A competitive advantage does not exist in a firm, but in a firm relative to a market. The segmental map of a market is criss-crossed by invisible contours of value that delineate alluring summits but also unexpected chasms.

A combination of marketing experience and market research should identify those segments where the best match can be made with the firm's capabilities as expressed through its range of products. It should be noticed that this match can be prompted by strategic goals rather than short-run profit maximisation. Low returns may be accepted from products that are breaking into segments or gaining knowledge to support future initiatives.

There is, though, a danger of making the whole process of market targeting seem overly precise and scientific. Equipped with the best information available, human judgement and even intuition remain at a premium. There are, as it were, many dark sides to the 'marketing moon'. Information about the nature of demand is always incomplete and out of date. Surprises abound and the best opportunities are often those that competitors have been unable to detect. Sometimes, new segments are discovered, or markets are redefined so that new segments emerge. Meanwhile, consumer tastes and incomes change, competitors shift their focus and external events intervene. A kaleidoscope of possibility continuously adjusts the demand frontiers for products and the potential for new products to find new targets.

Lucozade

Lucozade used to be packaged in a distinctive glass bottle with a yellow cellophane wrap. Its quaint slogan, 'May be drunk freely in sickness or in health' suggested a product for the bedside table. Predictably, sales were sluggish and weighted towards older age groups.

However, in 1980 brand owners SmithKline Beecham relaunched Lucozade in a 33cl can with fast, modern graphics and a young image of fitness and health. Powered by sports celebrity endorsement, sales quadrupled on some of the best margins in the soft drinks industry. A sleeping elderly brand was suddenly a youthful star.

Redefining markets

An effective analysis of market value opens the way for radical innovation in products and industries. This can allow firms to make a first landing in new market territory and to gain the strategic advantages of early incumbency and self-designed fit.

Kim and Mauborgne (1999) argue for the creation of unprecedented value profiles by thinking strategically across the traditional market boundaries. Over time, they observe, the strategies of competing firms tend to converge as all parties home in on the same core demand, the same features of performance, the same price levels and the same distribution channels. This tendency leads progressively to head-on competition with a relentless need to offer better overall performance at a lower price. The result is a collective erosion of added value that ultimately undermines all but the strongest firms.

The break-out from this cul-de-sac urged by Kim and Mauborgne is to deconstruct the sources of customer value and to challenge industry assumptions about how these are assembled in a product.

In Figure 19.4 the value factors in an existing 'industry standard' product may be radically re-specified to create new value.

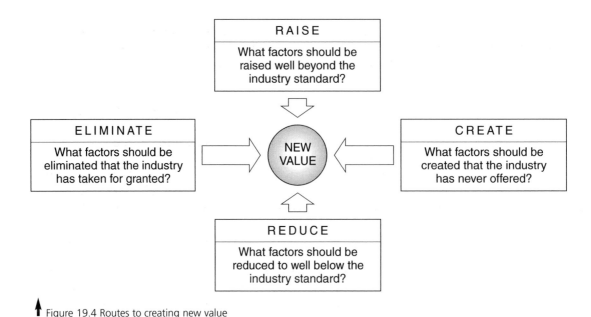

Figure 19.4 Routes to creating new value

Reprinted by permission of Harvard Business Review.
Adapted from 'Creating New Market Space' by W. C. Kim and R. Mauborgne, January/February 1999.
Copyright © 1999 by the Harvard Business School Publishing Corporation; all rights reserved.

This model has foundations in the work of Porter (1985) and the idea of a value chain (see Chapter 6) that identifies generic activities in the total process of production. It also draws on Ohmae (1990), who agues strongly for avoiding head-on competition with a strategy of innovation through better understanding of what exactly customers value.

Cost and value relationships are not just important as an aggregate, but as the building blocks of the unique value proposition offered by every product. Kim and Mauborgne highlight the specific value factors that influence consumer behaviour within a given industry. These can then be radically recast to offer the customer distinctive and superior value.

This may involve breaking down the barriers between industries that divide the value drivers of product experience. Although customers may buy a discrete product, they are usually looking for an integrated experience.

Home Depot

This highly successful US DIY chain amalgamated value from private contractors and the conventional hardware store. Customers are offered a combination of low-price warehouse-style shopping together with in-store expertise and advice that enables them to do jobs for themselves. Gone from the value equation are the costly locations and merchandising of hardware stores, and gone is the costly personal service of private contractors. These elements of the total home improvement 'product' are stripped out because the new configuration of value – Home Depot – makes them redundant: for many customers, they now fail to add net value.

For example, passengers on a train want far more than just transport between scheduled stops. Many want parking facilities, convenience shopping, good food and drink and productive use of the journey time for work or relaxation. Orchestrating and managing this total experience are challenges with new possibilities for adding value.

Within any industry, clusters of firms form strategic groups, convergent in serving key segments of the market. The architecture of value can be redrawn by designing new combinations of benefits between different strategic groups. Again, it is bringing together elements of high added value in more than one strategic group that creates new market space. For example, a hotel might discover that a high-quality restaurant characteristic of the 'five star' category could be linked to attractive but more modest accommodation in the 'three star' range. A new market might be opened among those who want an affordable overall package yet have a sophisticated interest in food and drink.

Kim and Mauborgne explore the principle of innovative value creation across different kinds of market barriers. In effect, any industry assumptions, explicit or tacit, may be open to challenge and the breaking out of new market space. The functional/emotional spectrum in product value is an example. Industry convergence tends to push the range of product offerings to one end of this spectrum. Car manufacturers have been prone to assume that while emotional and aesthetic statements underpin luxury cars, the small car market is about economy and convenience. But when Ford designed the Ka, they wanted a product that was young and stylish, more feminine, explicitly modern and yet still economical. The Ford Ka broke from the small car 'pack' and created new space in a heavily mapped market.

PART **D**

OPERATIONS
explained

20 The behaviour of costs

Overview

Business is a creative and transformational process. Every product is a template for combining scarce resources in such a way that they add value. This means that a firm's value of output – in the form of products – must exceed its corresponding cost of inputs. Since the difference is profit, it follows that the firm aims for the total gap between value of outputs and cost of inputs to be maximised. This simple proposition conceals an infinite complexity of ways and means, the mastery of which is the stuff of strategy.

The gap between total costs and total value provides the firm with strategic manoeuvring room. In the competitive arena of the marketplace, price must be set between cost and value: but where? Should the firm shelter in a niche market with comfortable margins of profit and consumer surplus, or should it venture out into the mass market where wafer-thin differences between cost, price and value can make or break the enterprise? It is clearly essential to explore the drivers of cost and value and their interaction within different markets.

Costs explored

Any use of a scarce resource is a cost. A resource is scarce if it has competing uses: in other words, it has an opportunity cost. Almost all resources are therefore scarce. In a market economy, firms compete for control of resources by their ability to add value. It is therefore essential to understand and calculate costs.

For convenience, costs are quantified in terms of money. As discussed later in this chapter, there are some important costs that are difficult to quantify and some costs that most firms do not choose to measure. However, the calculation of most costs is a legal requirement as well as a necessity for effective decision making.

In this sense there are two basic perspectives in looking at costs. An accountant would recognise direct costs – those directly incurred by the product itself – and indirect costs – that do not arise directly from the productive process but are necessary for its support. For the purposes of analysis, direct costs, such as materials, will tend to vary with output and sales, while for indirect costs, such as marketing, this relationship will be much weaker. This linkage with output is the basis of the second perspective used particularly by economists. Variable costs change proportionately with output, while fixed costs are incurred regardless of the output level. In practice, this is not a precise distinction. Costs such as materials and wage labour will vary fairly closely with output, and costs such as rents or insurance will not vary at all. However, other costs will show a more irregular relationship. Electricity or transport costs, for example, would tend to increase with output but in a pattern that could be complex or stepped. Usually, such costs are allocated as variable or fixed – in whole or in part – according to their dominant characteristic.

The behaviour of costs is critical to output and sales decisions. Costs are the 'floor' on which the higher 'stories' of price and value are built. Costs are the starting point for profit. Covering costs yields zero profit: all income above cost contributes towards profitability.

It is easy to assume that the cost of any product is known to the producer. But the distinction between variable and fixed costs quickly challenges this assumption. If many key costs do not vary with output, how are they to be related to any particular unit of output? The obvious solution is to use a measure of average cost that includes variable cost and a proportional fraction of fixed cost. This poses two problems. First, it means that the cost of a product has no definitive status but depends on the level of output (since any change in output gives a different fixed cost loading). Second, there is the problem of fixed cost allocation to any specific product line. Since most firms make more than one product, how can fixed costs – many of which are shared in common between products – be allocated to one given product?

A system of allotment known as absorption costing is the only solution. The idea is to use the most appropriate criterion for attaching fixed or overhead costs to *cost centres,* such as departments, workshops or production processes. If a cost centre is the only beneficiary of an overhead (e.g. a computer facility), then its cost is simply allocated accordingly. But when the benefit is shared between cost centres, then a criterion for apportionment must be decided. For example, monthly rent in a factory might be £10 000, apportioned by use of floorspace. If a cost centre uses 25 per cent of the available floorspace then it will be apportioned £2500 per month. Its apportioned share of other overhead expenses will also be added. The resulting total overhead is then absorbed by the flow of products passing through the cost centre. For example, if a packing department carries a monthly overhead of £6000, with 12 000 products being processed, then each product 'absorbs' an £0.50 overhead cost.

Other overhead costs might be apportioned using direct labour costs or machine hours, or any other relevant criterion. What it is important to recognise is that the whole process of allotting overheads is based on estimation and human judgement. If an accountant changes the way in which overheads are allotted, then the 'cost' of a product also changes. Add to this the fact that any major change in the level of output will impact on both fixed and variable costs and it becomes clear that unit costs are a useful guide rather than a definitive calculation.

The contribution principle

When a firm considers its plans for the output of existing or new products, its generation of cost data is clearly crucial. In this process there is an important distinction between the short and the long run. The economic short run is the period within which fixed capacity cannot be altered. Beyond this point lies the long run, in which all factors of production as inputs can be changed. In practical terms, this might mean that a factory could, in the short run, work more shifts or drive its machines harder, but could not install new machines or build an extension.

Given the difficulties of identifying a full cost (variable cost plus allotted fixed overheads) for individual products, an alternative approach is to use marginal or contribution costing. In the short run the firm's fixed overheads must be paid regardless of any judgements about cost or decisions about price. The marginal cost, or the cost of producing one more unit, is the variable cost incurred. This value is the total of the variable costs incurred at each relevant cost centre. Provided that the price obtained exceeds the marginal cost, then a *contribution* is made towards the fixed overheads. This contribution is clearly not a profit since no loading for the fixed overheads has been absorbed. The final step is to take the total contributions from all products and subtract the fixed overheads: what remains is profit.

This approach has the advantage of using only real data that can be calculated with a high degree of accuracy. Marginal cost and contribution cost isolate the leading edge of change. They are powerful values for budgeting and key indicators in management accounts (see Chapter 30).

The contribution concept is also a very useful tool in making decisions about the acceptability of price. Suppose a hotel with 40 rooms charges £50 per person per night. In breaking down this charge, variable costs amount to £15, allotted fixed overheads are £25 and profit is £10. Now suppose that a group travel organiser asks for ten rooms but can only offer £30 per night. On the face of it the hotel should refuse since this price implies a loss of £10 per room. Yet, assuming that the ten rooms would otherwise be empty, a price of £30 makes a £15 contribution to fixed overheads. Turn away this booking and the hotel has ten empty rooms and £150 less in total contribution.

Of course, if this special price were offered to all guests, then the hotel could only make losses. Yet equally, when filling spare capacity on special terms, it follows that all sales with a positive contribution will increase profits (or reduce losses). By a reverse application of this concept, a profitable multi-product firm may find its least successful products are loss-making when apportioned their share of fixed overheads. But provided these products are making a positive contribution then, in the absence of any better alternative, they should not be withdrawn.

Since almost all firms do have some spare capacity, the principle has wide-ranging applications. Indeed, where a product has a price inelastic core of demand, it may be possible to increase profits by deliberately charging a very high standard price and then selling off spare capacity on special terms at much lower prices, where only a contribution to fixed overheads is achieved.

The marginal cost principle carries certain dangers. It can be tempting to reduce price or offer discounts while contribution is still positive. Eroding real profitability can be concealed in the process. And although managers have the advantage of using real-cost data, contributions can disguise profit and loss. Attributable fixed overheads, were they to be calculated, could easily overwhelm an apparently healthy contribution.

Utilising and changing capacity

A firm's capacity is the maximum level of output that can be achieved using a given stock of fixed assets (e.g. land, buildings and installed equipment). In practice many firms operate with a lower 'soft ceiling' to output, at around 90–95 per cent capacity. This avoids the surge in marginal cost that often occurs as capacity is approached, and allows leeway to cope with unexpected orders or marketing opportunities. But operating with substantial spare capacity carries a heavy penalty. Because fixed overheads are spread across less output, unit costs increase, thus either shrinking margins or pushing up prices. The severity of this effect depends on the proportion of total costs represented by fixed overheads.

Capacity is a very real strategic problem. The growth of sales – and hence output – is projected both in budgets and in longer-term planning. But capacity takes time to adjust and may involve discontinuous changes such as relocation. Sales forecasts are subject to margins of error that widen rapidly as the period projected gets longer. Inadequate capacity can choke off a successful growth pattern, but excess capacity is a financial deadweight. The same problem in reverse applies to a firm in the process of contraction or retrenchment. A partial solution to these problems may lie in outsourcing or subcontracting any excess demand and filling spare capacity with subcontracts for other firms.

In the long run, a strategic decision must be made to expand (or contract) capacity. This usually involves significant capital investment on which adequate returns must be made. A basic attraction in expanding for most firms is the shape of the generic long-run average cost curve. Imagine that a firm could expand its capacity through an infinite range of size graduations, and for each size or scale of operations it plotted its average total cost of production, based on the optimum variable cost and the relevant fixed costs payable. The result would be a long-run average cost curve (LRAC) with a shape similar to that in Figure 20.1.

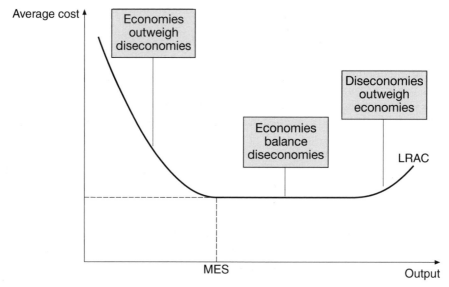

Figure 20.1 Typical long-run average cost curve

Every change in scale carries economies and diseconomies. These can be complex and interactive in their operation, but can be analysed through the categories shown in the table.

Economies and diseconomies of scale

Economies of scale	Diseconomies of scale
Technical, e.g. increased capacity costs proportionately less to install	**Organisational,** e.g. more complex structure makes communications slower and may reduce cross-functional co-ordination
Purchasing, e.g. bulk buying power cuts unit costs	**Motivational,** e.g. urgency of purpose lost; sense of alienation from senior management
Marketing, e.g. lower proportional rates for advertising or distribution	**Entrepreneurial,** e.g. weaker responses to opportunity; reduced flexibility and increased bureaucracy
Managerial, e.g. ability to employ specialist managers	
Financial, e.g. obtaining finance at lower cost	
Entrepreneurial, e.g. spreading risks avoids costly disruption when unfavourable events occur, such as a sales dip or a customer failing to pay	

Initially, at least, as a business grows in scale, the economies outweigh the diseconomies. The result is that the LRAC curve slopes downwards, often quite steeply and over a very wide range of output. This phenomenon explains the relatively low unit cost and very large scale of production for many basic goods and services – from lightbulbs to insurances, from cars to phone calls. So powerful can be the effect of scale on unit cost that firms may price products to earn low or negative returns while they penetrate the market and gain the market share necessary for a competitive cost base.

As firms grow in scale, however, there comes a point where diseconomies balance economies: in other words, there are constant returns to scale. Since this is the smallest scale of operation to benefit from minimised long-run average cost, it is known as Minimum Efficient Scale (MES). Firms in the industry operating on a scale below MES face a cost disadvantage compared with those achieving full economies of scale. To secure a competitive advantage it is likely that such firms will differentiate their product or rely on some non-contestable asset.

Something approximating to constant returns may prevail over wide ranges of output (or capacity). Many firms will expand under these conditions because the industry is young and demand is increasing, or because they are gaining market share.

Eventually, though, a scale is reached where diseconomies start to outweigh economies and with a rising cost base, profitability is likely to be eroded. In practice, diseconomies are a trap in which large companies can easily be caught. Managers get no warning that net diseconomies are emerging. Capacity increases by discontinuous leaps that are often driven by acquisitions or market opportunity. There may be optimism that initial diseconomies are only 'teething problems' that will soon be overcome.

Bic

The Bic Crystal throwaway ballpoint pen was launched in 1958 and has been produced ever since. As a product, it is a true classic and is even displayed in London's Museum of Design. It is also an icon in demonstrating the economies of scale.

At Bic's highly automated factory outside Paris in France, two million Crystals are produced every day. The machinery that makes the pens is immensely expensive but the scale of production is so great that each pen carries only a few pence in overhead costs. Direct material costs are low, direct labour costs are minimal. The rest of the 20–25p paid by the consumer is mainly accounted for by marketing and distribution.

The main source of demand is ironic – because the pens are so cheap, consumers take little trouble to look after them. Few pens ever see their ink exhausted. Most are simply lost!

Source: BIC (UK)

However, once net diseconomies are established, they can be difficult to reverse without drastic – and costly – reorganisation. Since diseconomies arise mainly from problems in human resource management and business organisation, they can advance and recede for a wide range of complex reasons. In many cases diseconomies actually set in well before they are recognised or understood. (For discussion of how such problems may be overcome, see Chapter 24.)

21 Mass production to lean production

Overview

Production aims to add the most value at the lowest cost. To approach this goal means that waste in all forms must be driven out of the production system. Lean production carries no 'fat' or waste, no matter how well concealed.

When mass production methods were first developed in the early 20th century, the gains in efficiency were so great that any waste in time and materials was easily overlooked. With large and expanding markets eager to enjoy the fruits of this new abundance, the lack of flexibility in production seemed to pose no problem.

Only in the second half of the century did business thinking move beyond the mindset of mass production and consider the possibilities of a more intelligent system. The seeds of this second revolution first took root in post-war Japan.

Efficiency and effectiveness

Efficiency is concerned with the relationships between inputs and outputs. Improving efficiency – in the simplest terms – means getting more from less. Within this overall context, the term 'efficiency' can be qualified to give it several distinctive and useful meanings. Technical efficiency is achieved when a given input to a process produces the greatest possible output. Productive efficiency is different in that it introduces cost. A firm is productively efficient when each unit of output is produced at the lowest possible cost.

Both these measures of efficiency are likely to be monitored by the operations management in a firm. Internally, the measurement of unit cost over time is a key approach. In the short run only variable costs are controllable, so average variable cost is the key indicator. This in turn is largely dependent on average materials cost and average labour cost. Notice that it is marginal cost – the cost of producing the 'last' unit – that is always driving average cost. Marginal cost is always a more volatile and telling series: it is in marginal cost data that problems (and opportunities) first show up. Finally, in the long run, when investment decisions and other fixed costs enter the picture, it is average total cost that must be analysed since this determines the cost base for true profitability.

Most firms, and especially those that are relatively labour-intensive, will want to investigate labour productivity. This is measured by output per person hour or the labour hours required for each unit of output. The measures are most meaningful when explored over a longer period or benchmarked against competitors. As an external criterion for the measurement of efficiency, benchmarking has risen sharply in importance and is discussed more fully below.

Clearly, operating efficiency is only one aspect of efficiency in the firm's overall performance. The process of adding value includes productive efficiency, but also depends on effectively meeting the needs of markets in relation to competitors. This is separately measured by return on capital employed (ROCE) or the added value ratio. A wider understanding of effectiveness would include the extent to which strategy has been successfully implemented and corporate aims fulfilled.

It should also be recognised that the firm, in its calculation of efficiency and effectiveness, usually only counts costs that the firm must pay: this frequently ignores social and environmental costs. Likewise, cutting costs can raise difficult ethical questions relating, for example, to redundancies or the use of cheap labour in poor countries.

Mass production

Ford and the Model T

Perhaps the first and ultimate icon of mass production, the Model T Ford, was launched to immediate success in 1908. The previous year Henry Ford had expressed his desire to 'build a car for the great multitude ... so low in price ... everybody will be able to afford one, and everyone will have one. The horse will have disappeared from our highways, the automobile will be taken for granted.'

Ford was among the first to recognise how a generic product could be designed for a low cost and low price entry into a mass market. He pursued his vision of maximised scale economies through the new techniques of mass production. The Model T was an unprecedented success even before Ford's first assembly line was opened at Highland Park, Michigan, in 1913. This cut the labour input to each car from just over 12 hours to 2 hours and 35 minutes. Within six months the factory was producing 1000 cars per day, with the unit labour input down again to an hour and a half.

These gains were not all appropriated as profit. Between 1908 and 1916 Ford reduced prices by 58 per cent despite overwhelming demand for the product.

Mass production is the basis on which many of today's largest business corporations have been built. Its core insight was that for many everyday products the source of utility among consumers is sufficiently similar to allow very long production runs of a standard product. This volume of output can exploit the economies of scale and technologies of flow production.

The 'Fordist' mode of production is thus based on some immensely powerful but rigid conditions. Its use of costly, inflexible plant means extended changeover times (the period necessary for altering the type of output) and infrequency of new products. Uninterrupted production and the high cost of 'downtime' require substantial buffer stocks of materials and components. Intensely repetitive, highly specialised work suits a command-and-control organisational style with little if any discretion passed down the line.

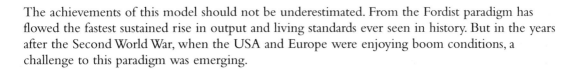

The achievements of this model should not be underestimated. From the Fordist paradigm has flowed the fastest sustained rise in output and living standards ever seen in history. But in the years after the Second World War, when the USA and Europe were enjoying boom conditions, a challenge to this paradigm was emerging.

Lean production

Toyota, the Japanese car manufacturer, was the first large firm to develop lean manufacturing techniques. Inspired by Taichi Ohno, the early adoption of two concepts by the company particularly stand out. The Japanese word *kanban* means cards or tokens that trigger the delivery of materials between stages in the production process. Different types of *kanbans* authorise production for stock, conveyance of materials from stock and receipt of external supplies. These simple systems were (and are) important because they expressed the goal of driving out waste (or *muda*) from the productive process. The other key feature was the embrace of quality throughout the organisation.

Deming's famous lectures to managers and engineers in Japan during 1950 stressed the need to 'manage for quality': a potent mix of management commitment, continuous learning and statistical control. This, he believed, would rebuild Japan's industrial base, transform its reputation for quality and conquer export markets all over the world. Acceptance of his advice soon proved Deming to be substantially correct. Toyota, in particular, became the most dedicated exponent of his philosophy, making quality the priority of everyone at every stage from product design to final delivery.

All this was powerful enough, but its transmission into overwhelming competitive advantage was ensured by treating the customer as the final and most important element in the production process. In this vision, the firm becomes a continuous value stream of purchasers drawing resources into the final task of meeting the customer's needs.

What, then, is the essence of lean production? Consider trying to make an urgent but complex journey by public transport. Not only would you need several changes between routes and services but you would also have to change between different modes of transport as well. As a passenger you would be 'processed' along fixed routes at fixed times that are geographically indirect and that require significant lead times at change points and terminals. You may not have wanted to go via London but you must. If the road ahead becomes congested, then your bus waits in a traffic jam without attempting to find a better route – or anticipating the problem or learning from the experience. When you finally arrive, it is not at the door that you wanted but at a bus or rail terminal some way away.

By contrast, as the driver of a car you can make a more direct journey, select from a flexible range of routes and take action to avoid delays. Your journey need include no interchanges or time-consuming waits for connecting services. It is door to door. You make mistakes but you can learn from them and let that knowledge build into a kind of expertise.

While public transport has other advantages, the analogy serves to illustrate some essential differences between mass and lean production. The first big difference between the two approaches is in their relationship to the customer. Mass production 'pushes' output through the process, stockpiles it and 'pushes' it to the market and the customer. Lean production starts with the demand of the customer which 'pulls' products through the process exactly as required. All queues and stockpiles in the system are eliminated. When a customer places an order, a seamless series of events is triggered that pulls resources through the system without costly accretions of waiting time. This sensitive and intelligent system routes and reroutes the production flow for maximum efficiency, snaps at every opportunity to drive up quality and cut down waste, and learns constantly from mistakes. It makes a formidable competitor.

Driving out waste, designing in quality

The first step in driving out waste is its identification. This judgement springs from the customer. Waste is all uses of time and other resources that do not generate value for the customer in the marketplace. Accurate matching of resources with the true wants of the customer is the foundation of quality. Toyota and other lean producers start with a portrait or specification of quality derived from careful unravelling of what their target customers really value. A rigorous statement of this standard then becomes the internal benchmark for quality at all stages of production.

This is the first dimension in our understanding of quality. The second is conformity to specification. This is the basic matter of reliability and fidelity in the product. Failure to reach specification quality implies waste and scrap, returns and reworking, complaints and damage to reputation. Philip Crosby (1979) famously observed that 'Quality is free.' Quality, that vital edge that cuts into markets, can be financed by the savings from eliminating quality failure.

Quality had exploded on to the management agenda in the USA after an NBC programme, *If Japan can, why can't we?*, broadcast in 1980. This was a time when US and European markets were suffering from deepening import penetration by Far Eastern countries, and particularly by Japan. Yet the original gurus of quality were not Japanese but American: W Edwards Deming and Joseph M Juran. Both had been passionate advocates of quality during the years after the Second World War, but were largely ignored in their own country. American business had plenty of easy markets at the time and it was Japan, with its devastated infrastructure and damaging reputation for poor quality, that accepted and internalised the quality message.

Too often in the West, quality has been confused with up-market specification or luxury. Ironically, and perhaps significantly, it was Japanese manufacturers for the mass market who used quality to win export success in the West. It needs to be stressed that there is no reason why a budget-priced product or a product aimed at the lowest socioeconomic groups should not be of a high quality.

The ten years after that NBC programme are often quoted as the period of a 'quality revolution'. Yet the achievement of consistent high quality proved an exacting journey for many firms. A chasm in philosophy and practice lies between corrective systems of quality control and preventive systems of quality assurance. The traditional approach was based on eliminating defective products before they reached the customer. Quality control was maintained by physical inspection and statistical sampling. It fitted the mechanical paradigm in being imposed and procedural: staff were required to perform appropriate checks as part of their job description.

In this sense, waste, instead of being designed out, was built into the system. A quality assurance system has two quite different principles. First, quality is designed into the product, not just in its specification but in the process of its manufacture. In this approach quality starts with the requirements of the customer and its assurance is agreed throughout the organisation. Second, staff learn to take responsibility for controlling the quality of their own work. Usually working in cells or teams, quality becomes a quest that is inherent to the culture of the workplace.

Many firms now seek formal accreditation of their quality assurance systems (ISO 9000), partly as an external evaluation of their own procedures and partly to ensure credibility and confidence among their customers. Since the 1980s, a growing proportion of these firms have attempted to make quality a default reflex throughout the organisation, to infuse quality in every layer of their culture. This vision of total quality management (TQM) moves beyond any specified standards towards expressing a holistic philosophy of integrity and excellence that everyone in the organisation represents. Quality becomes a matter of mindset, where the standards of any one part of the organisation reflect on the standards of every other part.

This indivisible approach to quality depends on commitment from management at all levels, and especially from top management. It can mean, quite literally, that an empty cigarette packet in the car park is as unacceptable as shipping to the customer a faulty product. Responsibility for quality meshes through the organisation along horizontal and vertical lines of commitment. A quality chain links each successive process or department, each as the customer of the next. Meanwhile, all employees are accountable to their line managers for the quality of work within their area of responsibility. With the trend towards multiskilling and flexible working, this becomes an interlocking and penetrating continuum of accountability. The use of quality circles is an instrument of continuous improvement (see below), but is also a sharing or 'infection' mechanism in the culture of total quality.

Time-based management

In business, time carries costs in two senses. First, resources are in the control of a firm because of the returns being generated over time. The earnings of resources deployed by a firm are strictly related to time and judged accordingly. Time is a fundamental dimension of achievement. Second, time is an axis of opportunity. Chances to secure a contract, enter a market or achieve a breakthrough depend for their value on timing. Often, a small time gain wins a large strategic gain. Lean production is dedicated to eliminating waste. Time is a key currency of waste.

Time-based management puts this concept into action. Think of the customer 'pulling' the product through the value-adding process with every connection taut in terms of time. Capacity in the necessary buildings, plant and equipment is available at the right time, while the arrival of materials and the availability of staff are synchronised to avoid waiting. Flexibility is ensured by resetting and reprogramming machines, but this changeover time is cut to the barest minimum. Finally, the whole process is taken at the maximum speed consistent with quality, and the product is released to the customer on or before the due date. Although lean production is usually discussed in relation to manufacturing, it is also relevant to service industries ranging from retailing and banking, through to public services such as education and health.

Holding stock (as materials, work-in-progress or finished goods) carries a range of operational costs such as storage, wastage and insurance. But the biggest negative of stockholding is the opportunity cost of capital tied up. Traditionally, firms would order their materials and components from many different suppliers with the award of large orders dependent on minimum unit cost. These consignments arrived in periodic deliveries and formed substantial stocks. In order to guard against a stockout (running out of stock), with all its costly implications for downtime of production lines, large buffer stocks were often maintained. The inevitable result was a high average stock level.

Since the 1980s there has been a quickening trend towards just-in-time (JIT) stock management. This treats all stocks as a form of waste that can be eliminated by tighter and better-managed links in the total supply chain. Most firms now operate with a smaller number of preferred suppliers with whom they can develop a long-term relationship that is mutually advantageous. Electronic ordering systems allow frequent deliveries of stock 'just-in-time' for the production process. Since suppliers themselves cannot afford large stocks, the JIT logic feeds backwards up the supply chain. The whole production process becomes taut in terms of time. Storage and opportunity costs shrink. Like a relay race, the 'baton' is stock delivered smoothly to the right place at the right time.

Just-in-time stock management becomes a just-in-time manufacturing system when every stage in the production chain, from the final customer back to the first supplier, is held in a tension so that resources spend no time queuing for their next deployment. This seamlessness creates an urgency and focus in the whole process that would otherwise be lacking. It demands tight co-ordination between links in the chain both internally and in the relationships with suppliers.

The just-in-time approach to management aims to drive out not only buffer stocks of physical goods, but also buffer stocks of work, customers and time. In practice, huge amounts of slack time are built into the production process of most goods and services. Queues of customers or work-in-progress arise from mismatches of capacity with demand. The answer may lie in improved scheduling or flexible capacity (see below). Even more wasteful, but quite common, are chronic queues where a backlog first builds and then persists when demand and capacity are back in balance.

There is also an important distinction to be made between value-adding and non-value-adding activities. Value is added by activities that build benefit for the final customer – for example, manufacturing or packaging. Non-value-adding activities may have some value for the firm but have no value to the customer. Checking, storage, stocktaking and paperwork are all examples. In UK manufacturing these non-value-adding activities can occupy 90–95 per cent of total production time. A goal of lean production is therefore to shorten or design out of the process these activities. The most radical solution in this context is business process re-engineering (see Chapter 24).

Time-based management is also essential to product development. Traditionally, this has tended to follow a linear pattern where each stage has been completed before the next is started. Lean design or simultaneous engineering involves running these multiple processes of development concurrently where possible, thus shortening the time to product launch. This achieves better use of specialised resources and may gain vital strategic advantage in entering a market ahead of competitors.

Value analysis

Value is constructed from costs. Every cost is a throughput of scarce resources and should be adding net value (see Chapter 5). Often, this addition to value is direct: the operation performed by the cost centre (any department, process or equipment for which costs can be separately identified) makes the product more valuable. In other cases, a cost is incurred for the value of its interaction with other costs as part of a total system. Such costs are more difficult to analyse because neither the cost nor its value can be isolated from the system of which they are part.

Value engineering is embedded in the design stage of new product development. Popularised in Japan, it is a cross-functional process to eliminate all costs that fail to add value. An interdepartmental team aims to cut unnecessary elements of expense, reduce the number of components and simplify the production process. Co-ordination between departmental teams is usually improved at the same time.

Value analysis occurs after a product has entered the market and again involves cross-functional teams. Their task is to identify and analyse a product's sources of value and then to find ways of sustaining or enhancing that value, but at lower cost. Just the process of analysing the origins of value can be very useful. A firm may have a good knowledge of a product's functional value without fully understanding its emotional value to different groups of buyers. For example, coloured back-lighting for digital displays in a hi-fi system may serve no functional purpose and add extra cost. Yet it could be a key source of appeal in its target market and a vital form of differentiation from its competitors.

It is also important to recognise systemic value. A hotel found that the cost of offering a night-time service of drinks and snacks was clearly loss-making; but when placed in the context of the hotel's total offering, it was found to add value with its connotations of reassurance and luxury. As a result of effective value analysis, a firm can often add further value to its products while eliminating significant sources of cost.

22 *Kaizen* and the new flexibility

Overview

An essential feature of lean production is the commitment to continuous improvement in every aspect of the productive process. This should permeate the culture of the organisation and needs to be recognised as a primary duty of all staff.

Benchmarking is an important technique in the search for improvement and needs the active commitment of all employees.

Meanwhile, flexibility is the defining feature of organisations successfully undergoing transformation from a mechanistic to an organic model. This helps firms to respond quickly to rapidly changing markets and to innovate ahead of competitors. Softening organisational structures allow staff greater autonomy, while training and development move beyond mastery of skills to embrace critical thinking and continuous learning.

Kaizen or continuous improvement

A unitary culture of common commitment is also very important to what is perhaps the core mechanism in the practice of lean production, namely *kaizen* or continuous improvement. Although *kaizen* is usually associated with cutting costs, it also embraces ideas for adding value at zero or disproportionately low cost. Indeed, failure to recognise or implement opportunities to add value is itself another form of waste.

The idea that present methods and performance are never good enough and that the urge for improvement should be a restless and unending impulse does not seem exceptional. Yet the command-and-control mindset of Western management has kept, as Pascale puts it, 'leadership as head and organisation as body'. *Kaizen*, by contrast, needs the whole organisation to be curious, critical, thoughtful and optimistic. Rather than progress by infrequent, expensive step changes where mistakes are prohibitively expensive, *kaizen* embraces small, incremental steps to improvement that can be reversed if necessary, yet which cumulatively can become a revolution.

The idea of continuous improvement is not a bolt-on management tool. It needs to become active in the organisational 'bloodstream', a dynamic cast of mind shared by management and staff alike. Its institutionalised expression may be quality circles, staff meetings, suggestion schemes or other participative arrangements. These structures are usually non-hierarchical and cross-functional in character and can spawn both the creative exchange of ideas and a personal feeling of responsibility and engagement.

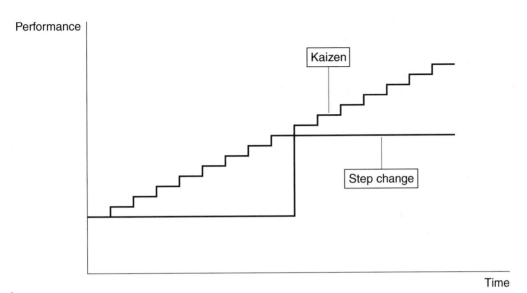

Figure 22.1 Step change and *kaizen*

'Never forget the gold in the workers' heads' is an old Toyota saying that reflects the close involvement of the workforce with operational realities at every level. Once employees are no longer 'cogs in a wheel' but critical agents of a firm's purpose, then their knowledge and ideas about efficiency and quality become a stream of value or a kind of 'gold'.

While a framework for collecting and rewarding staff ideas is essential, the *kaizen* principle is ultimately a way of thinking and responding. Impulses for improvement may gather anywhere in the organisation at any time. The need for staff to conceive, express and share ideas as a reflex suggests a very flat organisational structure with a culture of trust and experiment (see Chapter 32).

Richer Sounds

Julian Richer founded his chain of hi-fi stores in 1978 and has achieved the distinction of holding the world retail record for sales per square foot. As a high-profile entrepreneur he has advised a range of large companies, and was involved in assisting Asda in its revival before the Wal-Mart acquisition.

Richer's formula is based on selling quality hi-fi in low-cost locations with a highly motivated staff and exceptional customer service. He is a passionate advocate of *kaizen*, believing that continuous improvement and continuous learning are the life-blood of any business. As he says: 'There is never a perfect way – there is only the best way until you find a better way.'

The company maintains a decisive balance between central control and staff empowerment. Head Office requires the use of current best practice throughout the company. But in the areas of their work where prescription is unhelpful, staff are empowered to devise their own solutions. This particularly applies to customer service.

Meanwhile, the flow of ideas for improvement is channelled through a colleagues' suggestion scheme and a network of Colleagues' Representatives who quiz senior management. Energy is pumped into the suggestion scheme through fast responses and (modest) rewards for every contribution received. The scheme has the highest participation rate in the UK. Richer comments: 'A good suggestions scheme is like having an oil well in your back garden.'

In addition, once a month every branch or department holds a meeting, usually in the pub, and staff are given £5 each to spend on drinks. Creative brainstorming is the agenda and the proceeds of subsequent suggestions are shared.

Benchmarking

Developed under the shadow of Japanese imports, benchmarking has become an important tool for the improvement of operations. It is a simple idea that means the continuous effort to identify and emulate best practice.

Xerox ←

The pioneer of benchmarking as a serious technique was Xerox. Back in 1980 the Xerox corporation was faced by serious loss of market share to Japanese competitors. The company found that Japanese models were as good or better than the Xerox product, yet sold for less than a Xerox machine cost to produce.

The firm's response was to identify Japanese best performance against a range of criteria and to drive up the Xerox rating to match or exceed that standard. By the mid-1980s Xerox products were reaching world-class standards in terms of both cost and quality.

At first, benchmarking was mainly concerned to close the gap between US and European companies and their Japanese competitors. It soon became a more sophisticated tool where the terms of reference were global and 'world class' became the essential criterion. Instead of being industry-specified, benchmarking became based on a process comparison across industries. If, for example, customer service was the subject of concern, then the best practice in customer service should be benchmarked, regardless of the industry.

Benchmarking can be applied to any area of business practice that is measurable. As the firm clarifies its strengths and weaknesses, the process can be related to the best known practice. Benchmarking must be specific and not too broad in its specification. At the same time, the process must avoid so many criteria that it becomes bureaucratic or loses the urgency of a mission in the effort for improvement.

The technique of benchmarking follows a basic cycle as shown in Figure 22.2.

The selection of criteria depends on the areas of operations identified for improvement and the key points of competitive pressure. Some large firms find comparative data internally, perhaps in another division or subsidiary. External benchmarking can be based on partnering with another

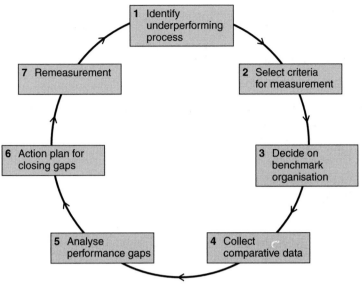

↑ Figure 22.2 The benchmarking cycle

organisation or on the use of mutual data banks shared between a number of firms. Targeted research in the industry and published secondary data can also be useful ways forward.

Analysis of data generally emphasises the gap between current and best practice. This leads to action plans for closing the gaps, and frequent reviews of progress made.

To be effective, benchmarking needs top management commitment with the active involvement of the workforce affected. It is not just another target or a way a driving employees harder. The process is most likely to succeed in an open culture where the idea of improvement is a norm and employees at all levels are routinely involved in thinking critically and setting goals.

The new flexibility

Lean production systems answer to their target market. This sounds a reassuringly stable idea, but it can actually imply being subject to whirlwinds of barely predictable, even chaotic change. We have already seen that the rate of change in markets is accelerating and that any map of consumer preferences is unstable and dynamic by its very nature. This makes product ranges and segmentation models contingent, transient statements that are always in the process of revision or reinvention. This is a world where the ground moves under moving targets and shooting has to be from the hip.

In such a world, the once impressive fortresses of mass production with their long runs of standardised output are clearly a retreating genre. Lean production drives out waste and it introduces flexibility. This is central to the paradigm shift from production as a piece of mechanics towards production as a self-improving and organic system.

Flexibility is about the ability to respond aptly and swiftly to change. Rigidity or even a state of equilibrium in the relationship between a firm and its market is extremely dangerous. As the quantity and nature of products demanded change, so the quantity and nature of the firm's output must change too. Firms that are slow to respond or that offer an inappropriate response will find their demand functions or value frontiers shrinking towards the origin. Conversely, firms that are faster than their competitors to respond, or that find a uniquely successful response, will experience advancing demand functions and new strategic options.

This kind of new flexibility challenges the old orthodoxy, where the search for scale economies locked firms into long cycles of inflexible behaviour. Increasingly, the goal is not only to produce at lower unit cost but also to respond far more flexibly to the marketplace where turbulence can be the norm. There are two levels of unpredictability that most firms need to address. The first is the shorter-run 'sawtooth' fluctuations in demand that occur on the 'surface' of most markets. These 'ups' and 'downs' in demand normally operate within outer parameters of probability, but can cause significant wastage without sufficient agility in response.

Second, there is the longer-term change in direction as the underlying trend shifts. This may happen very slowly at first and then later gather speed, or the change may be abrupt and even discontinuous where the new realities cannot be forecast through analysis of the past. Demand for an existing product may wither suddenly. A different version of the product type may soar in popularity, or an entirely different product may take its place. Such changes of direction can require all kinds of shifts, both in output volume and in the nature of the product.

There are three basic forms in which flexibility can be developed. These relate to the structure of the firm, the systems of its operation and the potential of its workforce. A traditional source of basic inflexibility has been the nature and structure of the firm itself. Ever since Peters and Waterman (1982) argued for the importance of focus in markets and operations, firms have been anxious to delineate their identity and sources of excellence. The core competence movement, spearheaded by Hamel and Prahalad (1990), has also been uncompromising in wanting to uncover the ultimate operational basis for winning a competitive advantage.

The idea of focus encouraged the ungluing of organisations with the emergence of a distinctive core and peripheral functions arranged around it. A diverse and contingent mix of outsourcing, subcontracting, alliances and partnerships has developed a new organisational flexibility where the concept of a fixed and rigid 'capacity' is no longer relevant. In a sense, part of the firm is actual and part virtual. Not only can the balance of these elements change, but the model allows a firm to break free from the traditional constraints imposed by its buildings, machinery, skills and experience. In some cases, the discrete nature of a firm dissolves and the business becomes a node of contracts and throughputs within a wider network of productive enterprise.

Flexible capacity is also more specifically achieved through the increasing use of smaller, often cell-based machinery that can be more readily reprogrammed and reconfigured. Traditionally, inflexible production lines are developing a more modular character where changes in the pattern of demand need not cause expensive disruption. Combined with faster change-over times in the function of machinery, this means that the old distinction between flow and batch production becomes blurred. A much wider range of products can be made with far greater flexibility in the range of output levels that are economic for any given product.

Schonberger (1990) stresses the need for organisational changes to fulfil the promise of lean production. A shift away from the conventional hierarchies of mass production, towards semi-autonomous work groups or cellular production, gives teams responsibility and ownership for an internal supply chain. Again, Toyota was one of the first major companies to adopt this new thinking when it reorganised its plants and equipment around the cellular principle.

Operational flexibility has to be matched with flexibility in the workforce. Until the 1980s there was a tendency to specify many jobs in terms of rigid hours and a single role and skill. Increasingly since then, various flexible forms of working have evolved. Staff may work longer hours at busy times and take time off in lieu later, while the use of part-timers has radically increased. The old demarcation lines between jobs and trades have been softened or erased as staff become multi-skilled. Cellular production, in particular, depends on multi-skilling as work is shared and many team members become interchangeable. Management commitment to training and development schemes is essential, especially in a rapidly changing work environment. This has led some firms to sponsor career-long education and learning programmes to encourage critical thinking and receptivity to new ideas.

These developments have met with mixed reactions from trade unions and the workforce. When associated with unsocial hours, insecurity and job losses, flexible working is understandably liable to fierce opposition. Its acceptance is far more likely when introduced in close consultation with staff, and linked to single status and enhancement in rewards and conditions of employment. Much also depends on achieving a change in culture (see Chapter 31) where the workforce ceases to see its interests as opposed to those of management and experiences, instead, a sense of commitment to a common cause.

PART **E**

HUMAN
RESOURCES
explained

23 From personnel to human resources

Overview

Every output contains a human input. Put another way, the costs of production will always include payment for human resources. Those payments represent a vital part of the rewards for work and provide the income to households that in turn funds customer demand.

Firms spend money on human inputs because they add value. In some cases, this added value is direct – for example, in many personal services such as hairdressing, where labour is explicitly involved. Often, though, labour inputs are hidden inside the value chain where they are no less significant. Increasingly in business, it is the complex contribution of human resources that creates and sustains competitive advantage. This may be achieved through exceptional productivity and correspondingly low unit labour costs. Alternatively, it may arise from the specialised skills and experience of staff who are able to offer superior quality of product and customer experience. Finally, it may also arise more subtly through people in teams or as part of a systemic whole where operational effectiveness and continuous innovation keep the value offering ahead of competitors.

The personnel tradition

Historically, the management of people has moved through stages that reflect the economic realities then prevailing. Before the First World War, the labour force was viewed as 'hands' that provided the repetitive manual labour then required at most stages in the productive process. Because it was literally a pair of hands rather than a person to fill a job, Henry Ford's complaint about the workforce is telling: 'How come when I want a pair of hands I get a human being as well?'

Labour as 'hands' was a commodity. One pair of hands was little different from another. A standard contract, standard wage rate and standard conditions found its opposite expression in the mass trade unions that developed over this period. Typically, the firm's organisational structure was hierarchical and its structure essentially mechanical. Indeed, given the repetitive nature of many jobs, the labour force was often viewed as 'human machinery'.

Modern personnel management dates from the early 20th century. This was a time of growing corporate scale and the emergence of office staff as a mass sector. Although in some firms philanthropy was an active driver of personnel policy, there was some widening recognition of a link between productivity and worker welfare. Firms with a Quaker background, such as Lever

Brothers and Cadbury, had long believed that the cause of employee welfare could advance both philanthropic and business ends. It was also during the 1930s that the 'Human Relations' school of management began to develop, spurred by the work of Elton Mayo (see Chapter 25). Evidence started to accumulate that the motivation and commitment of a workforce did not depend solely on pay and physical conditions, but also on psychological and social factors such as personal recognition and group cohesion.

Interestingly, too, firms were becoming more concerned with their public image. Large companies were employing more staff to deal with the public directly. This gave the quality of staff greater importance as the reputation of brands began to add value. The concept of public relations also dates from this period.

It was against this background that the early personnel departments were established by firms such as Marks & Spencer and London Transport. These were essentially service departments that codified and professionalised much of what had been *ad hoc* before. The typical personnel department had responsibility for recruitment, selection, training promotion and payment systems, together with a welfare and disciplinary role. During the mid-20th century, personnel management became a standard feature of corporate life, but it was usually tangential to the core business functions of production, sales and finance. In a world where factory work and even office employment were a graded commodity, the task of personnel managers was to supply the organisation with the units and hours of labour that it required.

The personnel department has tended to be regarded as a source of cost rather than added value. Its work has often been perceived as 'soft' when compared with the 'hard' nature of operations or finance. Significantly, many female staff have found career progression in personnel, while the Personnel Manager has often lacked a place on the board.

What is human resource management (HRM)?

Gathering in force since the 1980s, a growing challenge has confronted this model. This is the concept of human resource management (HRM) that, in many larger firms, has represented a sea-change in the perception and management of staff. Driven by accelerating automation and the advent of the knowledge economy, firms have realised that their critical assets are no longer real estate and machinery, but people – and the ability of people to think and to share ideas. As a famous aphorism in the *New York Times* (1995) put it: 'Microsoft's only factory asset is the human imagination.'

In a real sense, HRM tacitly demands the graduation of employees from 'pairs of hands' and 'filling jobs' to becoming the thinking and flexible agents of an intelligent organisation. In this model, people management is no longer a 'soft service' but instead becomes a 'hard' strategic centrality.

HRM acknowledges that in most firms employees represent a high proportion of costs. More significantly, it recognises that an even higher and often growing percentage of added value is dependent on the staff. In this context, HRM places a firm's workforce at the heart of the business and its strategy.

It is clear that competitive advantage is becoming more and more dependent on the people in the organisation. Often the major – even the only – differentiating factor in a firm is the knowledge, relationships and culture among staff. Advantages based on installed plant, technical processes, scale economies and even location all tend to lack longevity. No matter how substantial or advanced a firm's operational advantage, in the long term it is open to replication. But people-based advantages are extraordinarily complex. They can adapt, transmute, reinvent themselves in response to threat or opportunity. Replication by competitors of human resource advantages is extremely difficult.

Dig deeper into the roots of competitive advantage and the human resource factor shows at every level. Core capabilities – except where non-contestable – are ultimately embedded in people. Innovation, creativity, knowledge-sharing, teamwork and reputation all have their springs in people: individuals, groups and systems.

HRM analysed

The concept of HRM has applications at every level in the organisation. As always in business, the goal is to add more value. Specifically, this means that a key aim is to improve the ratio of cost to added value. This can be achieved by increasing the quantity or value of output for a given labour input. Sometimes it may also be possible to reduce the cost of labour, although leeway here is limited by the market forces of demand and supply.

Making people more productive is a long-standing management goal. In its simplest form, this means increasing the quantity or volume of output per time period. But more and more today, the measurement of productive output has a second dimension. Productive effectiveness embraces the quality of output, which in turn drives market value and ultimate customer loyalty (see Chapter XX). As products become more complex, jobs get more skilled, while the trend towards empowerment gives still more discretion. Meanwhile, many products contain an increasingly value-adding element of personal service. All of these factors highlight the importance of quality. And effectiveness has a broader meaning still. Teams are only valuable because they generate synergy. Put another way, the team effort is more valuable than the sum of its constituent parts working in isolation. Staff who contribute effectively within a team, share knowledge and offer creative ideas for improvement add further value. This reflects a systems interpretation of business that values organisational intelligence and recognises the interactivity of a more organic business model.

In recent years, this has all involved a fundamental rethinking of the proper role and mindset of people at work. The mechanical view of people as cogs in a machine requires little more than obedience and the proper application of skills learned for the job. Reconceive people as thoughtful agents of a shared purpose and the whole picture changes. If, as McGregor (1960) suggests, people naturally seek responsibility, then they need less supervision and control and more skills of leadership and task management. This implies a flatter, less hierarchical structure with more delegation and trust and wider spans of control (see Chapter 24). It also suggests the need for vigorous bottom-up communications and a sense of purpose understood and shared by all.

Advocated by Herzberg (1959), empowerment at work has been slow to arrive. Cultural tradition, as well as fear and suspicion among both managers and workforce, have been serious obstacles. However, the pace of change quickened in the late 20th century as competitive benefits showed through. Organisations have slimmed middle management and, assisted by information technology, brought the top and bottom of their organisational pyramids much closer together. Training and

A new freedom?

The years ahead should be a good time for dreamers and visionaries of the business world, for the barriers to innovation, the roadblocks to inspiration and imagination, are being knocked down one by one.

For individuals ... barriers to ambition (although not always to achievement of those ambitions) are being challenged and eliminated. ... Within corporations, people can aspire to greater achievements because of a weakening of hierarchy and a broadening of participation in problem-solving and even decision-making. Business is gradually shedding the shackles of an artificial status order that told people what their place was – and to stay in it.

Source: Rosabeth Moss Kanter When Giants Learn to Dance *(Simon & Schuster, 1989)*

development have expanded and intensified, with growing opportunities for employees to negotiate their own training plans. Many different forms of employee participation have emerged, including quality circles and autonomous work groups. These structures vary widely between industries and firms, but all aim to capture workforce ideas, take a team approach to problem solving and spread best practice.

Taken together, these trends represent a new philosophy of work that supports continuous improvement (*kaizen* – see Chapter 22) in each and every productive process. This highlights the growing need in HRM to develop an organisational culture that encourages curiosity, entrepreneurship, knowledge-sharing and teamwork. This is only likely to occur with the real and active support of top management. Maintaining the alignment between the resulting organisational energy and strategic goals is a challenge: the potential cumulative gains are building blocks of competitive advantage.

HRM as a strategic activity

A firm's strategy always had implications for the personnel department. HRM makes people management integral to strategy, and often the defining feature of the strategy itself. HRM as a key dimension of competitive advantage usually requires a cross-functional approach that builds teams into systems of knowledge and intelligence (see Chapter 26). This implies a strategy horizon that is long term and evolutionary. If successful, the human resource advantage will add value in itself and facilitate value adding in every business function.

The encoded nature of human resource capability is, by its nature, well defended against replication. Relationships between people are unique and organic. They are thinking and adaptable. That operate at individual, group and systemic levels. They are an expression of organisational culture that is probably the least easy feature of any to copy.

How, exactly, do human resource capabilities add value? First, well-designed, well-made relationships and linkages improve co-ordination and raise synergy levels. Sensitivity and thoughtfulness towards the external environment enhance and quicken the flow of information and ideas. Possibilities for creative thinking are opened and innovation can become more of a reflex and less of a special occasion. Meanwhile, the superior 'wiring' between people allows a faster and more complex response to stimuli of all kinds. Second, all these value-adding tendencies are amplified in their intensity and probability if staff feel committed and engaged, their energy aligned with the organisation's purpose. Except at the most senior levels, it is often not necessary for staff to articulate corporate strategy. But they must feel energised in a common cause that is the source of urgency and meaning throughout the organisation.

Finally, at the highest level, the human resource advantage is about organisational intelligence. Handy (1989) identified the 'Triple I' factors: information, ideas and intelligence. HRM can, by degrees, convert an organisation from a mechanistic to a neural paradigm (this concept is explored further in Chapter 24). But it is in the accumulation and sharing of knowledge and in the generation of ideas that future added value is likely to be found.

New HR configurations

In more and more industries the whole concept of a 'mass labour force' is changing. The very term 'labour' suggests undifferentiated low-skill work where any one employee is more or less the equivalent of another. As labour-saving technologies advance and the value added by knowledge increases, so firms tend to want on their permanent pay-roll committed staff who offer distinctive skills with the ability to adapt and learn.

Handy (1989) offers the Shamrock model, where the image of the three-leaf plant is used to distinguish three different types of worker in the new organisational pattern. The first group are the core workers – the professionals, managers and technicians who hold the most valuable organisational knowledge. They are permanent, committed, hard working and well paid. This core has shrunk in size over recent years: it is high cost and so must be high value-adding. The old tiers of middle management have largely been delayered, downsized, eliminated. Core staff operate in typically 'flat' hierarchies, or even non-hierarchical networks (see Chapter 24). They become partners and colleagues in the firm and are valued and partly paid by their performance. As the 'human capital' of the business they will be retained by all means affordable.

The second leaf of the shamrock is the contracted-out labour force, no longer working directly for the firm. This has grown very rapidly. It can hugely reduce the scale of organisational pyramids and take the firm out of activities for which it lacks any strong competitive advantage and where other specialised firms can do a more effective job. The management of subcontracting is a widening skill. Subject to necessary conditions, payment is by result – the work delivered. More and more firms are becoming assembly operations of a kind: in the chain of added value they are experts in one type of resource configuration. Continuously, they buy in and sell on.

The third and final shamrock leaf is the flexible labour force made up of mainly part-time and temporary staff. This is the residual world of commodity labour, where staff come and go and are paid at a market rate. Flexible workers seek acceptable pay, reasonable conditions and some conviviality from their work. It is usually in the interests of employers to offer basic privileges and adequate training so that quality and motivation are maintained. This is especially vital in industries with a direct customer interface. The danger is poor treatment of this sector leading to failures in quality and inconsistencies in delivery of the product.

24 Organisational design

Overview

Organisations are patterns for the contributions of people working together. They are found in every arena of human activity. Some organisations are formal, with agreed roles and relationships that are written down. Many others are informal. These are typically flexible and in a state of continuous change. Most formal organisations also contain some kind of informal organisation. The interaction between the two is often highly significant.

Every organisation exists for a purpose. This may be explicit in confronting a particular task or an ongoing series of tasks. Most business organisations are of the latter type. Some organisations have a purpose that is more implicit, such as a family or a group of employees inside a firm.

A business organisation aims to add value. In other words, to justify its existence, the organisation must achieve synergy. More value must be added by the whole than would have been added by the sum of the parts. In this sense, every organisation has an opportunity cost: what would the next-best configuration have achieved?

It follows that the design of organisations in business is a critical factor in their achievement of competitive advantage. An organisation is a powerful model and often takes on a life of its own. When people are connected, they work differently from when they work alone. An organisational structure determines the pathways of control, responsibility and communication. It is therefore a key influence on such factors as co-ordination, flexibility and speed of response. It also helps to shape the prevailing culture or characteristic patterns of behaviour by people as individuals or in groups.

The meaning of organisational design

Sometimes, an entirely new organisation is given a purpose-made design – a kind of operational blueprint. Usually, however, the design of an organisation evolves over a period, although it may be subject to occasional 'reorganisation' where its managers make an intentional and abrupt change to the structure.

In the search for effective business strategy, the design of an organisation is often a critical factor. In a real sense it is the internal architecture of the firm and, like the design of a building, this architecture has a major influence on what takes place within its parameters. At the most basic level, an organisation's design must facilitate its work. The pathways of leadership and responsibility specified must be effective in enabling the organisation to implement its strategy in pursuit of agreed objectives. To this end the design will decide the form and extent of specialisation. It will also determine the formal interactivity of people and greatly influence their informal relations.

Organisational design has a huge potential impact on the motivation of staff (see Chapter 25). The extent and nature of supervision are key factors. Intensive regulation usually demotivates, but so can lack of guidance. Similarly, good communication – downward, upward and lateral – is a vital function of organisational design. The routes for promotion through the structure with their differing levels of reward are also part of the motivational picture.

Much in the way of effectiveness relates to how people interpret their roles. Is a job closely described or is it open and flexible? Are staff expected to be dutiful and cautious or are they encouraged to be entrepreneurial and to take risks in return for opportunity? And are employees generally functional towards their work or are they likely to be creative? The answers to these questions and many others depend on the organisational culture (see Chapter 31) which is itself significantly predicated by organisational design.

There is a further dimension to the way in which organisations are designed. We often talk about products being 'smart' or even intelligent. From a simple thermostat to an advanced microprocessor, an increasing range of products have built into them an ability to respond to new instructions and changing conditions. Organisational designs have parallel implications. The insight and foresight shown by an organisation, the speed of its reactions and its capability to share and add to its knowledge are all to some extent programmed by the structure and systems represented by its design.

The classic hierarchy

When large-scale industrial business first developed in the 19th century, the military hierarchy of command and control was its natural model. Owners and entrepreneurs were the generals, managers were the officers and the rest of the workforce were soldiers in the lower ranks. The classic pyramid hierarchy that is still the basic pattern of many organisations today (Figure 24.1) has its origins in the structure of the Roman army.

Top management set organisational goals and corporate strategy. Senior and middle managers take strategic decisions that implement the overarching plan, while junior managers make tactical decisions that are more routine and concerned with the detail of operations. At the bottom of the hierarchy a mass workforce is supervised to carry out instructions. The essence of this model is its capacity to transmit authority through the levels in the hierarchy from the top to the bottom of the structure. Each superior delegates authority to the subordinates within his or her span of control but retains *responsibility* in the process. Although there may be some feedback from the 'bottom up', the thrust of communication is 'top down' in the form of commands.

The classical hierarchy is an essentially rigid and mechanical structure that transmits cause and effect through the organisational equivalent of 'rods and pulleys'. In its historical context, this is not surprising. The view of a business espoused by FW Taylor (1911) reflected the triumph of applied science in the 19th century. The foundations of modern management were avowedly mechanical and successful in mass manufacturing, where physical output was all-important and people were 'paid hands'.

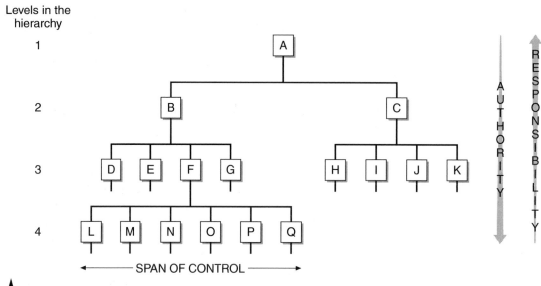

Figure 24.1 Classic pyramid hierarchy

In reality, the control-and-command model only seemed efficient because it embodied the leading edge of technology and applied the division of labour with an unprecedented intensity. It survived where labour inputs were essentially a commodity obtainable at fairly uniform and modest price.

Pyramids under attack

The discovery of the *Hawthorne effect* by Elton Mayo and his researchers in the 1930s was the earliest assertion that organisations contained complex human beings rather than quasi-mechanical components. Yet it was not really until 1960, when Douglas McGregor published his *Theory X* and *Theory Y* (for a fuller coverage, see Chapter 25), that the possibility of dismantling pyramids began to emerge.

Theory X was the stuff of hierarchical management. As a command-and-control structure, the traditional pyramid is based on the assumption that staff need supervision and coercion if they are to work effectively. It is further assumed that staff are uncommitted to the organisation's goals. They show no ability or interest in understanding them or in relating their own skills to the challenge of those objectives. Such a view validates an hierarchical structure with a strong chain of command and tight spans of control.

Theory Y is a contrast above all in assumptions. This is a participative vision of people who can internalise organisational objectives and independently apply their intellect and imagination to the tasks in hand. Of course, McGregor knew that Theory X frequently appeared to be the most accurate in describing employees' actual behaviour, but this was because the description was self-fulfilling. Treat employees as though Theory X *was* true, design your organisation accordingly, and by and large employees will fulfil your expectations. To break out of Theory X and enter the more productive world of Theory Y, a fundamental shift in assumptions is necessary. This was always likely to have profound implications for the classic hierarchy.

It was not until the 1980s that the challenge to 'tall' multilayered hierarchies really gathered force. By then a number of key trends were affecting business organisations across the Western world. First was the intensification of global competition. No firm could afford to carry any fat, and layers of costly middle management began to look like a luxury. Markets moved faster and became more complex as mass affluence allowed progressively finer segmentation. Meanwhile, as new technology drove down manufacturing costs, an increasing proportion of added value was dependent on the performance of people. Production was beginning to 'dematerialise' as value came to depend less on physical inputs and more on embedded knowledge. The combination of all these changes began to place classic hierarchies at a competitive disadvantage.

This is best understood in terms of the new demands acting on organisations in the late 20th century and beyond. To track shifting markets and to fulfil new patterns of demand, firms have needed to get much closer to their customers. This means 'flatter' structures where even senior management are closely in touch with the market interface. Bottom-up communications must become much faster and more sensitive. Organisations must be able to anticipate change and respond rapidly with flexibility and cross-functional co-ordination.

Meanwhile, as most jobs become more complex and highly skilled, staff increasingly work in team formations that share knowledge and experience. This in turn means that leadership becomes more dispersed in the organisation and that collective intelligence is needed at all levels.

General Electric

In 1981 Jack Welch became the youngest ever chairman of the US industrial giant, General Electric. Between then and his retirement in 2001, the business gained a strategic and motivational energy that carried its market value from $13 billion to $550 billion – and earned Welch a reputation as 'the greatest manager of the 20th century'.

He started with a tough approach to underperformance. Every business was required to be No. 1 or No. 2 in its market. Otherwise the message was 'fix, close or sell'. A decisive innovation was the introduction of the GE 'Work-Out'. This sprang from a wish to avoid the concentration of thinking at the apex of the organisation and to energise every employee level or grouping with the cycle of questioning, testing and learning.

The process involved staff in meeting to identify problems and making proposals for their resolution. Managers were required to give an immediate answer where possible, or anyway within one month. The result – popularised as 'picking the low-hanging fruit' – was a speed-up in recognising and solving problems. It also began to engage staff as critical and thoughtful co-learners in support of business objectives.

Action Work-Outs developed the system with workplace brainstorming among staff and management on a collaborative basis. A logical extension was Welch's notion of 'boundarylessness'. This involved a total cross-functionalism, where innovation and best practice were shared across every GE business. Knowledge was also propagated both upstream and downstream to assist suppliers and customers.

> Welch's central vision was to make General Electric into a thinking and learning organisation. Instead of the company's size being a managerial liability, it would become an asset through the scale and diversity of ideas generated and shared.

New organisational designs

These factors have led to a progressive meltdown of the tall pyramid. During the 1990s hierarchies became 'flatter' as delayering stripped out whole levels in the organisational structure, mostly from middle management. Correspondingly, spans of control have widened, with managers taking on a role of strategic leadership and mentoring rather than command and control. Delegation has increased at all levels, thus increasing the premium on trust and the maintenance of ethical standards.

There are, meanwhile, ways of making pyramid-style hierarchies more effective in meeting specific needs. The oldest solution is divisionalisation. Made famous by Alfred Sloan at General Motors, the organisation is typically split by brand, product range or geographical market. The divisions are decentralised in that they are each structured as an independent firm with its own functional management. The divisional heads are directly responsible for business performance, and report to head office where only the strategic planning and corporate finance functions are centralised.

The matrix pattern

A more recent development is the matrix or project-based structure.

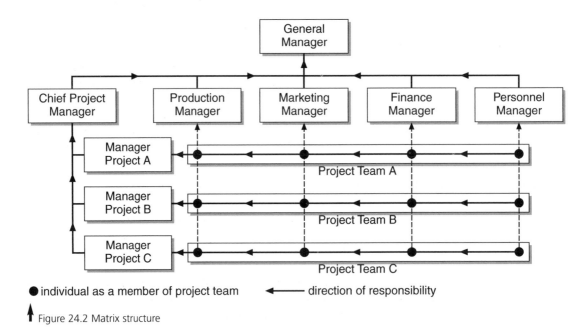

● individual as a member of project team   ◄─── direction of responsibility

↑ Figure 24.2 Matrix structure

This creates lines of horizontal linkage across the traditional functions. A team or project manager might engage selected staff from, say, the production, marketing, R&D and finance departments. Staff in this grouping would then have responsibilities to both their line manager and their project manager. The matrix structure is flexible and can appear at different points and in different forms within a formal structure. It can create synergy and originality by linking departments and can direct the right resources towards meeting a particular challenge or opportunity.

Since the mid-1990s the matrix concept has lost some of its earlier popularity. The main reason has been the complexity of responsibilities created. Divided loyalties, loss of focus and an excessive administrative load can seriously reduce the effectiveness of staff. Many firms are now looking for simpler and clearer structures that give managers a compelling sense of direction.

The federal organisation

A more radical counterpart to divisionalisation is the federal organisation described by Handy (1989). In this model – borrowed from the political concept – the process of delegation is effectively reversed, with the company's 'states' or divisions or constituent enterprises yielding to a small headquarters a portfolio of strategic tasks. Most of the dynamism, innovation, knowledge and capabilities are to be found in the federated parts of the total organisation. The centre accepts operating freedom for its member companies, yet keeps control over truly 'federal' affairs: key appointments, group strategy, major investment.

The emergence of federal patterns is, according to Handy, the result of information overload. Amplified by new technology, the flow of information from conventional divisions implies a large and costly headquarters staff. The federal model allows the centre to shrink, often drastically, to a spare, concentrated form where it performs a critical but very limited role for which it has a unique competitive advantage. In effect, this applies the principle of subsidiarity where every decision should be taken as far down any organisation as remains consistent with efficiency. Indeed, in business, decisions may actually gain in effectiveness as they move further 'down' the organisation yet get closer to the customer.

Front-end/back-end structures

An important shift now developing is towards a business-orientated model that mimics the strategic pattern of the business itself. Called a front-end/back-end structure, the front-end serves the designated target markets while the back-end is responsible for the productive processes in which the firm has distinctive capability. Inside this structure, markets drive the value chain as internal 'suppliers' compete with out-sourcing options for each contract. Thus, the market interface detects and delivers to segments of opportunity where there is a strong strategic fit with the firm's

---

Hewlett-Packard

Since it started out in the 1930s, HP had operated successfully as a highly decentralised organisation, spawning over 80 separate units for product development and manufacture. Global marketing was divided by country, with an additional structure for global accounts.

Carly Fiorina, the Chief Executive appointed in 2000, quickly shifted to a front-end/back-end model, with front-end marketing units focused on corporate and consumer sales plus two production-based back-end units assigned to computers and printers.

Reactions were mixed. Some stressed the simplicity and effectiveness of the new structure. Others disliked the loss of independence enjoyed by the old operating units.

capabilities. As products are 'pulled' through the organisation, out-sourcing is adopted wherever the opportunity cost of in-house provision gets too high.

It should be recognised that removing traditional hierarchies can have negative effects, too. Staff may find themselves overstretched and stressed by a rising volume of work. Quality may suffer and mounting pressures may deny opportunities for discussion and reflection. A culture of functionalism can result where 'hitting targets' and 'getting the job done' become all that matter. These are dysfunctional outcomes of flatter pyramids that need active management to prevent them. In some cases the solution may lie in new structural forms altogether.

Reengineering

Unsurprisingly, the whole concept of the functional hierarchy with its vertical departments is being questioned even when enhanced by matrix bolt-ons and semi-autonomous divisions. In essence, the traditional model is producer led. It is designed to 'do a job', such as insure cars or make plastics, and this job is then tacitly assumed to be justified and always to be justified. In fact, organisations are prone to take on a life of their own that becomes hard to challenge or reconceive.

This was a task taken on by Michael Hammer and James Champy in their best-selling *Reengineering the Corporation* (1993). The concept is simple. Firms over time develop patterns, pathways and structures that are largely taken for granted. A discontinuous leap in operating performance is often possible if real value-adding processes are isolated and radically redesigned without regard for the past – or the present. Activities failing to add value are eliminated. Reengineering starts from zero assumptions and builds from the ground up.

The approach quickly became popular in the world of corporate management and some dramatic success stories emerged. However, the early 1990s was also a period of severe recession. Reengineering became closely linked with downsizing and job insecurity. Many firms underrated or ignored the human implications of dislocative change and neutralised any efficiency gains through loss of employee trust and damage to morale. In later writing Hammer and Champy have defended the core concept of reengineering but recognised the greater stress needed on human motivation and self-respect.

Re-conceiving organisations

We have seen that organisations are becoming 'flatter', with fewer levels in their hierarchies and wider spans of control. This has implied more responsibility for all staff who are connected by much shorter lines of communication. Top management have tended to become more informal and more accessible to their staff, a trend popularised by Tom Peters (1987) as 'management-by-wandering-about' (MBWA).

The traditional large firm was built like an ocean liner. It moved slowly but powerfully with in-house provision for most of the complex services on which a business depends. Today, a radical rethink is under way about the whole nature and structure of organisations.

The authority to make decisions is being pushed closer to the front line as the business units within a firm gain greater autonomy. Strategic opportunities now move rapidly and often unpredictably into and out of reach. Smaller semi-independent units need fast reactions along short lines of communication if they are to compete effectively. More and more services are contracted out as headquarters get smaller. Instead of standing on the bridge of an ocean liner, managers find themselves co-ordinating a flotilla of powerboats.

Intense and increasingly global competition has been the driving force in all these changes. As firms analyse their internal value chains they look for strategic focus around their core competencies. The logic here is important. When a business begins to disaggregate its activities, its competitive advantage is far greater in some than in others. Where disaggregation does not damage performance, it makes sense to outsource all activities where competitive advantage is minimal or non-existent. This in turn allows the firm to concentrate its energy on areas of particular expertise where competitive advantage is sustainable and strong.

The result has been a rapid decline in the traditional all-purpose, all-function firm. The first stage in 'unbundling' was to contract out peripheral services such as catering, maintenance or transport. The next stage has been more radical and has caused cracks across the edifice of many large firms. Corporate fragmentation has taken two main forms.

First, the firm may indeed extend the process of deconstruction by strategic activity. Here, the firm withdraws from significant areas of its own value chain. These might include design, manufacturing, marketing, distribution, installation or customer service. With the sale or direct outsourcing of the activity, the firm creates new suppliers and customers reflecting the new configuration of added value.

The second way in which firms have split is by strategic business unit. A large firm is usually a configuration of value-adding activities linked with varying degrees of intimacy. These are held together by mutual synergy. One adds competitive advantage to another: they add value as a systemic whole. If this mutuality fails to add value or begins to destroy value, then pressure builds for units to be pulled apart. This could mean fast-growing, emergent businesses or former acquisitions that no longer 'fit' being sold on the open market or through a management buy-out. It can also mean major divisions or large 'chunks' of the firm becoming independent.

Splits of this kind are driven by a reversal of the common argument for mergers. Instead of the synergy intended from combining two operations, shareholders hope to benefit from unlocking organisational energy and market value when business units break apart. In practice, they may later remerge with another group whose strategic fit is better.

The reality of resource ownership often lags behind the logic of its control. Over time firms develop a kind of institutional or 'gravitational' glue that holds them together. It often takes some determined management to prise apart activities that yield no synergy.

Organisational remaking is never permanent, but is contingent by its very nature. Markets and external conditions are subject to continuous change, creating new tensions and new opportunities. Previously unseen faultlines appear as the process of splitting and merging continues.

Virtual organisations

In this postmodern world (see Chapter 35), organisations lose the discrete identities that they once appeared to have. The firm becomes a contingent alignment of capabilities seeking to build competitive advantage in a dynamic environment. This blurs boundaries between firms and may lead towards the virtual corporation.

This occurs when a firm outsources almost everything. All that remains is the ability to outsource and take responsibility for the resulting product. The firm becomes a kind of 'switchboard' (Moss Kanter, 1989) routeing flows of value towards their target market. This is a perfectly viable business model and can be well illustrated by the role of managing contractors in the construction industry. A business always makes sense if it is able to add value with a sustainable competitive advantage.

Conclusion

An organisational structure determines the pathways of control and command. It maps the chain of responsibility between individuals and groups. It decides how the various business functions, such as marketing and finance, should be configured and co-ordinated. It has a major impact on the pathways of communication that animate an organisation and enable it to pursue its aims. And, finally, the structure shapes the prevailing culture that expresses and, in turn, moulds the characteristic patterns of behaviour – or 'the way things are done'.

The whole trend away from rigid hierarchies towards leaner, faster and more intelligent organisational forms has been driven by a mix of technologies and markets. The new information technologies have, by their very nature, the capacity to disperse decision making. Meanwhile, the value added by personal service and knowledge accumulation has grown apace. A new agility and creativity have become necessary if firms are to maintain and build defensible competitive advantage.

25 Models for motivation

Overview

In human resources terms, motivation means the degree of energy and commitment with which a person performs a job. This is important because it determines the quality and quantity of output – and hence the added value – arising from the cost of employing that person.

Until the late 20th century the emphasis in motivation studies was usually on the quantitative measures of productivity, where the quality of output was standardised and subject to inspection and checking. In recent years, the quality of work performed has become increasingly important in adding value, while many jobs have grown in complexity and variety. Motivation has also gained greater significance as delayering and moves towards empowerment have increased the responsibility carried by many staff.

The old notion of employees as 'hands' suggests an external relationship to the business, in which money was paid in return for hours or output. This model is still relevant where jobs are well defined and repetitious, but wherever higher levels of skill, responsibility or discretion are required, then staff are increasingly expected to be thoughtful representatives of the firm and its strategy. A more internalised relationship to the business is being sought where motivation towards best performance is at a premium.

FW Taylor

In the 19th century – and to a diminishing extent ever since – labour was essentially a commodity, classified by economists as a factor of production. Scarcely related to the idea of the individual, labour could be hired at a going rate. The value of labour to the employer depended on how hard and how effectively people worked.

There was a widespread assumption that since workers were naturally lazy, their motivation would largely depend on discipline and the threat of punishment. For the most part, effectiveness had been studied very little and depended on local circumstances and tradition. Whereas craft skills were learned and practised within distinctive codes, the output of factory hands and labourers was often thought to depend on sheer numbers in the workforce rather than the exercise of management skill. It was against this background that Frederick Taylor began thinking about productivity.

His ideas found their fullest and most famous expression while he was Consulting Engineer at the Bethlehem Steel Works at Pittsburgh. Here, he developed the 'science of shovelling'. In an immense yard, 500 men were employed to load and unload by shovelling a range of bulk materials. Taylor observed that each man had his own (unstandardised) shovel that he applied to all types of material, regardless of density. The weight of material on the shovel blade varied from 3.5 pounds for light 'rice coal' to 38 pounds for heavy iron ore. The question that he then asked was deadly in its cogency and was to resonate down the whole of the next century:

> **Now, is 3.5 pounds the proper shovel-load or is 38 pounds the proper shovel – load? They cannot both be right. Under scientific management the answer to this question is not a matter of anyone's opinion; it is a question for accurate, careful scientific investigation.**

It emerged that 21.5 pounds was the optimum shovel-load. The company bought specialised shovels, the men were specially trained and payment was made by results. It was not long before employment was cut by 72 per cent and costs by 50 per cent. Significantly, wages for competent workers were 60 per cent higher than before.

The Human Relations School

Today, the idea that people as employees have complex needs seems uncontroversial. Yet back in 1932 it took an experiment in scientific management to trigger recognition of this reality. Elton Mayo (1880-1949) was an Australian academic who was involved in a series of social experiments (1927-32) at the Hawthorn Plant of Western Electric in Chicago. One of the most famous involved the isolation of a work group to test improvements in lighting. Gains in productivity were achieved by the test group, but were *also* achieved by a control group whose lighting conditions were unchanged. Further investigation exposed the significance for workers of being made to feel 'special' and a focus of management attention. Subsequent experiments uncovered the power of informal social networks among staff where work norms could be more influential than official policy.

Mayo's perspective has been criticised (Pascale, 1990) for its paternalistic assumptions and limited view of capabilities among the workforce. However, the recognition that complex motivational factors are vital to work performance was a crucial catalyst for later thinking about human behaviour at work.

Maslow's hierarchy of needs

A deeper view of human needs was popularised by the US psychologist Abraham Maslow (1908-70). His celebrated 'hierarchy of needs' model (1943) proposes that needs are broadly layered in such a way that only when one need is fulfilled does the next need in the hierarchy become an active motivator. Thus, only when basic physiological and security needs are met, do affiliation needs become a source of motivation. Two key implications for managers follow. First, to rely on money as an all-purpose motivator is ill conceived, since beyond a certain level of reward, employees will be more powerfully motivated by other more complex needs. Money alone becomes a weak motivator and fails to prevent frustration. Second, the hierarchy points to the higher needs of people at work, the fulfilment of which is motivating and likely to add value.

Maslow's hierarchy of needs remains a foundation of motivational theory, but has been subject to some important criticism. The relative importance of needs arguably varies between individuals.

For example, esteem and ego needs may be more powerful and more urgent than the fulfilment of affiliation needs. The rigid order of the hierarchy is also open to question as some individuals may pursue higher-level needs in advance of satisfying needs at lower levels in the hierarchy. It is also important to recognise that the ranking of needs is unlikely to be innate. Cultural and soci forces shape the evaluation by individuals of their priorities in terms of needs.

Alderfer (1972) built on Maslow's model in proposing a spectrum of needs across three levels.

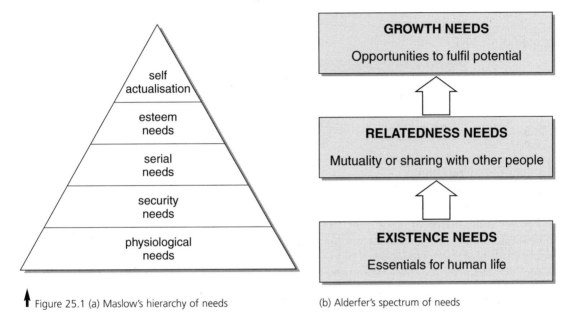

Figure 25.1 (a) Maslow's hierarchy of needs   (b) Alderfer's spectrum of needs

Alderfer accepted the idea that as one level of need is satisfied, the next level is activated. But he argued that if one level is thwarted then the level below becomes proportionately more important, with corresponding risks of conflict and frustration.

Herzberg

Thinking about the motivation of employees became known as the Human Relations School. Frederick Herzberg (b. 1923) carried out a particularly famous piece of research in the late 1950s, when he surveyed professionals and managers in Pittsburgh to determine their perception of positive and negative factors at work.

In *The Motivation to Work* (1959) he identified a basic distinction between motivational factors and 'hygiene' or maintenance factors. The latter covered salary, working conditions, interpersonal relations, administrative arrangements and job security. Herzberg found that while deficiencies in these factors were a source of job dissatisfaction, the factors were not in themselves a motivational force. By contrast, the key motivators were achievement, personal development and recognition. The absence of these factors would not in itself cause dissatisfaction, but their presence would cause job satisfaction and personal motivation.

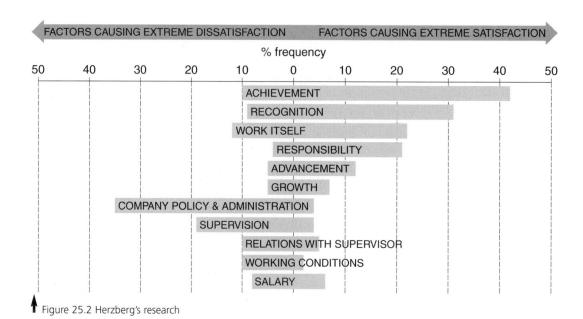

Figure 25.2 Herzberg's research

Herzberg's ideas were reinforced by McClelland (1961), who highlighted achievement, affiliation and power as the drivers of motivation. The relative strength of the criteria varied between individuals, but where achievement was the primary need, there was the likelihood that employees would work hard, seek responsibility and welcome challenges that were capable of fulfilment. While such characteristics were often perceived as desirable, it did not necessarily follow that the achievement-driven individual would be the most effective manager. In some roles, the affiliation or power-orientated person might be more suitable (see Fiedler's contingency theory of leadership, Chapter 26).

Herzberg sustained and developed his position in 'One More Time: How Do You Motivate Employees?' (*Harvard Business Review*, 1968), where he criticised the tendency to seek motivation through various kinds of positive incentives designed to reward performance. These, he argued, represented the motivation of the manager and not the employee. To generate true motivation, firms needed to change the nature of the *job* so that it became a source of the motivators that Herzberg had identified.

Controversy has continued in relation to the role of money as an incentive. In many contexts it seems to remain a central motivator, yet salary emerges as a 'hygiene' factor in Herzberg's model, a status confirmed by subsequent research. The explanation may lie in the distinction between the motivation to *hold* a job and the motivation *within* that job to work hard. For most employees, pay is strongly motivational in the desire to hold a job, but once working within that job, the motivational factors identified by Herzberg come into play.

Southwest Airlines

For Europeans, the concept of the low-cost, low-fares airline with no meals and no advance seat reservations is relatively new. In the USA, Southwest Airlines have been successfully exploiting the formula for much longer. To make it work, employees must be special: they are special to the company and the company must be special for them.

Southwest differentiates itself in the market through the combination of cheap fares and high quality customer service. Employees as people (not schedules or landing slots) are at the centre of the company's purpose and identity. Since the need is for highly committed and skilled staff, recruitment is exceptionally selective. From around 150 000 job applicants each year, only 5000 are selected. Successful candidates are strong characters, outward-going and humorous – and effective in a team.

Chief Executive, Herb Kelleher, aims to give every employee the consistent experience that they matter. To this end, he attempts to know each employee by name and ensures that he and other senior managers are directly accessible to staff. The company's philosophy puts the staff first, the customers second and the stockholders third. This is based on the belief that customer value and profitability depend on motivated and fulfilled employees.

McGregor's Theory X and Theory Y

Do people at work seek responsibility and want to meet their higher needs? Or do they respond best to discipline and the threat of punishment? Douglas McGregor (1906–64) set these two visions of motivation side by side in Theory X and Theory Y.

Theory X

- The average human being dislikes work and will try to avoid it.
- Most people must be controlled and threatened with punishment if they are to strive for organisational objectives.
- Most staff prefer to be directed and want to avoid responsibility.
- They have little ambition and want security above all.

Theory Y

- Making an effort at work is as natural as play or rest.
- People will use self-direction and self-control in pursuit of objectives to which they are committed.
- Most people will accept and seek responsibility.
- Most people have powers of imagination, ingenuity and creativity that are often wasted.

In *The Human Side of Enterprise* (1960), he offered Theory X as the managerial belief that employees are inherently reluctant to give of their best or to use their higher faculties. By total contrast, Theory Y expounds the view that people naturally want to work, to accept responsibility and to be creative. McGregor argued that Theory X was widespread in organisational life throughout America.

Theory X is certainly a common view of human nature and often seems confirmed by the behaviour of employees. But McGregor argued that it was the very expectation of Theory X that creates such a culture. Far from being natural, Theory X is the manifestation of management assumptions. So, if assumptions change in favour of Theory Y, then so will employee behaviour.

McGregor's view has been criticised for its oversimplified polarity. Theory X and Theory Y, it has been argued, are points at opposite ends of a spectrum. Not long before he died, McGregor was working on a vision that built his beliefs into the idea of a strong and effective organisational culture: Theory Z. This was developed by William Ouchi (1981), who argued that US firms overemphasised individualism while needing more stress on a family-style culture where co-operation, trust and loyalty were the pillars of competitiveness.

Meanwhile, Theory X and Y have remained a seminal model in the world of management. In a sense, Theories X and Y represent two rival interpretations of human nature. They also, to some extent, underpin the classic conservative and liberal world views. They are archetypes, but are powerful because each encapsulates a fundamental set of assumptions. Perhaps McGregor's most important insight was to recognise the tendency of such assumptions to become self-fulfilling in their outcome.

Vroom's expectancy theory

An influential goal-directed model of motivation was offered by Vroom (1964) based on his expectancy theory. This proposes that the force of motivation to act in a particular way depends on the value attached to the desired outcome, discounted by the expectancy that the outcome will be derived from the action. More formally:

$$\text{Force (motivation)} = \text{Valence} \times \text{Expectancy}$$

where *valence* is the value of an outcome and *expectancy* is the perceived probability that the action will be followed by the outcome.

Vroom's model bases the determinants of motivation on the subjective judgements of individuals. In the context of work the valence of actions will vary widely among different people and over time. Likewise, expectancy levels will be distributed across a spectrum of judgement that may be influenced by types of leadership and shifts in organisational culture. The message for managers is that to increase motivation depends on the experience of work being valued and expected to yield rewards.

Porter and Lawler (1968) endorsed Vroom's essential finding but qualified and extended his model. Effort and work performance, they pointed out, do depend on motivation but are also affected by appropriate ability and skills and by the clarity of the work role concerned. Unless motivated work is based on capabilities and clearly directed, it will not translate fully into the desired performance.

They also focused attention on the link between performance and job satisfaction. If rewards are intrinsic (e.g. the satisfaction derived from achievement), then expectancy values are independent of the organisation and likely to be high. Where rewards are extrinsic (e.g. the prospect of promotion), then the style of management and the prevailing culture become critical. This is further qualified by the worker's perception of equity. To the extent that a reward is perceived to be less than fair, its motivational value is reduced. This again highlights the importance of subjectivity in understanding motivation.

Empowerment

There have been a range of responses to the link between motivation and increased intrinsic rewards from work. Early initiatives stressed job rotation and job enlargement, which provide employees with the chance to vary or extend the scope of their duties. More radical but much more difficult to implement have been ideas of job enrichment and empowerment.

Schemes for job enrichment followed Herzberg's work and were often embedded in systems of cellular production. These have involved giving significant stages in a total production process to a relatively autonomous work group. Important decisions concerning the scheduling, distribution and day-to-day management of work then become the responsibility of the group. In the context of individual workers, job enrichment has also meant enhanced responsibility for a specific process, work station or facility. The aim has been to increase motivation through a sense of ownership for and identity with the work.

Empowerment takes this thinking a step further in attempting to give employees a sense of owning their job and its meaning in the value chain of which it is part. An early advocate of this approach was Rosabeth Moss Kanter (1977). Her research confirmed McGregor's assertion that corporations tend to waste the potential talents of employees and place a bureaucratic premium on predictability in staff. Kanter highlighted the powerlessness experienced by many workers and frontline managers (especially women) in their jobs. To avoid the resulting dissatisfaction, demotivation and alienation she recommended unblocking the career pathways of hitherto 'powerless' groups, flattening hierarchies and giving much greater autonomy to work groups.

Meanwhile, Peters and Waterman (1982) developed and publicised the Seven-S framework where structure, systems and strategy form the skeleton of the business, which is only animated by the 'soft S' factors — staff, style, skills and shared values. Later Peters (1987) insisted that these soft drivers of value would truly thrive only in a climate of empowerment. With widening spans of control, trust in staff was not just desirable but essential. With echoes of McGregor's Theory Y, he argued that there was no limit to what people can achieve if they are given proper training and real power in human scale groups. Expressed in references to 'front line heroes' Peters argued that pride at work must be nurtured and achievements openly celebrated. It is through their staff that firms can be entrepreneurial, flexible and creative.

Once again, the idea of motivation is deeply engaged with the organisational culture (see Chapter 31). A pioneer in the exploration of this link has been Edgar Schein (1980) who identified a *de facto* 'psychological contract' between employer and employee. In its appearance and in its legal existence, a contract of employment relates a set of duties and responsibilities to a rate of pay and other extrinsic rewards. Yet in reality, argues Schein, there is an additional and concealed psychological contract on both sides. The employing organisation expects various intangible qualities in its employees, such as loyalty, determination or energy. Equally, the employee has a range of hidden or implicit expectations: a sense of belonging, affirmation of self-respect and personal growth are typical examples. Effective motivation requires a reasonably accurate match in the psychological contract. A mismatch will lead to conflict, alienation and under-performance. Precisely because it is not explicit, this kind of match depends on embedded values and the prevailing culture.

26 Leadership and teams

Overview

Organisational structures are inhabited by people. It is how people behave within the structure and not the structure itself that adds value. It is therefore essential to gain some insight into the forces acting on people and the dynamics of their complex interaction.

People in an organisation can be viewed as individuals, as members of groups and as components or elements in a system. The men who did the shovelling in FW Taylor's experiments were evaluated and rewarded as individuals whose contributions were standardised and repetitive. A century later, staff are valued for their individual and their interactive contributions that are becoming less standardised and less repetitive. Organisations and employees are becoming less like 'wheels' and 'cogs' and more like organisms that use multiple sources of intelligence to exploit their changing environment.

The purpose of this chapter is to explore how the influence of leadership, the interactivity of teams and the shared values of a culture can become a source of competitive advantage.

What is leadership?

'Without a leader, nothing happens.' Michael Hammer's blunt comment is an exaggeration, but points towards the essence of leadership. Leadership is about articulating a goal, choosing a pathway and energising others to follow. It is a universal phenomenon, appearing in all societies and in all organisations and social groups. Warren Bennis, the American leadership guru, offers the following definition of leadership:

The capacity to create a compelling vision and translate it into action and sustain it.

The relevance to business is immediately obvious. Every firm depends on people working towards strategic and tactical objectives. Leadership is the inspirational, motivational and organisational force that makes this happen. All writers agree on the importance of the leader setting a direction or vision for the organisation. This reflects what the organisation is 'about', its underlying purpose. In this sense, the leader clarifies the organisation's prime values that are the weightings of meaning attached to every decision, explicit and implicit. But values alone are static, a potentiality for shaping actions but not one resolved. Leadership transforms values into a vector of urgency, a force of intention towards a clear goal. For top leaders, this goal will necessarily be broad but it can be forged into operational objectives as it is understood and embodied in the organisation.

The vision needs to be challenging but still believable. It needs to be framed in terms that have emotional as well as cognitive meaning. As Peters (1987) agues, a leader must articulate an empowering vision towards which followers can feel a sense of personal *ownership*.

A vision is about change: it carries a strong sense of 'tomorrow'. Yet leaders start with today as they explore and evaluate the organisation's present circumstances and scan the horizons of external change. Their job is not to be 'framed', even seduced by the *status quo*, but to insist on the right to think outside present boundaries and to conceive a future that is different.

This future will still be rooted in the relationship between core capabilities and target customers. How can this critical alignment be redesigned to add more value? So what is at stake in a vision is an organisation's identity and the identity of the demand that it aims to fulfil. This also provides leaders throughout the organisation with benchmarks for judging success. The vision confers credit. Performing activities outside the remit of vision is normally a form of ineffectiveness. The vision selects and calibrates performance indicators so that progress can be measured and rewards allocated.

The other dimension of the leader's role is to motivate and energise followers. Often this springs from the leader's own energy and passion in pursuit of a shared vision; but the leader must also release energy from people at all levels in the organisation. This is not a simple question of training or empowerment or clarity of strategic intent. It involves a kind of emotional orchestration where people feel at once understood, needed and challenged. The task of leaders at every level is to ensure that a harmony exists between the vision and those responsible for its implementation.

In this effort, much depends on making the vision 'emotionally contagious'. Winning over the minds of staff takes time and may or may not be easy. But winning their hearts can be faster and more powerful in its action. This is where the leader's empathetic connection with followers is important. The vision can be transmitted far more easily down the organisation's 'neural wires' if attuned emotionally to followers' perceptions and underlying needs.

A vision also needs to be memorable or 'sticky' (Gladwell, 2000), adhering to the consciousness of followers and thus prompting their actions. In this sense, the framing of a vision should be in the language and the imagery of followers and not leaders. Many visions are expressed in bureaucratic and managerial terms that stir no one to act. By contrast, Honda's famous vision is instructive: 'We will crush, squash, slaughter Yamaha'. This is 'sticky' and stirring.

Leadership style

There have been many studies of leadership styles and their relative effectiveness. The most basic criterion of style is the extent to which the leader invites the participation of followers in decision making. At one end of the spectrum, authoritarian leaders allow little if any participation and distance themselves from the group. They communicate 'top-down', supervise events closely and expect unquestioning obedience. By contrast, democratic leaders urge group participation in decisions and identify closely with their followers. Communications form a dialogue upwards and downwards, with independence of thought encouraged among the group.

A different but linked approach to style is offered by the contingency theory of leadership. Fred Fiedler (1967) distinguished two types of leader, one who is task motivated and one who is relationship motivated. Task-motivated leaders tend to be more authoritarian in their preoccupation with a successful outcome to the job in hand. Relationship-motivated leaders tend to be more democratic with their desire to interact with followers and understand their point of view. Fiedler found that neither style was 'right' but that their effectiveness depended on the contingent circumstances. John Adair (1973) recognised task, team and individuals as essential but competing priorities for leadership (see Figure 26.1), arguing that while these interdependent 'circles' of need overlap, their relative size will vary according to the needs of the situation.

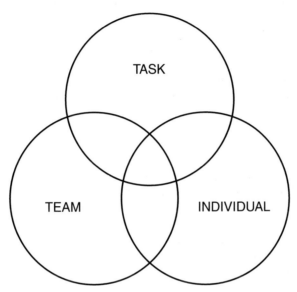

Figure 26.1 Adair's leadership model

Just as no one style of leadership is definitively successful, so it is argued that there is no one ideal type of leader. Douglas McGregor (1960) considered that effective leadership depended on the way in which a complex set of variables was configured. These included the qualities of the would-be leader, the attitudes and needs of followers, the type of organisation and tasks, and the characteristics of the external environment. A leader could thrive in one set of circumstances and yet fail in another. This suggests the need for leaders of many types, with leadership potential existing in a wide range of people.

What makes a leader?

The old debate about how far people's behavioural characteristics are the result of nature and how far of nurture is echoed in the question of whether leaders are born or made.

Until the 1930s it was generally believed that leadership depended on a genetic trait or natural gift. Since then the view has developed that people differ in their leadership potential, but many can learn to be proficient in the essential skills.

What are the characteristics of an effective leader? There is no final or definitive answer, but there are some common characteristics to which most writers attach importance. These mirror the functions of leadership and relate to the processes of *envisioning* and *energising*.

The ability to envision effectively a scenario for the future depends on an open-minded and holistic perception of the organisation and its environment. Most members of an organisation have an 'elevation view': that is, they enter the organisation at ground level and perceive each department, division or branch as they encounter it. Leaders need the realism and insight of the 'elevation view', but also the holistic panorama of a 'plan view' or a view from above. Only by taking the two views together can the organisation be properly understood in terms of its possible future.

Envisioning itself embraces a range of situations varying from a group process of strategic analysis to the hunch of a lone leader. Often it arises from the restless energy of asking tough, potentially disruptive questions, of spotting weaknesses and wasted potential, and leaping forward to a possible future and painting it as a compelling vision. Sometimes the vision will simply be the next step along a waymarked path. In other cases it may involve a discontinuous jump that could not be extrapolated from the organisation's history.

In energising the organisation towards the envisioned future, leaders usually need passion, courage and staying power. Leaders need credibility and integrity. They must be capable of fulfilling stated intentions and have an honesty of character that gives their assertions a moral force. Charisma can be a motivational short-cut, injecting a kind of adrenaline into the organisational bloodstream. However, there is no long-term substitute for aligning the needs and aspirations of the workforce with the goals of the organisation and developing everywhere a contagious mood of positive thinking.

The new leadership

In a classical hierarchy, strategic leadership is provided by the chief executive and senior management at its apex. More specific, day-to-day leadership flows through line management, with each level in the hierarchy assuming leadership functions in relation to the level below. Flatter structures push leadership functions lower down in the hierarchy while putting greater emphasis on the leadership of teams. As organisations become less hierarchical, more organic and more intelligent in their functioning, so leadership becomes more dispersed and more team related. This makes it important for almost all employees to gain some leadership skills if they are to function effectively.

Peter Senge (1990) sees a broad shift away from the traditional Western view of leaders as 'heroes' directing powerless followers who lack any vision of their own. Instead, he sees leaders as designers and teachers in organisations where people expand their capabilities and learn continuously. Leaders of this kind help people to find meaning in complexity and to share models that signpost action.

Evaluation

Leadership is a crucial factor in building and sustaining competitive advantage. In some cases it is concentrated at the top or in the centre of the organisation, in which case there is a danger of a vacuum when the founder or the senior executives leave. More sustainably, leadership can become dispersed and renewable, needing at most a flow of vision and questing energy from the top.

Thus, the best leaders envision the future and empower it to happen. Rather than detailing strategy, they set a pattern of strategic thinking. They persuade the individuals and groups around them to buy into their goals and energise people to achieve more even than they ever thought possible. The importance of this leadership process extends from the top of an organisation through every layer downward and outward until the lowest-status member of staff has a clear picture of what they seek to achieve. Given the extent to which the quality and configuration of leadership become drivers of ultimate performance, it is no wonder that Warren Bennis calls leadership studies a 'heavy industry'.

The logic of teams

Warren Bennis (1989) remarked: 'Devising and maintaining an atmosphere in which others can put a dent in the universe is the leader's creative act.' A key part of the leader's role is the orchestration of people, not just to perform their tasks but to achieve something important – usually collectively. Although every organisation necessarily contains individuals, it is made up of groups. Human beings lived and worked in small groups long before the arrival of civilisation, and remain genetically disposed to find their role and identity in groups of various kinds. Primary groups are in the style of family groupings based on frequent and closely shared purpose. Secondary groups are a coalition of primary groups such as might be found in a factory or office headquarters.

Formal groups – those created by the organisation – often overlap in their membership and are complemented by informal groups that form spontaneously and lack official status. As Mayo's research (1928–32) established, informal groups have a powerful influence on the performance of formal groups.

Teams are groups with a common purpose. It follows that a firm is a complex configuration of teams that should be working to both a local and a common corporate purpose. Interest in teams has increased rapidly since command-and-control organisations began to give way to more intelligent structures where almost all employees need to reflect, confer, make decisions and act creatively together.

Teams have about them an essential logic. To fulfil objectives involves a multiplicity of tasks, most of which are interdependent and fall into domains, stages or groups. Teamwork is the efficient response. It extends specialisation through flexibility in allowing staff to exploit their strengths. It gives the team what psychologists call a 'transactional memory', where everyone knows who can most effectively perform a task and who is the holder of necessary knowledge. Teams provide encouragement and motivation for their members, while as entities they can produce results that are worth far more than the sum of their parts.

A key application of teamwork has been the development of cell production. This groups people and equipment in semi-autonomous 'villages' arranged to allow a complete stage of work to be accomplished rather than the product needing to move through a series of separate workstations. The team is motivated by its responsibility for a complete unit of work and exploits the dynamics of mutuality where interaction and 'togetherness' generate synergy.

Schonberger (1982) traces the development of cell production from experiments in Britain in the late 1960s and early 1970s. The idea was taken forward by Volvo in its purpose-designed Kalmar factory where improved quality and productivity were achieved using cell production. Toyota then developed the concept, applied its principles across the company and spread the system to suppliers.

Teams again represent a move away from the 'cogs-in-a-wheel' view of the workforce towards a wired vision of the organisation, where complex and continuous interaction is essential between people with complementary talents.

Teams need their own leadership and usually function best with considerable autonomy. Simultaneously, teams must often accept their linkage to other teams to form a chain of internal customer/supplier relationships. This can make teams explicitly part of a value chain where teams may even be in competition with external suppliers.

Group dynamics

The dynamics of groups are extremely complex. Different personalities, beliefs, value systems and attitudes engage with unpredictable results. Much depends on the group's formal role, the pressures of the task and the norms of the organisation.

Selecting and constructing winning teams is a highly skilled job. Given the leaps in quality and productivity possible through successful team formation, the process has become a potential source of competitive advantage. Meredith Belbin carried out some of the pioneering research into team effectiveness at Henley Management College (1967). This showed that teams with complementary strengths performed best, and that individuals contribute best in the roles that they find most natural to them. Belbin also found that particular strengths in individuals were often linked to 'allowable weaknesses'. These characteristic weaknesses did not need to undermine the team as they could be counteracted by corresponding strengths in other members. As he put it: 'Imperfect people can make perfect teams.'

Like their parent organisations, teams develop a distinctive culture, a unique pattern of uniformity in ways of being and doing. This cultural encoding assists the team's effective functioning by heightening members' sense of solidarity and enabling them to anticipate one another's likely behaviour. But it also carries a risk of 'framing' the team within boundaries of thought and action that become reinforced over time. Innovation can quietly die as team approval gravitates towards a familiar equilibrium.

This tendency is made more dangerous by the phenomenon of 'groupthink', where individual objections and doubts are withdrawn or never expressed in the face of group convergence on the decision 'everyone supports'.

Teams can avoid becoming stagnant and self-referential if there is a circulation of membership. In some firms, employees enter a kind of internal market for the membership of teams, and the teams themselves are increasingly contingent, forming and reforming as need suggests.

Teamwork of this kind is another interesting feature of the post-Fordist organisation, where intelligent soft circuits replace the inert geometry of control-and-command.

Gore Associates ◄

Famous as makers of the water-resistant fabric Gore-Tex, this private company in Newark, Delaware, also manufactures hi-tech coatings, containers and tubing for a wide range of applications. But the most surprising feature at Gore is the lack of hierarchies, titles and command-and-control relationships. A loose-knit 'free-form management style' is achieved by casting each operating unit in the style of a small entrepreneurial start-up.

As the business grows – and Gore is a very successful, high-growth company – the units split, amoeba-like so that they never contain more than about 150 employees. This size, which is widely found as the upper limit for human-scale organisation, ensures that every employee can feel a sense of personal engagement with the work and the company. Furthermore, the grouping size is small enough for staff to know one another's strengths and weaknesses and where to find the right expertise and knowledge. The ultra-flat structure allows teams to network, spreading co-operation, insight and intelligence.

PART **F**

FINANCE
explained

27 The meaning of finance

Overview

Finance has a tendency to seem dry and opaque. It need be neither. Finance is about value expressed in terms of money. Business involves attempts to add value. Firms therefore need to obtain resources with a value and transform them into products with a greater value.

How does a business obtain resources? How does it use those resources? How can their transformation be measured? Chapters 27 to 30 will address these questions.

What is finance?

Finance is money – a medium of exchange that is generally acceptable in the settlement of debt. Debts are incurred when a buyer agrees to purchase goods or services from a seller. Sometimes that debt is settled immediately, but it may be allowed to remain outstanding – typically for a period of up to three months. Money depends for its value on its power to settle debts. It follows that money is a denominator of value: the buyer uses a sum of money to obtain specified resources from a seller. Resources are only sold because the money sum agreed as their price exceeds the opportunity cost of their ownership. Thus, finance in the form of money provides access to resources.

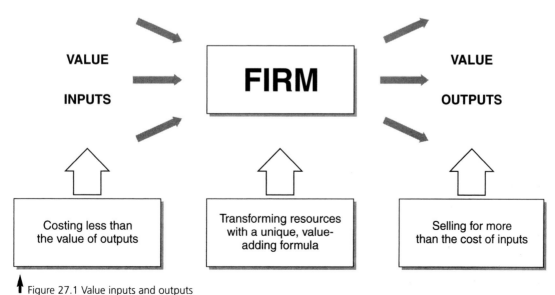

Figure 27.1 Value inputs and outputs

Every firm is a value processor. In effect, a firm is a system for reconfiguring resources so that their value on exit is greater than their value on entry. Such a system is like a complex template designed to achieve the necessary 'mixing' or configuring of resources. Each firm's system is unique and the extent to which it is difficult to replicate defines the sustainability of its competitive advantage.

Tesco

Think of Tesco, a highly successful retailer of food and household goods, that turned over £26.3bn in 2002. In effect, it is a vast distribution system, purchasing goods from thousands of producers and supplying them at a higher price to its customers. This process is like a complex piece of wiring. A thicket of fine-gauge 'wires' combine to supply a relatively small number of outlets with a complete range of 'messages' in the form of value propositions. As a business system, it gains competitive advantage from the efficiency of its architecture, a record of innovation and the power of the Tesco brand.

The essential flow of resources on which a business depends is generated by sales revenue. In other words, the firm's trading activity generates a circulation of money as the direct and indirect costs of inputs are financed by the sale of the resulting output in the market.

Each firm or system also contains some resources that are not processed but are *processors*. These are the firm's fixed assets, which are owned by the business over the long run and funded by capital. In some industries, such as oil extraction or car manufacturing, these fixed assets are very costly and require large inputs of capital. In other types of business activity – professional services or forms of e-commerce, for example – fixed assets can be modest and require only small-scale capital funding.

Thus, a business can be mapped in terms of value by the stock of fixed capital that it represents and by the flow of resources that passes through its ownership. The optimisation of these stocks and flows relative to corporate objectives is the subject of financial strategy. The use of money in measurement provides a uniform standard of value that allows comparisons and judgements to be made in the deployment of resources.

Obtaining finance

A business is usually financed to a significant degree by its owners. In smaller companies, this equity (or shareholders' investment) is generally supplied by a few key individuals, often members of the same family. In larger, public companies there are many smaller shareholders, but the bulk of the equity is in the hands of financial institutions. Share capital is risk capital: it represents a direct stake in the enterprise. Shareholders are therefore responsible for appointing directors and, ultimately at least, for ensuring the effective management of the enterprise. They share in profits and losses and benefit or lose from changes in the firm's market value. Unsurprisingly, they seek net returns well above the prevailing rate of interest.

As well as using risk capital, most firms also obtain loan capital. This typically takes the form of debentures, bank loans and venture capital. Rates of interest depend on the perceived risk. This can be dampened by providing lenders with security in the form of pledged assets.

Using finance

From the moment that funds enter a firm's bank account – from any source – they incur costs. In the case of loan capital, the cost is transparent. Share capital, though, carries no charge as such. It is the owners' funding; it belongs to the company: it is the company. In reality, of course, share capital, like all capital, carries an opportunity cost. Funds that are owned by shareholders must achieve earnings that at least cover their opportunity cost if they are to remain at the firm's disposal.

Rent free?

Reports appear in the media pointing to the advantage enjoyed by retailers who own the freeholds of their own stores and therefore pay no rent.

Such reports fail to point out that the freeholds represent a commitment of resources. This carries an opportunity cost that must be covered by the relevant earnings.

The long-term task of directors acting on behalf of shareholders is to generate returns on risk capital that exceed its opportunity cost. It is this surplus that is true added value and reflects the firm's competitive advantage (see Chapter 7).

A basic principle in a market economy is the mobility of capital. Investors will always tend to place their funds where, after allowing for risk (see Chapter 30), the highest returns are anticipated. Thus, the prospect or the reality of supernormal returns will attract capital just as the absence of such prospects or the failure to make normal returns will release capital.

This is best understood using the concept of opportunity cost. Imagine that capital is perfectly mobile. The finance will flow into all those business opportunities that appear to offer the best returns. The tendency of these flows would be to ensure that the marginal return on capital was equal to the opportunity cost of capital. The logic of this proposition is simply clarified: if the return on the last pound employed by a firm was above its opportunity cost, then other pounds in the next-best employment should be flowing in to the firm in order to benefit from the differential. Equally, if returns on the marginal pound have fallen below its opportunity cost, then the pounds below this threshold should leave the firm and switch employment to that next-best use. Equilibrium would be reached among firms when returns on every marginal pound were equal to their corresponding opportunity cost.

It follows that an imputed cost must be attached to shareholders' funds that correspond to the firm's opportunity cost of capital. In the real business world the relative performance of firms varies widely and changes continuously. Differentials in prospective earnings act like magnetic fields in their pull on resources, gaining and losing intensity. Equilibrium in this real model is impossible. Even as resources attempt to track earnings, the picture moves and the leading edge for returns appears through a different window of opportunity.

This turbulence does not prevent coherent patterns emerging in the distribution of resources. Consistent poor performance in one company or in one sector does weaken the hold on resources. The lack of retained profits prevents organic growth, while losses shrink the equity base.

Share issues become difficult or impossible. Loans are likely to be expensive and studded with conditions. And as the share price falls, the risk of hostile bids increases. Strong performance generates the reverse pattern. Retained profits swell. New share capital is easily attracted, while loan finance is available on better terms. As the share price rises, the prospects for acquisitions improve.

Kingfisher

In the 1990s Kingfisher owned B&Q (282 stores), Comet (255 stores), Woolworths (783 stores) and Superdrug (705 stores). The business year to 1998 was highly successful, with sales and profits at record levels. Dividends were increased, the share price soared and the company was ready for expansion. The Chief Executive's salary package was worth £1.2m.

	1995/96	1996/97	1997/98
Turnover £ million	5 281	5 815	6 409
Operating profit £ million	317	416	519
ROCE %	17.0	23.9	24.6

Source: Adapted from Kingfisher Annual Reports, 1996–98

Sears

Sears was a major retail group that included Selfridges, Freemans (mail order), Miss Selfridge, Richards, Wallis, Warehouse, Adams, Shoe Express, Shoe City and Dolcis.

Worsening results led to the sale of the shoe businesses and the break-up of the Sears group. Selfridges was de-merged to form an independent company while Freemans and the clothing fascias were sold to new owners. The Chief Executive resigned.

	1995/96	1996/97	1997/98
Turnover £ million	2 016	1 952	1 819
Operating profit £ million	106	89	59
ROCE %	10.5	8.7	5.6

Source: Adapted from Sears Annual Reports, 1996–98

In practice, this attraction and release model for resources is obstructed and diverted in many ways. Personalities and company politics intervene, stakeholders pull in different directions while markets themselves work imperfectly. An important factor is the 'friction' underlying the allocation of resources. Every configuration of business assets develops its own inertia. Each decision to deploy financial resources carries some cost for its reversal. A threshold is formed that must be surmounted by any force for change. Resistance to change often has invisible dimensions that represent human and cultural allegiances. Patterns of human commitment to every *status quo* are soon established and are surprisingly difficult to undo.

There is also the question of sunk costs. When a firm uses its financial resources to build a factory and install machinery, it has a fixed asset to its name. Yet most of the money spent is effectively non-recoverable. Any quick sale of the factory and its equipment would be unlikely to yield more than a small fraction of the original costs. These costs are 'sunk' in the enterprise and form a substantial barrier to exit from the market or industry.

28 Key financial statements

Overview

Business activity involves decisions about configurations and flows of resources that lead to the sale of products in a market of some kind. Records of these decisions and transactions are kept in the firm's internal accounting system, where they are systematised and aggregated to form financial information. This is the material from which a financial strategy is constructed, but it also contains vital indicators of corporate performance that bear on strategy across all functions of the organisation.

Almost all of the detailed data is likely to be confidential. However, all companies are required by law to publish summarised accounting information at regular half-yearly or yearly intervals. This chapter and the following chapter will together explain the significance of unpublished and published data, and will show how published accounts can be used to clarify and evaluate strategic performance.

Financial data

Dixons

Unusually among very senior managers, the CEO at Dixons has a computer on his desk. At a moment's notice he can access the day's takings so far at any of his stores – a very headline indicator that does not distract him from a host of other more time-loaded variables. Dixons' strategy unfolds by the month, week, day, hour.

Because financial data represents the mobilisation of resources, its emergence tells an unfolding story about real events in the real world. This needs continuous monitoring and analysis. Often this will relate to historic time, so that knowledge and experience are accumulated and projections made into the future. But every organisation also needs its financial 'control room' where real-time and recent-time data are scrutinised for pathways of digression away from projections and plans.

Unfortunately, like any emergent pattern, financial meanings are difficult to construct ahead of their confirmed identity. This does not reduce the importance of trying. From one manager trying to interpret a surge in sales for a particular product, right through to financial analysts in the City attempting to advise investors on underlying profitability, extrapolations matter.

New Labour

1–2 May 1997 was the night on which New Labour hoped to win power and Tony Blair aimed to become Prime Minister. The polling stations closed at 10 pm and the first result was declared before 11 pm in Sunderland South. An instant computer analysis based on the swing to Labour suggested that Blair would indeed win with a landslide Commons majority of about 200 seats.

As subsequent results were fed into the computer, the extrapolated majority moved upwards and downwards, but eventually settled close to the actual outcome at 179 seats.

For the Conservatives, John Major had seen the end approaching well before the election.

Sir Richard Greenbury at Marks & Spencers was less well informed.

No pilot can afford to ignore the instruments on the flightdeck of an airliner. Similarly, no manager can afford to ignore the indicators that are derived from financial data. These are dependent for their meaning on the mapped pathways of strategy and business planning and on the conceptual underpinnings of the indicators themselves.

Next

George Davies was the architect of the concept that is still Next. He was also the company's first CEO.

On 24 February 1982 the doors opened at the first four branches of Next. Four hours later, at lunchtime on that critical Saturday, Davies phoned each of the four managers to ask them for results. Would sales be in line with the targets? Unable to conceal his excitement and anticipation, Davies collected the answers.

His smile betrayed all. Every store was ahead of budget. Next was in business. There would be no turning back.

We have seen that there are two financial perspectives on a business organisation. One views the business as a configuration of resources with a value, while the other highlights the flow of resources to which value is added (or from which value is subtracted). Each of these views is represented in the formal accounting statements required from companies.

The profit and loss account

Two very basic and related questions to ask about any business over a given period are:

• What was the total sales revenue?
• How much were the corresponding total costs?

The profit and loss account sets out to answer these questions through a sequence of logically ordered arithmetic that isolates each significant total in the process. We will look briefly at a model statement for a fictitious company and then at a real example.

Creative Kitchens Ltd

Profit & Loss Account for year ending 31 December 2002

	£m	£m
Turnover		60
Cost of sales		<u>25</u>
Gross profit		35
Distribution costs	12	
Administrative expenses	<u>8</u>	
Net (operating) profit		15
Non-operating income		<u>1</u>
Profit before interest and tax		16
Interest expense		<u>2</u>
Profit before tax		14
Taxation expense		<u>4</u>
Profit after tax		10
Dividends payable		<u>5</u>
Retained profit		<u><u>5</u></u>

The Companies Act 1985 allows two main types of format for the profit and loss account, but the version shown here is fairly typical of listed (public) companies. It should be noticed that while the extent to which accounts are consistent and comprehensive is governed by law, their detailed presentation and choice of exact terminology still vary from one firm to another.

Although the logic of the profit and loss account is straightforward, there are some important concepts underlying its narrative and some key relationships to be explored.

The opening value for turnover or sales revenue represents the value of all sales in the period arising from the firm's normal trading activity. This is obviously a headline figure, with comparisons between years giving an idea of the firm's growth (or contraction) and its share of the relevant market. As explained below, however, it needs interpreting carefully.

Cost of sales is a term that refers to the direct costs of production. Its largest components are normally labour and materials and these must be carefully matched against the corresponding sales to ensure accounting accuracy. Gross profit (as we have seen in Chapter 20) is the reservoir of surplus that contributes towards overheads or indirect costs and the firm's net or operating profit. The gross profit margin (gross profit as percentage of sales) is a key indicator of front-line profitability. Typical values vary widely by industry, and gross margins are most usefully analysed between firms and over time.

Overhead expenses are usually split up. Distribution expenses are shown separately, while administrative expenses is a catch-all category that includes salaries, rent, insurance and depreciation. The deduction of these overhead expenses from gross profit allows the calculation of operating or net profit (or loss). In strategic terms, this is the key profit value since it captures the surplus earned by the ordinary trading activities of the enterprise. The operating margin (operating profit as percentage of sales) is the definitive measure for the rate at which profit is being extracted from sales. Analysis of its value over time and in comparison with competitors is useful, but we have seen that much depends on the intended strategic balance between margin and sales.

Below operating profit comes a series of adjustments and deductions that highlight a 'staircase' of profit values, each with distinctive significance. Non-operating income may arise from financial fixed assets or investments (see below) made in other companies or in government stocks. When this is added, we reach profit before interest and tax, which is a key total when considering the company's ability to meet interest payments on loan capital. Interest charges arise from long-term loans, any debentures (secured loans equivalent to a business mortgage) and bank overdrafts. Only after the deduction of interest are company profits liable for corporation tax, which is paid a year in arrears.

When tax is paid (at 19–30 per cent according to turnover), the remaining profit after tax is then available for 'appropriation'. The directors normally declare a dividend (per share) payment of which typically uses up 30–50 per cent of the funds. The remainder automatically becomes retained profit for reinvestment in the business. This is usually the largest source of funding for expansion and should directly benefit shareholders by increasing the value of their assets and the market value of their shares.

Interpreting the profit and loss account

In asking about the fundamental purpose of the profit and loss account there are two different views. Advocates of one perspective argue that its proper goal is to reveal the firm's operating performance. This puts the emphasis on the firm's essential transformative process in converting the cost of inputs into the sale of outputs. The input of non-operating income and one-off items, such as income from the sale of property, would be downplayed. The opposing view supports the all-inclusive concept that regards the profit and loss account as a comprehensive statement embracing all transactions that affect shareholder value. This view sees the firm as a total financial entity where all flows of value need to be highlighted.

Firms generally report increases in sales as an achievement suggesting the success of their current strategy. Conversely, a fall in sales is often perceived as evidence of decline or failure. Even assuming a rise in real turnover (i.e. after allowing for inflation), it is useful to make some evaluation on a like-for-like basis. This means identifying sales in the financial period ended that originated from the same trading units as sales in the previous year. For example, a retailer might increase aggregate sales by opening new branches, while sales in ongoing branches actually declined. Alternatively, the retailer may have acquired a competitor and presented aggregated accounts that disguise changes in underlying performance.

When adjustments for comparability have been made, the value of sales raises more questions. Should we equate higher sales with progress and lower sales with decline? The touchstone must lie in strategy. A niche trader may be more concerned with margins than with sales. Such a firm may know that the size of their niche market is limited. Its strategic goal is to dominate that niche, protect its integrity and take high margins. The goal is not to expand or to increase sales, but to sustain the competitive advantage that makes that strategy work.

By contrast, a supermarket chain such as Tesco clearly seeks market share. With scale economies in place, it rolls out its formula more and more widely. Low margins, together with low costs, provide the wedge for market penetration. Sometimes, too, firms expand or contract in response to external changes over which they have little if any control. Fashion trends, economic cycles, political events and demographic changes are some examples of forces that critically impact on business (see Chapter 13). Reacting to the external curtailment of a market by shrinking output and sales can be an adaptive response essential to efficiency and survival. Countervailing opportunities for expansion may or may not be discovered.

The profit and loss account, as its name suggests, is essentially about how a business generates and deploys a surplus (or makes and absorbs a loss). The accounts provide information about the quantity of that surplus, but its *quality* is left to interpretation. Quality of profit depends on judgement but the key criterion is sustainability. One-off gains such as property disposals represent low-quality profit because they are not sustainable and do not spring from the firm's distinctive capabilities. Even mainline operating profit varies in quality. Abnormal factors may have improved profit over a limited period. A key competitor may have withdrawn while no new competitor has yet appeared. A key source of competitive advantage may be about to crumble. The stream of profits earned needs careful strategic analysis to test its underlying strength and sustainabiltity.

Finally, notice that UK accounting data does not make allowance for inflation and that amounts are stated in the money terms of the relevant year. This is a common source of distortion in comparisons over time. For example, even with inflation running at around 2.5 per cent per annum, a firm that reports a rise in sales over five years from £50m to £55m has actually seen a real *decline* in sales of 2.8 per cent. It is therefore important to convert money amounts from earlier years into the constant purchasing power of the current (or a given) year so that *real* values can be compared.

The balance sheet

A balance sheet is like a financial X-ray through a business enterprise. In relation to a stated date, it lists and values the resources in the ownership of the firm and states how that total value has been funded. This explains the idea of 'balance'. All assets in the business represent a use of funds. Those uses of funds must have corresponding sources of funds or liabilities. The balance between the two 'sides' must occur by definition. The key categories of assets and liabilities are the components of the balance sheet

---

Liabilities

- **Shareholders' funds** means the money in the business that belongs to the owners. It logically embraces the value of all assets on the balance sheet, less what is owed to creditors. A distinction is made between share capital raised from the issue of shares and all other increases in the value of shareholders' funds, such as the retention of profits.

- **Long-term liabilities** are amounts owed that are not repayable for at least 12 months.

- **Current liabilities** are amounts owed that are repayable within 12 months and include trade creditors, short-term loans and bank overdrafts.

Assets

- **Fixed assets** are resources that will stay in the business on a long-term basis and, in most cases, contribute to the process of adding value, e.g. land and buildings, plant and machinery, equipment and fittings. As well as these tangible fixed assets, some firms also have intangible assets, such as patents and copyrights, while others may include a valuation for brands.

- **Current assets** are resources that are passing through the business in the process of production, e.g. stock, debtors and cash.

The format for the balance sheet follows a basic pattern that is intended to clarify the structure of assets and liabilities and the relationships between them. As with the profit and loss account, the terminology used varies between companies but the essential meanings do not change.

A typical example of a balance sheet is shown below (continued overleaf).

Creative Kitchens Ltd

Balance sheet as at 31 December 2002

	£m	£m
Fixed assets		22
Current assets	14	
Creditors: amounts falling due within one year	<u>6</u>	
Net current assets		<u>8</u>
Total assets less current liabilities		30
Creditors: amounts falling due after more than one year		<u>10</u>
Net assets		**20**

Share capital	5
Reserves	15
Shareholders' funds	**20**

Notice that investments by the firm appear as fixed assets if they are held on a long-term basis, and as current assets if they can be turned into cash at short notice.

In this vertical format net current assets are also the value of working capital. Current liabilities (creditors: amounts falling due within one year') are stripped out to highlight the net value of current assets that must be financed in the long term. The balance sheet *could* then balance on total assets less current liabilities and capital employed (shareholders' funds plus long-term loans). However, public companies focus on the shareholder interest by deducting 'creditors: amounts falling due after more than one year' and balancing net assets against shareholders' funds.

Interpreting the balance sheet

The balance sheet reveals how resources are being used in the business and the structure of their funding. Taken over successive years and allowing comparison with other enterprises, the balance sheet is a rich source of financial analysis. It is also usually open to a range of interpretations.

A key area of interest in any firm is liquidity and the availability of working capital. We have noted that every firm has a stream of cash coming into it and a stream of cash going out. This circulation of cash is like the bloodstream of a business, where fixed assets are the 'skeleton'. Cash is essential for the firm's interaction with the economy around it. It is needed to buy materials, pay wages and salaries and settle a vast range of bills or debts that the business incurs through its consumption of resources as inputs. It may also be needed to fund investment in fixed assets. To meet these needs, sales generate cash. In addition, a firm may draw new cash from share issues and loans. Monitoring and broadly balancing the inflows and outflows of cash is the purpose of the cash flow forecast and the management of working capital (see below).

In balance sheet terms, the critical variables are current assets and current liabilities (creditors falling due within 12 months). It is important to recognise that in providing working capital, current liabilities are a source of finance. Put another way, a business only provides long-term finance for working capital to the extent of the shortfall of current assets over current liabilities.

Textbook theory expects current assets (the sources of liquidity) to exceed current liabilities (the sources of demand for cash). The current ratio (current assets ÷ current liabilities) measures this relationship. In practice, the ratio has no ideal value but rather reflects the conventions of the industry and the particular patterns of trading for the business. For some firms a prudent value may be up to 2.0, but in other cases – such as retailing – negative working capital or a value below 1.0 is perfectly sound. Likewise, the tighter liquidity measure of the quick or acid test ratio (current assets – stock ÷ current liabilities) shows typical values of around 1.0 but varies widely. As with most ratios, the more telling data emerges with comparisons over time and between competitors.

Cadbury-Schweppes plc

Abbreviated balance sheet as at 29 December 2002

	£m	£m
Fixed assets		5 815
Current assets	2 052	
Creditors: amounts falling due within one year	2 585	
Net current assets		(533)
Total assets less current liabilities		5 282
Creditors: amounts falling due after more than one year		(1 996)
Net assets		**3 286**
Share capital		257
Reserves		2 763
Minority interests		266
Total capital employed		**3 286**

However, financial data are never static. Even allowing for external pressures, the raw material of ratios is not 'given' but 'made'. Although working capital is traditionally the basis of solvency and a cushion against risk, it has come under pressure in the drive for lean management. Just-in-time stock control, tight credit management and rapid reinvestment of cash have all tended to push down liquidity ratios. This may not matter if the firm is more athletic in its use of resources and sustains a healthy cash flow.

The cash flow statement

The cash flow statement is the third major accounting document that every company must produce. As its name suggests, it catalogues all inflows and outflows of cash arising from any aspect of the company's financial operations. In effect, it translates all events reflected in the profit and loss account and the balance sheet into the terms of cash movement.

The statement follows an essentially standard format.

Creative Kitchens plc

Cash flow statement for the year ending 31 December 2002

	£m
Cash flow from operating activities	17
Returns on investment and servicing of finance	(1)
Taxation	(4)
Capital expenditure and investments	(3)
Acquisitions and disposals	2
Dividends paid to ordinary shareholders	(5)
Cash (outflow)/inflow before use of liquid resources and financing	**6**
Management of liquid resources	1
Financing	(4)
(Decrease)/increase in cash	**3**

The cash flow statement at Creative Kitchens shows only the main definitive headings and more detail would be provided both on the face of the statement and in the notes.

'Cash flow from operating activities' is unlikely to correspond with operating profit, since profit is calculated by matching revenues with costs, neither of which are fully reflected by cash movements in the period. The largest source of discrepancy usually comes from the depreciation allowance entered in the overhead expenses. This is a real cost in that some part of the value of fixed assets has been 'used up' during the financial year but no corresponding cash outflow occurs. In effect, the cash expenditure was recorded in earlier years when each fixed asset was purchased. It should also be noticed that changes in stock, debtors or creditors can all contribute to recorded profit without any cash movement.

'Returns on investment and servicing of finance' covers any income from investments and the cost of servicing debt. 'Taxation' is usually a deduction but can be a refund, while 'Capital expenditure and investments' includes net spending on fixed assets plus any financial investments. 'Acquisitions and disposals' is a net value followed by the use of cash for 'Dividends paid to ordinary shareholders'.

The total now reached is a value for net cash inflow or outflow. This is followed by 'Management of liquid resources', which refers to the net purchase or sale of short-term liquid financial assets that is typically part of treasury management in large public companies. Finally, the value for 'Financing' is again a net figure reflecting changes in issued share capital or long-term debt. The last total indicates the actual increase or decrease in cash over the accounting period.

Cadbury-Schweppes plc

Cash flow statement for year ending 30 December 2001

	£m
Cash flow from operating activities	1 101
Returns on investment and servicing of finance	(117)
Taxation	(178)
Capital expenditure and investments	(319)
Acquisitions and disposals	(714)
Dividends paid to ordinary shareholders	(214)
Cash (outflow)/inflow before use of liquid resources and financing	**(403)**
Management of liquid resources	29
Financing	373
(Decrease)/increase in cash	**(1)**

Source: Adapted from Cadbury-Schweppes Annual Report 2002

Free cash flow

Some companies are now explicit in targeting 'free cash flow', which essentially means the cash available for directors to use at their discretion after deductions for capital investment. In practice, the term is used with various technical definitions so that dividend payments, for example, may or may not be included. The value of free cash flow is important because it pinpoints the amount of finance that is 'free' of capital spending and can be used for debt repayment, acquisitions or increasing the total cash balance. It also has use in valuing the company as a total investment and this is explained in Chapter 29.

'A true and fair view'?

Published accounts are based on a multitude of professional estimates, of which the potential for cumulative error is considerable. The valuation of fixed assets is particularly problematic. In many cases there can be no realistic test of their market value, which would anyway depend on the 'package' of assets for sale. The value of intangible assets such as goodwill, brands or intellectual property is necessarily subject to uncertainty. In any case, companies vary widely in their practices for recording – and not recording – intangibles.

Another problem area is profit. Naturally, data relating to profit is perceived by users as lying at the heart of accounts. Investors will tend to look at profit after tax, while analysts are more likely to focus on operating profit since it reveals the generation of profit from 'ordinary activities'. A number of questions then arise. How 'ordinary' was this profit? The accounts must be examined to find out how far it is derived from continuing operations and how far from those sold during the year. Is the operating profit the outcome of a reasonably typical trading year, or is it the product of special circumstances? The quality of profit in this sense is a vital concept in interpreting accounts.

Since accounts are such a visible and public statement about a firm's financial position, the data as published needs more than technical interpretation. While accounting data is supposed to offer 'a true and fair view' of the company's affairs, a good deal of perfectly legal window-dressing is possible. This allows directors some leeway in presenting their firm's financial affairs in a favourable context. For example, the cash and stock levels are shown on the balance sheet at a fixed date and this can be manipulated to suit the directors' purposes. Finally, as the abrupt collapse of Enron in 2001 indicated, the auditing process is less secure than many had imagined. International accounting firms that carry out major audits can have conflicting interests that make impartiality difficult.

29 Evaluating performance

Overview

No single ideal measure of business performance is universally recognised. This reflects the diversity of purpose in undertaking business activity. Stakeholder perspectives differ widely, while there is a tension between evaluating performance over the short and the long run. While there is an almost limitless range of goals that a business might wish to pursue, there is one central requirement that comes before all others: namely, to add value. Without meeting this condition a business process is merely destructive and undermines all other objectives. It is also unsustainable.

Performance indicators

Because finance represents value, the tools of financial analysis can be used to assess business performance. The classic approach is to measure the return on capital employed (ROCE): operating profit ÷ capital employed × 100. This exposes the percentage return on every pound of capital invested and allows comparison with other types of investment. It looks at the enterprise as a whole and does not differentiate between equity and loan capital.

ROCE values vary widely over time and between firms and industries. Although 15–25 per cent is a working average figure, risk is a vital determinant. The nil risk opportunity cost of capital is the yield on government bonds. Earnings above that level will carry a degree of risk that rises with the prospective rate of return.

What are the financial drivers of ROCE? There are two basic variables: the margin of profit and the rate of sales. We have already looked at the net or operating profit margin. The rate of sales generated by the capital in the business is measured by the capital turnover ratio (sales ÷ capital employed). This ratio asks how many times the value of capital employed was turned over during the financial year. An important identity emerges:

$$\text{Operating profit} \times \text{Capital turnover ratio} = \text{Return on capital employed}$$

or

$$\frac{\text{Profit margin}}{\text{Sales}} \times \frac{\text{Sales}}{\text{Capital employed}} = \frac{\text{Operating profit}}{\text{Capital employed}}$$

Cadbury Schweppes and Tesco ←

Financial years ending in 2002

		Cadbury-Schweppes	Tesco
Sales	£m	5 298	28 337
Operating profit	£m	866	1 484
Capital employed	£m	5 282	11 129
Profit margin	%	16.35	5.63
Capital turnover ratio		1.0	2.37
Return on Capital Employed	%	16.4	13.33

These two components of ROCE – profit margin and relative turnover speed – do not only vary in line with performance. Their linked values reflect the nature of the industry and the firm's position in the market. For example, a specialist engineering firm with a heavy fixed asset base might achieve high margins but a slow turnover relative to capital employed. A supermarket chain with its mass market and fast throughput of goods would have a low margin but a high ratio for capital turnover.

These two ratios can prompt further investigation into the roots of ROCE. The operating profit margin is the starting point for a ratio analysis of the profit and loss account, while the capital

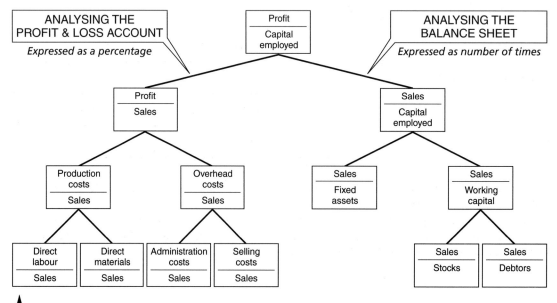

Figure 29.1 Pyramid of ratios

turnover ratio leads to ratio analysis of the balance sheet. Taken together, these strands of analysis form a pyramid of ratios as outlined in Figure 29.1.

Comparison of these ratios over time and, if possible, on an inter-firm basis can pinpoint barriers to better performance.

Shareholder measures

Since shareholders own the business and, as such, are the final arbiters of strategy, it follows that some key performance indicators isolate the shareholder interest. A firm's return on equity relates profit to shareholders' funds only (profit after tax ÷ shareholders' fund × 100). While operating profit is a key guide to the underlying success of a firm's strategy, profit after tax is the money actually available to the ordinary shareholders. This ratio therefore measures the direct return on the shareholders' investment.

This same focus is sharpened further by calculating the EPS or earnings per share (profit after tax ÷ number of issued shares). The value for EPS has to be disclosed by companies in their accounts. Changes in this value are watched closely in the financial media since it is an important driver of share price. However, in analysing EPS trends it is essential to distinguish between changes in the level of profit and changes in the number of shares issued.

A stock market view of a firm's performance is given by price–earnings ratio ('the P/E ratio'), which measures how many years' current earnings per share are represented by the share price. For example, a firm whose EPS is 150p might have their shares priced at 120p. The P/E ratio is 8:1 in other words the shares are priced at eight times current earnings. A high P/E ratio suggests market confidence in the firm's prospects, with a high and sustained value of earnings into the future. Conversely, a low P/E indicates poor levels of confidence in a firm's future.

EPS and P/E ratios (2003)

Company	Earnings per share	P/E ratio
Cadbury-Schweppes	28.7	12.3
Tesco	13.5	15.8
ARM	3.2	25.9

P/E ratios are very useful but there are strong qualifications. First, share prices are often very volatile and influenced by waves of buying and selling. P/Es can rise and fall from day to day without any real change in the firm's prospects. Second, the earnings data used are always out of date and, in any case reflect earlier performance. A particular firm's P/E ratio may be more useful in the context of averages for the relevant sector.

Shareholder value

From the 1980s an increasing number of firms took the view that improving shareholder value should be their explicit and overriding objective. This could be achieved in two ways: one was through the payment of dividends and the other was through increases in the share price. Management in pursuit of these goals has been at the heart of the shareholder value movement.

Cadbury-Schweppes ◄─────────────────────────

Managing for value

Our primary objective is to grow the value of the business for our shareowners.

Managing for value is the objective philosophy which unites all our activities in pursuit of this objective.

The objective is quantified. We have set three financial targets to measure our progress:

1 to increase our earnings per share by at least **10%** every year
2 to generate **£150 million** of free cash flow every year
3 to **double** the value of our shareowners' investment within four years.

Our approach to this task is holistic. We seek simultaneously to develop better strategies, upgrade our business culture and align our reward structure with the interests of our shareowners.

NB Company's emboldening.

Source: Cadbury-Schweppes Annual Report 1998

This approach has a two-pronged logic. In so far as the shareholders want short-term benefit from their investment, they want dividends. The relative rate of dividend payments is measured by the dividend yield (dividends per share ÷ share price × 100). This ratio answers the question: how rewarding is the investment in cash terms relative to its value? Notice, however, that a rise in the share price depresses dividend yield, while a collapse in the shares can flatter even reduced dividends with an impressive yield!

The shareholders' long-term benefit depends on the stream of earnings to be generated by the business in the future, and on which the share price also depends. Strategy based directly on shareholder value therefore targets the share price as well as the payment of dividends. In practice, however, share price makes a mercurial, even whimsical, performance indicator. As the collapse of the dot.com boom in 2000 indicated, shareholder value through the prism of share price can be ephemeral and largely illusory.

Yet the concept of shareholder value is based on the Efficient Markets Hypothesis. In essense, this asserts that, at any given time, a company's share price already has factored into it all publicly available information about the prospect ahead – whether favourable or unfavourable. A problem with this view is that bull and bear markets can take on a life of their own where prices become driven by expectations of further rises or falls rather than the company's underlying performance.

The main counter-argument is that senior managers should build strategies for long-term added value rather than any short-term efforts to 'manage' their share price. This view does not deny the centrality of shareholder value but suggests that the long-term creation of added value must lead strategy and that the indicators of relative success will follow.

Which performance measure?

As a measure of performance, ROCE has some serious problems. The ratio is intended to explore the link between the resources in a firm and the profit or surplus that they generate over a period. But is capital employed on the balance sheet a realistic guide to the value of resources in the business? The 'capital employed' denominator for ROCE does not pretend to equate with the value of the business as expressed, for instance, by its market capitalisation (number of shares issued × share price).

Capital employed and market capitalisation

Company	Capital employed £m	Market capitalisation £m	Market capitalisation/ Capital employed
Cadbury-Schweppes	5 282	7 266	1.38
Tesco	11 129	15 489	1.39
ARM	86	846	9.84

Data based on 2002/03 accounts and share prices in June 2003

The difference between capital employed and capitalisation is, however, a gulf full of questions. Suppose that a pharmaceutical firm carries out some promising R&D and enters on its balance sheet some valuation of this intangible fixed asset. This would be perfectly legitimate, but it increases capital employed through an increase in the shareholders' funds. Then suppose the same firm decides to value its over-the-counter brands and capitalises these as fixed assets. What else now fills that gap between capital employed and the firm's market value? Perhaps it is research staff, or teamwork, or customer networks, or leadership? Or it could even be such extreme intangibles as knowledge or culture or organisational energy.

In theory, each of these 'assets' could be valued and entered on the balance sheet. For a given moment in time the firm's capital employed could tally with market value. Yet precisely because these assets are so intangible, their value changes from day to day, as reflected in the company share price. After all, it is not the value of the firm's property or plant that makes the share price fluctuate. It is the prospective value of the complex mesh of intangibles wrapped round those tangible assets that is unstable. It is unstable in relation to markets, competition and the external environment.

From this impasse, there is no easy escape. ROCE remains useful as a general performance indicator, especially when taken in a time series for one firm or in comparisons between firms subject to the necessary accounting adjustments. But the basic problems with ROCE spring from the whole concept of 'capital employed'. When modern accounting conventions were developing in the 19th century, the typical business enterprise was a relatively small manufacturing unit. In this world, labour was a commodity, brands were unimportant and the assets of value were indeed those shown on the traditional balance sheet. Capital employed and the value of the business were not the same, but they were not different by any great order of magnitude.

Over the second half of the 20th century the realities changed as the tertiary sector expanded, goods and services became less homogeneous and value was conveyed in emotional propositions. The hard geometry of tangible assets increasingly melts value into the soft contours of networks, knowledge and creativity. In the 21st century the formal balance sheets drawn up by corporations look more and more like stage scenery, while value flows through dialogue among the actors.

The idea of economic value added (EVA) breaks with the convention of relating returns to assets or sums of capital and, instead, treats every use of resources as a cost. EVA is generally defined as operating profit after tax less a charge for the cost of the capital used to generate that profit. This residual or 'economic profit' is also the supernormal return earned by a competitive advantage and explained in Chapter 7. As such, it is at the heart of our understanding of how competitive markets work.

Kay (1993) measures EVA as a ratio between one pound's worth of input cost (including capital cost) and the corresponding output value. A firm with a ratio of 1.0 is putting resources through a neutral cycle and neither adding nor subtracting value. Yet such a firm would report a positive return on capital since, by definition, it was able to meet the whole cost of its capital employed. Only when the economic added value ratio moves above 1.0 has a firm added any real value and demonstrated a competitive advantage. This approach is arguably far more transparent and logically rigorous. It exposes firms that are coasting on the margins of shareholder acceptability and signals resources towards their most efficient use.

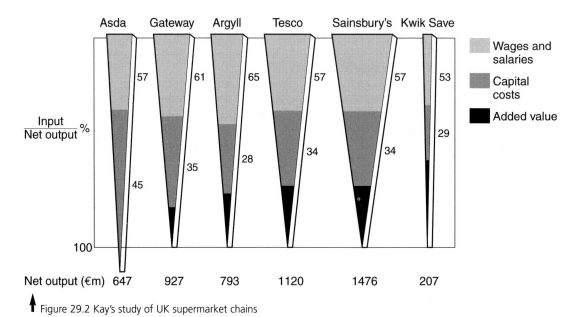

Figure 29.2 Kay's study of UK supermarket chains

Source: Adapted from J Kay The Foundations of Corporate Success *(Oxford, 1993)*

Asda is the marginal firm with an added value ratio of 0.95. Kwik-Save was then the king of added value, but across a narrower flow of sales than J Sainsbury in second place. It is interesting to notice the reversal of fortunes over the ten years since this study.

The shareholder value approach to performance has been widely criticised. Kay (2001) believes that it encourages short-term thinking and distracts managers from the real task of developing distinctive capabilities that translate into value-adding strategies. Not only are share prices fickle, but they reflect the perspective of the moment. Targeting a transient perception is quite different from the real outcomes pursued by long-term strategy.

However, in terms of management, the shareholder value concept can be effective in aligning strategy and even organisational culture with the imperative to add value. In practice, the emphasis is often on increasing earnings per share, free cash flow and the *value* of the shareholders' investment. Success in improving these variables of real strategy should – all other things being equal – be reflected in a rising share price. The potentially less favourable implications for stakeholders who are not owners of equity will be discussed in Chapter 37.

The balanced scorecard

Measures of financial performance relate to the outcomes as distinct from the drivers of business success. They also refer backwards to a completed trading period rather than forwards to the strategic challenges ahead. The balanced scorecard developed by Kaplan and Norton (1992, 1996) is a performance tool designed to link financial outcomes with measures of the 'softer' variables on which those outcomes depend. It is used in a range of customised forms by many of the largest companies in the USA and Europe.

The process starts with establishing for the business a strategic mission from which objectives can be derived. It is these objectives that are then targeted by the scorecard, which frames key criteria for continuous improvement. The essential framework for the scorecard is shown in Figure 29.3 overleaf.

In each quadrant of the scorecard there are likely to be a number of specific objectives and corresponding performance indicators. The firm's progress towards its strategic mission can then be monitored on a broad front that includes both financial ratios and their critical drivers. The scorecard may be seen as 'balanced' in that it captures financial and non-financial indicators, it addresses the long run as well as the short run and it helps resolve the perspectives of key stakeholders.

Financial perspective		Customer perspective	
How do we look to shareholders?		How do customers see us?	
GOALS	MEASURES	GOALS	MEASURES

Internal business perspective		Innovation and learning perspective	
What must we excel at?		How can we continue to improve and create value?	
GOALS	MEASURES	GOALS	MEASURES

Figure 29.3 Kaplan and Norton's balanced scorecard

30 Financial management

Overview

As processors of resources, firms need active financial management. Like a traffic routeing and signalling system, financial management is essential to enabling desired events to happen. It has several dimensions. The inward flow of cash and the availability of finance up to the planning horizon are first responsibilities. Then the right amounts of finance must reach the right parts of the business at the right times. This involves decisions about the allocation of fixed and working capital. These financial commitments must be properly managed so that they yield the largest possible surplus of value over cost. Finally, the capital structure of the enterprise needs managing for the right balance between stability and returns.

It is a mistake to see financial management as somehow separate from business management. Because the currency of business value is money, the generation of value depends on a configuration of finance. This pattern of 'money-tagged' resources is highly dynamic. It needs planning, steering, switching and checking across timescales ranging from an hour to a decade. Financial management is a focused life support system to strategic management, where one significant error can allow a perfectly good business to die.

Capital structure

We have seen that every firm is built from a mix of equity and loan capital. Whether a business is at the start-up stage or wishing to expand and diversify, borrowed funds have some important advantages. Of course, where share capital is difficult or impossible to raise, then loan finance is the only option. Similarly, a risky venture in which the owners have confidence may find borrowing, even at high rates of interest, the only realistic plan. The provision of venture capital often works on this basis. Funding also has major implications for ownership and control. The significant equity holders in a firm may not be able to increase their investment yet equally they may not want to dilute their control. Loan finance is again the obvious answer.

However, loan capital also has a fundamental financial attraction. A business can only survive in the long term if it has some sustainable source of competitive advantage. This in turn implies returns above the opportunity cost of capital. The minimum level of opportunity cost for capital is the long-run interest rate. Thus, a firm with a competitive advantage and the ability to obtain loans at commercial interest rates will find that every pound borrowed covers its own cost and contributes a surplus to swell profit before tax. This surplus is equivalent to the true rate of added value (as explained in Chapter 5).

The relationship between debt and equity in a firm's capital structure is expressed in the gearing ratio: loan capital ÷ shareholders' funds × 100. It is clear that a high gearing ratio can provide ordinary shareholders with greatly enhanced rates of return on their equity. The limiting factor is risk, since the mechanism of gain cuts two ways. While the business generates rates of return above the rate of interest payable, loan capital is advantageous, but once returns fall below this rate, the logic moves into reverse with serious implications.

Red Bus and Green Bus ⟵

Green Bus is a well-established operator that has grown through the investment of retained profits. While shareholders' funds amount to £90 million, borrowing has been limited to £10 million at a 5 per cent interest rate.

Red Bus is a smaller and aggressive competitor that has grown quickly through borrowing. With just £4 million in shareholders' funds, the company's long-term loans total £6 million, also at a 5 per cent rate of interest.

This information is summarised below:

	Green Bus	Red Bus
Equity	£90m	£4m
Debt (long term)	£10m	£6m
Capital employed	£100m	£10m
Gearing	10%	60%

The table below shows the implications of falling profitability over the next three years. Assume that each firm's capital structure remains unchanged.

Year 1 ROCE = 22%

	Green Bus	Red Bus
Operating profit	£22.0m	£2.2m
Interest expense	£1.0m	£0.4m
Profit before tax	£21.0m	£1.8m
Tax @ 25%	£5.25m	£0.45m
Profit after tax	£15.75m	£1.35m
Return on equity	19.7%	67.5%
Interest cover	22.0	5.5

Year 2 ROCE = 12%

	Green Bus	Red Bus
Operating profit	£12.0m	£1.2m
Interest expense	£1.0m	£0.4m
Profit before tax	£11.0m	£0.8m
Tax @ 25%	£2.75m	£0.2m
Profit after tax	£8.25m	£0.6m
Return on equity	10.31%	30.0%
Interest cover	12.0	3.0

Year 3 ROCE = 2%

	Green Bus	Red Bus	
Operating profit	£2.0m	£0.2m	
Interest expense	£1.0m	£0.4m	
Profit before tax	£1.0m	–	
Tax @ 25%	£0.25m	–	
Profit after tax	£0.75m	–	Risk of insolvency
Return on equity	0.94%	–	
Interest cover	2.0	–	

With equal but high rates of return on capital, highly geared Red Bus enjoys a far better return on equity than the low geared Green Bus. However, the interest cover at Red Bus is much lower. This becomes serious as ROCE falls. By Year 3 interest cover at Red Bus is down to 0.5. Now the whole operating profit plus a further £0.2m is needed simply to meet the interest expense. Return on equity is negative and there is a real risk of insolvency.

Notice that the minimum rate of return on capital necessary to meet interest expenses = rate of interest × gearing.

Interest payments are obligatory. High gearing means that as returns fall below the rate of interest, the funds earned by the relatively lower level of equity are disproportionately required to service debt. The resulting return on equity falls rapidly towards zero and may even become negative, so that any liquid assets in the business are then quickly absorbed. If returns deteriorate further, then the prospect of insolvency looms.

An added twist is the possibility of a rise in the rate of interest. Loan capital may carry fixed or variable rates. Where rates are variable the risks of high gearing increase. This raises the stakes for financial managers in balancing debt and equity, while a change in interest rates may itself alter a firm's choice of capital structure. Reducing gearing is unlikely to be easy at short notice, especially when returns are falling.

Next ←

From the moment of launch in 1982, Next was a success story. It had found its gap in the market with impressive accuracy. Its target customers were increasing in number and spending power. The 1980s' boom showed no sign of abating. Expansion was rapid and, via acquisitions, often discontinuous. With a growing freehold property portfolio, Next had little difficulty in securing large-scale loan finance.

The skies darkened rapidly after the enforced departure of the high-profile Chief Executive, George Davies. By late 1988 the house price boom had stalled in London and the South East. It was not long before prices moved into reverse. Interest rates soared from 8 per cent to 15 per cent. By 1990 the whole economy was entering the most severe recession since the Second World War. Among the hardest hit were younger home owners – the core market for Next.

Profit before tax collapsed from £62 million in 1988 to a loss of £47 million in the following year. Interest payments became a serious threat as the company's property assets lost value. With the share price as low as 16p, Next was fighting for survival.

Cost of capital

A basic consideration when raising business capital is its cost. Even to retain finance in a business, its managers must achieve some minimum rate of return. A firm that fails this test will, in the long run, lose its grip on resources. Such performance-related instability might begin with a change of top management, continue with a change of ownership and end in a wave of closures and redundancies.

When a business wishes to attract new capital, the likely cost must be related to the prospective returns. And for any given business with its track record and apparent prospects, there will be minimum rates of return necessary to attract either loan or equity capital.

Why is a charge payable for the use of capital? First, the use of capital always entails some degree of risk, which forms a variable part of the capital charge. Second, the value of money changes according to the rate of inflation, the expected level of which is built into interest rates. Finally, there is the opportunity cost of capital itself that forms a kind of 'hire charge' to any user.

The cost of loan capital is specified by the interest rate, although in the case of variable rate loans there is obviously a real degree of uncertainty. It is also important to notice that because interest is paid before tax, the after-tax cost of loan capital is significantly lower than it appears. For example, if a firm is paying a 30 per cent tax rate, then an 8 per cent interest rate has an after-tax cost of only 5.6 per cent (0.7 × 8 per cent).

Equity has a slightly more complex cost structure. The cost of share capital is not just the dividends paid, but is the opportunity cost of that capital. This is normally higher than the dividend yield (dividends per share ÷ share price) and reflects the value of the retained profits that fund the expansion of the firm and growth in future dividends. The opportunity cost of capital is the baseline for return on any investment. The extent to which the value of rewards to shareholders exceeds the opportunity cost of capital is the gravitational force that holds that capital within the company.

There are a number of ways in which the cost of share capital can be calculated. One of the best known and most useful approaches is the Capital Asset Pricing Model (CAPM). This identifies three elements in the cost of share capital, which are as follows.

1 Risk-free return

This is the rate of return available to investors without any risk. It is usually benchmarked as the rate of return on Treasury Bills (about 4 per cent in 2002).

2 Market risk

When a security in the form of equity shares is purchased, it has attached to it risk of two types. First, there is unique risk that is specific to the company concerned. This can arise from an almost infinite range of random causes. A supplier may fail, a customer may default on payment, an industrial dispute may occur or a talented CEO may leave.

This risk can be eliminated by investors through holding a multi-share or diversified portfolio. In this way, the adverse and favourable outcomes of unique risk become balanced by probability of occurrence. Statistically, it is only necessary to hold four securities to eliminate nearly three-quarters of this unique risk. A dozen securities reduces unique risk by about 90 per cent.

For this reason the cost of capital does not include any premium for unique risk: it is assumed to be diversified away. As indicated in Figure 30.1, what remains is an irreducible market risk – constituting about one-third of the total risk in holding a one-security (undiversified) portfolio. This risk affects all equities in the market. It is caused by macroeconomic events and uncertainties such as changing prospects for economic growth, movements in exchange rates or changes in the price of oil.

A wide range of studies analysing returns over many years has established that market risk (also called systematic risk) has a value of around 8 per cent, i.e. the return necessary to compensate for market risk.

3 Volatility risk

Surveys over time show that the value of some shares moves closely in line with the market as a whole. Others are more volatile, with their values less closely tied to this relationship and therefore carry a higher level of risk. Using regression analysis, shares are given 'Beta values' that indicate their degree of volatility relative to the market. 'Aggressive' Beta values significantly above 1.0 (e.g. British Airways at 1.22) imply a correspondingly greater degree of risk in holding the security.

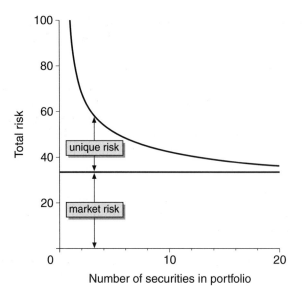

Figure 30.1 Diversifying against risk

Conversely, a 'defensive' Beta (e.g. ICI at 0.65) carries less risk than the market as a whole. A 'neutral' Beta, around 1.0, carries a level of risk approximating to the market as a whole.

Using this understanding of risk, we can now put together a formula specifying the minimum rate of return required by a given security. If Rf is the risk-free return and Rm is the return on the overall equity market, then:

Cost of capital (required rate of return) = Rf + β (Rm − Rf).

Put in words, this means that equity capital must earn a risk-free return plus a premium for market risk (Rm − Ri) adjusted for the likelihood of volatility in returns (β).

Since most firms finance themselves with both equity and debt, a weighted cost of capital model must be used (WACC). This relates the proportion of finance to its cost. For example, a company might be financed by £9m in equity costing a 16 per cent return, and £3m in debt with an 8 per cent rate of interest. The WACC would be: (75 per cent × 16 per cent) + (25 per cent × 8 per cent) = 14 per cent.

Research tests on the CAPM model (e.g. Ross, 1976) have questioned the nature of the trade-off between Beta values and expected returns, pointing to other variables that can be at least as powerful. Managerially, too, the elimination of unique risk is a doubtful assumption. While shareholders can use portfolio diversification to neutralise the risks specific to one enterprise, managers are far more dependent on the particular firm and may therefore set much higher risk thresholds to protect their own interests.

Investment decisions

There is a basic distinction in business between revenue and capital expenditure. Revenue spending includes meeting all the expenses involved in the running of the business (e.g. materials, wages, energy, administration, rent) where no long-term or fixed asset is acquired. Capital expenditure is concerned entirely with the purchase of fixed assets of all types.

Investing in fixed assets is of the most important tasks carried out by management. Where large sums are involved relative to the size of the firm, or when the asset has real strategic importance, then investment decisions can literally make or break the business. Sometimes these decisions are of the yes or no type. Do we buy a retail site or not? Often they allow a graduation of response. If new capacity is to be installed, should it be size A, B or C? Frequently, firms have a number of investment options that appear viable but have limited funding available. In all cases informed choices are necessary.

Investments in fixed assets yield long-term streams of benefit to the firm. These may be in the form of additional sales or reduced costs. To determine the value of these cash flows that arise in the future, several techniques are available.

The simplest method is to calculate the Annual Rate of Return (ARR). This is the aggregated net cash flows divided by the number of years in a project's life, expressed as a percentage of the initial investment.

$$\text{ARR} = \frac{\text{average annual return}}{\text{initial investment}} \times 100$$

The payback method is even simpler and measures the time taken for an investment to have financed itself. Both of these methods have serious limitations. ARR fails to account for the timing of cash flows. This is an important defect since money has a time value. Payback captures the time factor but ignores all cash flows after the payback date. An example clarifies the difference.

A company is considering two possible investments with anticipated cash flows as follows:

End of Year	Net cash flow (£)	
	Investment P	Investment Q
0	(10 000)	(10 000)
1	1 000	7 000
2	2 000	4 000
3	4 000	2 000
4	8 000	1 000
TOTAL	5 000	4 000

Note that the investments are not expected to have any residual value.

	Investment P	Investment Q
ARR	12.5%	10%
Payback	3.37 years	1.75 years

The more sophisticated approaches are based on discounted cash flow (DCF). This is based on the principle that if the opportunity cost of capital is the rate of interest, say 10 per cent, then £1 received in one year's time is worth £1 ÷ 1.1 = £0.909 today. (£1 at 10 per cent interest rate is worth £1 × 1.1 = £1.10 in one year's time; £1.10 in one year's time is worth £1 ÷ 1.1 = £1. So, £1 in one year's time is worth £1 ÷ 1.1 = £0.909 today.)

The value 0.909 is a discount factor applying to £1 receivable in a years' time with a cost of capital at 10 per cent. As such, it can be applied to any relevant sum. On the same basis, £1 to be received in two years' time is worth £1 ÷ 1.12. = £0.826, forming another discount factor. It is clear that tables of discount factors can be constructed for any opportunity cost or discount rate for any period of time. This in turn means that the net present value (NPV) of any cash flow stream extending into the future can be readily calculated. Notice that even at a 10 per cent discount rate (cost of capital), £1 to be received in 10 years' time has a present value of only 38.6p.

Investments P and Q: NPV calculations at 10% discount rate

End of Year	Investment P			Investment Q		
	Cash flow £	Discount factor	Net Present Value £	Cash flow £	Discount factor	Net Present Value £
0	(10 000)	1.000	(10 000)	(10 000)	1.000	(10 000)
1	1 000	0.909	909	10 000	0.909	6 363
2	2 000	0.826	1 652	6 000	0.826	3 304
3	4 000	0.751	3 004	3 000	0.751	1 502
4	8 000	0.683	5 464	1 000	0.683	683
TOTAL	5 000		1 029	4 000		1 852

On this basis, Project Q is now revealed as the better choice with an NPV that is higher than Project P by £823.

Clearly, the choice of discount rate is a deciding factor in the calculation. The minimum required rate of return or criterion rate must be the cost of capital to the company (see CAPM above), but the actual rate applied is usually higher, reflecting internal opportunity costs and strategic prospects over the life of the project.

Usually, projects under consideration require different initial investments. For this reason NPV alone lacks a basis for comparability, but the net discounted cashflow can be divided by the initial investment to give a profitability index. The alternative is to calculate the internal rate of return (IRR).

This is expressed as a percentage and is calculated as the discount rate necessary to reduce a project's NPV to exactly zero. Put another way, the IRR is the highest rate of discount that a project can sustain without showing a negative NPV. Its exact value can be found by iteration or the use of any business software package.

Investments P and Q: IRR calculations confirmed at 13.5% rate for Investment P and 21.7% rate for Investment Q

Year	Cash flow £	Discount factor	Net Present Value £	Cash flow £	Discount factor	Net Present Value £
0	(10 000)	1.000	(10 000)	(10 000)	1.000	(10 000)
1	1 000	0.881	881	7 000	0.821	5 747
2	2 000	0.777	1 554	4 000	0.675	2 700
3	4 000	0.684	2 736	2 000	0.554	1 108
4	8 000	0.603	4 824	1 000	0.455	455
TOTAL	5 000		(5)	4 000	4 000	10

NB The residual NPV values appoximate to zero.

The DCF approach has a useful wider application in efforts to value a company as a 'total investment'. Logically the value of a business is the total discounted value of its future free cash flows (see Chapter 29). Put simply, this amounts to the present value of all expected future cash flows less the current and capital cost of their generation.

Budgeting

Typically, a firm will have budgets for sales, purchasing, production costs, administration, capital spending and R&D. The implications of these budgets in terms of funds flowing into and out of the business are projected in the cash budget or cash flow forecast. Finally, the master budget shows the future profit and loss account and balance sheet expected to emerge from the detailed budgets agreed.

Effective budgeting acts as a powerful planning device that translates strategic objectives into the operational detail of resource movements. In large firms, the master budget is the top tier in a complex hierarchy of divisional, departmental and other sub-budgets. Taken together, these articulate the firm's intentions for the use of scarce resources in the period ahead. To allow for emerging circumstances, most firms have flexibility built into their budgetary system to take account of changing activity levels and shifting external pressures.

If they have been properly negotiated, budgets are an important source of motivation, embodying constraints and targets that are challenging but fair. Implicit within this scenario is the process of control. Each budget holder has a responsibility to work within the terms agreed and to be accountable for significant deviations.

To turn a budget from an inert statement into an active management tool requires the continuous analysis of variance. It is clear from the outset that actual and budgeted events will rarely coincide. As results begin to emerge, the variance between budgeted and actual forms a system of feedback loops

Midland Models Ltd ←

Labour cost variance for April 2003

VARIABLE	BUDGET £	ACTUAL £	VARIANCE £	%	A/F
Labour costs	10 000	12 000	+2 000	+20	A

Was the variance caused by a rise in labour costs or a higher volume of production?

Production was above budget in April by 25 per cent. The budget is now flexed by this percentage:

VARIABLE	BUDGET £	ACTUAL £	VARIANCE £	%	A/F
Labour costs	12 500	12 000	−500	−4	F

It is now clear that proportional labour costs have actually fallen. This in itself may be worth investigating further.

throughout the organisation. Variances are termed 'favourable' (F) or 'adverse' (A) and may be measured in both absolute and percentage terms. They can also be analysed to identify their underlying causes.

Minor variances are to be expected and can usually be disregarded. Significant or growing variances attract attention, while radical variances may prompt a rapid or even emergency response. Understanding favourable variances can be as useful as investigating adverse variances: widening opportunities may be signalled by better-than-expected results.

This approach is a classic example of 'management by exception', where managers avoid spending limited resources on systems that are working normally and instead are alerted to points of need by the identification of variances. However, it can become too formulaic. Hidden within 'normal' results can be countervailing variances and growing tensions that will later trigger abrupt or even discontinuous change. Viewed in isolation, the appearance of small variances in a system can seem insignificant, yet taken together they may have a vital message that is also emerging in other systems within the organisation (see Chapter 32).

Liquidity management

Given the importance of cash, every business prepares a cash budget in the form of a cash flow forecast. This can be updated as actual events unfold and provides a continuous projection of cash availability and cash needs. In this way any cash shortfall can be covered in advance. This might be achieved by converting stock, debtors or short-term investments into cash, or by arranging a bank overdraft or a short-term loan.

Financing cash outflows for a specific asset with a longer-term loan is another possibility. This releases cash for use as working capital. However, an expanding business usually needs an increasing level of working capital and will wish to avoid the pitfall of overtrading. This is likely to require an injection of share capital, although small enterprises have a tendency to rely on renewable overdrafts.

Yet there is a deep conflict or trade-off operating at the heart of the liquidity issue. Firms do need cash and must remain solvent, but the greater the liquidity of the form in which assets are held, the lower the likely rate of return. In other words, liquidity carries an opportunity cost and cash carries the highest opportunity cost of all. It follows that financial management involves a continuous tension between the maintenance of adequate liquidity and the opportunity cost of holding liquid assets.

In practice, it is quite common for firms to accumulate cash balances that exceed their liquidity needs. Given that most firms have no competitive advantage in making financial investments with cash, the directors may decide to purchase their own shares. Such share buy-backs effectively return cash to shareholders and tend to increase the share price. What happens is that the same profit before tax gets generated by a smaller number of shares, so pushing up earnings per share (EPS) and – all other things being equal – the share price. This may in itself also act as a deterrent against any hostile bid for the company.

Some firms, however, have a strategic purpose in building a 'cash mountain'. Although it is costly to hold, cash does give firms a hungry and mobile quality. Acquisition opportunities can be seized without the difficulties and delays of arranging external funding. Besides, many firms now work with a contingent status for their strategy and its associated assets. Liquidity does not end at the frontier between current and fixed assets. It is a relative concept that can be applied to all uses of funds within the business. Avoiding the arthritic tendency of over-commitment to highly specific fixed assets has become a way of facilitating flexibility and fast changes of direction. The growth in leasing and out-sourcing, and in joint ventures and partnerships can all reflect a need for greater agility and quick reactions to opportunities and events.

Risks and risk management

Every business seeks a return on its resources, but every business return involves a risk. This means simply that there are always downside outcomes to any uncertainty. Risk is the possibility of adverse events and forms a negative weighting to all prospective returns.

But just as firms specialise in their chosen sources of return, so they will also specialise in their chosen acceptance of risk. For example, an innovative electronics business might be willing to take the risk of an unconventional product launch failing, but would wish to avoid the risk of an adverse change in exchange rates. Risks falling within a firm's specialised area of competence are far more likely to be acceptable than those falling outside. This is because the firm's competitive advantage in the field may mean that the risk is relatively lower for that firm than for any other. Moreover, the risk may be heavily offset by the corresponding chance to harvest an opportunity.

In facing risks and aiming to optimise returns, firms use various techniques for risk management. The process starts with the identification of risks to which the firm is exposed. These risks can then be evaluated in terms of probabilities and degree of exposure. Even quite a high risk of a manageable loss may be preferred to a small risk of a loss devastating to the business.

Risk management itself involves deciding how to handle the risks identified. Some risks will be retained unavoidably as part of the core business. Many of these can be reduced through taking precautions and ensuring that if 'Plan A' fails, 'Plan B' can be adopted without excessive cost. Investment project management, in particular, needs the point-of-no-return to be clarified so that 'Plan B' alternatives can be evaluated while still feasible.

Another approach is to diversify the firm's portfolio of business activities so that risks are mutually offsetting. Of the remaining risks, some are small relative to the firm's size and can be carried or absorbed. Others are transferred to another party through the insurance market or by hedging where, for a fee, the risk attached to a future transaction is greatly reduced or eliminated. Buying into agreed exchange rates or fixed prices for a commodity are common applications of hedging.

Sensitivity analysis

In analysing strategic risk, it is important to isolate the key variables on which success depends. Sensitivity analysis tests the implications of deviations in actual events away from those assumptions. For example, a premium ice cream producer plans a major investment that is expected to yield a favourable rate of return. Key assumptions include the level of sales, selling prices, labour savings and the final cost of the project. The sensitivity of cashflows to deviations from these assumptions can then be explored. For example, while a 5 per cent reduction in projected sales may only reduce cashflows by 10 per cent, a 5 per cent fall in price caused by the entry of an aggressive competitor will cut net cashflows in half. In this way managers are alerted to the most dangerously sensitive variables and can assess the probability of deviations from forecast.

PART G

AGENDA
explained

31 Culture and context

Overview

The traditional mechanical model for management made little if any allowance for the shared assumptions of employees or the corporate culture. Instead, hierarchical organisations have traditionally tended to assume that effective management depends on making objectively correct decisions and communicating them downwards so that appropriate actions take place.

It is now clear that culture is influential across every aspect of organisational behaviour and can make the difference between corporate success or failure. There is limitless diversity in the forms of culture, but some definitive types can usefully be identified. No particular culture is 'ideal', but a culture can assist or obstruct strategic purpose. It is likely that the features of a successful culture are shifting in line with the trend towards distributed decision making and intelligence. This makes autocratic or imposed cultures less likely to succeed; but it may increase the importance of a culture in shaping behaviour when it is no longer directed by an all-knowing echelon of senior management.

Another important factor is context. The significance of symbols, rituals and myths has always been recognised in national life and is becoming better understood in the nurturance of corporate culture. Context, arguably, can profoundly change the way people think and act.

What is corporate culture?

A first visit to the home of a friend or colleague is always instructive. From the moment of arrival the visitor is bombarded with statements about meaning, value and precedence. Symbols and contextual alignments abound. Protocol may be high or low profile, but its existence is undeniable.

Of course, many of these messages are lost on the visitor. Some are only dimly recognised, others are assigned inappropriate levels of importance. But almost always an impression is formed – and it is an impression of a living culture, a pattern of behaviour and meaning that has usually developed over a considerable time. Regardless of any desire to the contrary, judgements are made. Are the visitor and host cultures compatible, even for a short time? Will there be awkwardness, corners to smooth or even jarring, perhaps embarrassing collisions? Or does the culture feel comfortable? Is it stimulating, opening horizons of thought, feeling and symbolism that the visitor might wish to adopt? We have all had these experiences; we have all read and misread cultures and can often remember the consequences.

Business organisations are really no different. Beneath the official image, every company has layer upon layer of semi-hidden and hidden agendas. Even when entering a business site, the sign outside, the car park, the reception area and the responses of people are immensely revealing of the likely work and life patterns beyond the doors marked 'Private'. Consider a corporate website or Annual Report and Accounts. Certainly there are hints of the underlying culture, but we know we are looking down the lens of a very partial camera. Actually, one slogan on the shopfloor, one coffee in the canteen, one glimpse of the Chief Executive's office may all be far more significant.

A culture is a shared pattern of meanings that acts as a template in constructing reality. This is worth thinking about carefully. The scale and complexity of 'reality' when it means the whole world with its embodiment of reason, emotion and meaning are far beyond any individual or organisation to grasp. Our patterns of life must be simplified, localised and, to some degree, routinised. Only then can we operate effectively. But the decisions that we make necessarily represent an arbitrary construct. We bring the potential chaos of reality under control by saying: 'This is how it's done'. Thus, a template falls across the swarming options and a culture is in the making.

Many published definitions of organisational culture have been offered, mostly with close-knit similarities. Ralph Stacey (1996) says:

> **The culture of any group of people is that set of beliefs, customs, practices and ways of thinking that they have come to share with each other through being and working together.**

Schein (1991) defines culture as 'a pattern of shared assumptions invented, discovered, or developed by a given group.' More exotically, Hofstede (1991) refers to culture as 'software of the mind'. And finally, in earlier writing, Schein (1985) famously condensed the idea into 'the way we do things around here.'

Considering its immense significance, it seems extraordinary that business culture was relatively ignored by management theorists for so long. Entrepreneurs have always recognised its power. Famously, Josiah Wedgewood at the dawn of the Industrial Revolution used to inspect the work of his employees and break substandard pots with his stick. The Cadbury family in the 19th century were well known for temperance, ethical standards and care for their employees.

The work of Elton Mayo at the Hawthorne plant (see Chapter 25) did detect the importance of informal cultures among working groups and stressed the difference between official and unofficial norms. The famous study by Trist and Bamforth (1951) of coal-cutting methods highlighted the systemic importance of social groups in terms of resulting productivity. Much of the work on motivation that followed tacitly recognised the workings of culture, especially McGregor's Theory X and Theory Y.

However, it was not really until Athos' and Pascale's *The Art of Japanese Management* (1981) and Peters' and Waterman's *In Search of Excellence* (1982) that culture became a subject of study. The authors' combined development of the McKinsey Seven-S 'management molecule' acknowledged American achievements in the 'cold triangle' of structure, strategy and systems, but gave special emphasis to the 'warm square' of skills, staff, style and superordinate goals. It was the rationalist paradigm of scientific management that had occluded the 'soft Ss' in which culture is embodied. In particular, the positioning of superordinate goals at the heart of the model signalled a new interest in culture.

Culture and performance

Superordinate goals are above all the shared values that drive an organisation. As Pascale put it: 'Great companies make meaning.' His celebrated analysis of the Japanese company Matsushita Electric (owners of the Panasonic and Technics brands) showed how these shared values can permeate every aspect of corporate life and can bind together an organisation's constituent individuals and groups in a powerful common cause. The cold triangle of hard Ss might deliver a strategy and good products, but it does not ensure either fit with a congruent culture or the organisational energy unleashed by those superordinate goals.

Because culture is the arrangement of meaning, it shapes every aspect of organisational life. Attitudes to customers, work practices, communications, flexibility, learning and innovation are just some of the key factors that find expression through a firm's culture. Moreover, Schein's 'the ways things are done round here' can be the right way or the wrong way in achieving fit between a strategy and a culture. Because culture is neither measurable nor tangible, it can seem a matter of decoration, even idiosyncrasy; yet because it is actually the collective signature of the people who give an organisation life, culture can be make or break.

A strong culture with good fit regularly forms the underlying basis for competitive advantage. A firm may be said to have a superior reputation or relationship network or record of innovation, but all of these depend to some extent on the embedded forces of culture. Indeed, culture helps to explain the dynamic sustainability of competitive advantage. Like a kind of corporate DNA, culture is almost impossible to copy. Much of the structure, systems and even strategy of a winning company are open to efforts at replication, but the supporting culture, like a local ecology, remains unique.

The Body Shop

With **MAKE YOUR MARK**, we are mounting the largest human rights campaign we have ever done. We will access dozens of countries with millions of customers who will make their mark with a thumbprint to recognise the courageous work done by human rights defenders. **A campaign like this is part of the DNA of our business.** Not only does it fire up our day-to-day lives but it embodies our conviction that business should be about social responsibility as well as profit.

Source: The Body Shop Annual Report and Accounts, 1998

Culture can also greatly influence the competitive performance of nations. Pascale (1981) found that American culture tended to place most stress on the 'hard Ss' of structure, strategy and systems with their more overtly scientific and quantitative bias. By contrast, Japanese culture could excel on 'hard S' criteria but also express excellence in the management of the 'soft S' values. Germany has a long-standing culture of excellence in precision engineering that reaches deep into the education system and popular attitudes. Italy's design workshops and salons are a unique culture in their own right, while a highly exacting home market provides a test bed for exports. In a more general context, it is likely that American values of individualism, self-reliance and enterprise contribute to the high US rate of business start-ups and innovation at all levels.

Culture formation

Cultures form over time. They are shaped by shared events and experiences, by charismatic leaders and by certain defining moments that are often recounted as stories that become semi-mythologised. High-profile cultures have been forged by company founders who give them the vibrancy and timbre of their own personality: Thomas John Watson, President of IBM in the 1930s and Richard Branson, the founder of Virgin Group in the 1970s are famous examples. Sometimes, the defining leader is the 'saviour' or architect of turnaround: the CEO who rescues the company and reorientates the organisation with superordinate goals that start cutting strategic success. The leadership of Archie Norman at Asda in the 1990s is a striking example.

Cultures are also made by the exigencies of the industry and the nature of the product. Primary sector activities, such as mining or farming, are good examples, but equally, service industries such as healthcare or security follow the same pattern. The market is also a maker of business cultures. Competitive advantage depends on intense closeness to the customer, where market fit must be maximised and where every nuance in the pattern of demand needs to be detected ahead of the competition.

However, there are times when the cultural convergence of competitors and shifts in the market allow the creation of strategic space by challenging the dominant 'way things are done' and doing them differently. UK banking in the 1980s was ripe for such a initiative.

First Direct

Clearing banks had always laid stress on their network of branches and the air of probity and permanence conveyed by their buildings and interiors, by their staff and the subtle rituals of discretion and privacy. This was all customary and seemed natural. Banks had needed visibly to acknowledge that looking after other people's money was a grave responsibility.

But this culture was also a liability. For an increasing proportion of customers, banking meant queues in uninspiring places, lost lunchbreaks and encounters through a security screen with a rules-driven staff. The functionality of the new relationship that many customers wanted with their bank was already established through the cash machine.

Midland Bank – or HSBC today – launched First Direct in 1989 as the pioneering branchless bank entirely based on telephone communication. In this new banking culture, customers received an automatic overdraft facility and had 24-hour access to advisory staff and their account details. Quickly, a new customer base was built and First Direct became a powerful brand in an emergent strategic space. With the launch of internet brands in the late 1990s, the culture of banking evolved even further from its traditional roots.

Real, inward culture, however, is not easily changed and efforts to construct new cultures are often problematic. Very easily the 'genes' of the old culture enter the new and subvert the strategic purpose. Entirely new staff are often needed to make cultural innovation or renewal work.

Cultural typologies

To understand an organisational culture and to evaluate its strategic contribution requires placing that culture in some kind of typology or map. Perhaps surprisingly there is no definitive model for the analysis or mapping of organisational culture. To some extent this reflects the multidimensional nature of cultures and the lack of any definitive axes on which they can be placed. The answers about culture depend on the questions being asked.

Miles and Snow (1978) classified cultures by their typical reaction patterns in confronting strategic choice. *Defender* cultures were found in clearly defined markets, where the preferred strategy is to consolidate or gain market share. The priority is not innovation outside the market, but the protection of vital interests inside the market concerned. *Prospector* cultures have the opposite preferences, exploring, testing and pioneering new markets. Being risk tolerant, they thrive on uncertainty. *Analyser* cultures are not committed to the status quo or to breaking frontiers, but to analysing each scenario on its merits. Finally, *reactor* cultures take their cues from competitors and prefer imitation to innovation. Strategically they may lack focus, but may be effective opportunists in seizing their moment.

Deal and Kennedy (1984) related the taking of risks to the timing of feedback on strategic decisions. After analysing hundreds of US companies, they found four key cultural types. First, a *macho* culture takes high risks and stresses fast returns. Individuals risk everything on decisions and quickly become heroes or has-beens. Second, the *work hard/play hard* culture keeps risks low among its staff but still brings quick feedback on results. Both of these short-cycle cultures tend to be less hierarchical and to take decisions quickly.

The third group, *bet-your-company* culture accepts high risks but with long timescales on the feedback of consequences. Common where crucial investment decisions are involved, staff work closely together to reach the right decision. Fourth and finally, the *process* culture offers low risk to its staff but with slow feedback. Typically bureaucracies with a formal hierarchy, organisations of this type often become focused on *how* work is done rather than *what* work is done. Employees are cautious and rules orientated. In different ways each of these cultures is resistant to change and dependent on hierarchical structures.

Perhaps the best-known typology was developed by Harrison and Handy (1978, 1993). This is based on patterns of authority and the way that work is done.

The power culture

This is typically based on a powerful founder or entrepreneur who emanates authority in a web-like pattern. Flexible and energetic, organisations of this type have few formal procedures and let trusted people get on with their job. Power cultures can find growth a problem if it leads to breaks in the 'web'.

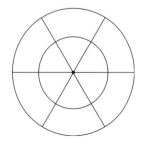

The role culture

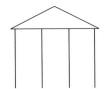

This is the classic rationalist bureaucracy. It is divided into clear operating functions co-ordinated by a layer of top management. Role cultures place emphasis on rules and procedures and power depends on official position. They can be effective in stable conditions but find rapid change threatening.

The task culture

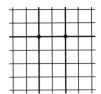

The task culture is shaped and driven by the practical needs of the job in hand. Managers allocate expert staff and relevant resources and then rely on teamwork to complete the task. The net or matrix-type structure can be adaptable and efficient, but may come under pressure if the business falters.

The person culture

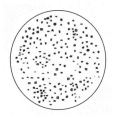

This is a culture of individuals who choose loosely to associate themselves for mutual benefit. Structure or organisation is kept to a minimum and there is an absence of hierarchies or position power. A person culture can work in some professional fields but can be broken up by changing events.

It is clear that no one typology is 'correct' or necessarily more useful than another. All classifications of this kind must oversimplify reality and sets up boundaries that are artificial. However, because a model improves understanding, it often inspires and initiates change that might otherwise have occurred later or been less effective.

Context and culture

⌐ Carpets and Christian names ◄────────

The Headmaster of Stantonbury Campus – a cutting-edge comprehensive school in Milton Keynes – was asked, what was special about his school?

'Carpets and Christian names,' came his significant answer.

Culture creates context and context reinforces culture. Every human environment is rich in symbolic meanings. Indeed, meanings in the environment are so ubiquitous and so familiar that they mostly go unnoticed. Over time the environment becomes an affirmative statement of the dominant culture, filled with signifiers that act like beacons in guiding people's behaviour. When someone outside an organisation first enters its culture, they instinctively use this guidance system

---

Stanford prison experiment, Zambardo *et al.* (1973)

A group of psychologists at Stanford University, led by Philip Zambardo, decided to simulate a prison environment in the basement of a university building. The experiment was rigorous and authentic. A group of selected volunteers were divided at random into the roles of guards and prisoners.

Guards were given uniforms and dark glasses. The prisoners were given a realistic arrest in their own homes, handcuffed, charged and brought blindfolded to the 'prison'. Here, they were stripped and issued with prison uniforms and identification numbers before being locked in their cells.

The psychologists were then taken aback by the speed of events. The guards became increasingly authoritarian and repressive. A prisoner revolt was crushed while arbitrary and often humiliating punishments were enforced.

Both guards and prisoners fell into roles that were quite unlike their normal selves. Tension mounted and four of the prisoners became so disturbed that their release was necessary. Intended to run for two weeks, the experiment had to be halted after six days.

Was it the inmates or the environment of prisons that made them such unpleasant places?

Source: adapted from M Gladwell The Tipping Point *(Little, Brown & Co., 2000)*

---

but often make errors in its interpretation. If the newcomer remains, they quickly become socialised into the culture and their conscious perception of the signifiers fades with familiarity. Meanwhile, they are no less influenced by the culture and the context.

People tend to expect consistency from other people and from organisations. In this they are often disappointed. We are strongly influenced in our thoughts, feelings and behaviour by context: the interactive circumstances and environment wrapped round every scenario.

Advocates of the context argument point to the apparent success of zero tolerance policies on the New York subway and in the dramatic reduction in the 1990s of that city's overall crime rate. Both these campaigns were initially focused on tackling symbolic features of the crime context: graffiti on the subway trains and minor public disorder offences in the city streets. These and similar efforts, it was argued, changed the context from one that was lawless and disorderly to one that was lawful and orderly. People with a propensity to commit crimes became much less likely to commit them.

This puts a very different perspective on crime from the usual liberal/conservative divide: improved welfare and more effort to resolve social problems versus more policing and tougher sentences. The context argument cuts across this debate and urges more modest changes that may prompt people to act differently.

The same principle could be important in many business applications – for example, ensuring total quality in operations, discontinuously upgrading customer service, restoring morale after retrenchment or implementing a merger. In the long term there needs to be a culture change but this may be signalled by a change in context.

Cultural change

Organisational cultures – as patterns of belief and behaviour – need to change. Reality in the form of the business environment does not stand still and nor does the nature of strategic fit. To maintain or develop its competitive advantage, a firm may have to reorchestrate its strengths and redefine its mission. This will almost certainly require changes in the supporting culture.

Being slow to form, culture is usually slow to change. In evolving markets with stable competitive structures, this may pose no problem. But where markets are fragmenting and re-forming at speed and competitive activity is intense and unpredictable, then culture may have to change under duress. Indeed, when a business comes under new leadership or new ownership, cultural change is often the first priority.

Kurt Lewin (1951) proposed a model for change that starts with the 'unfreezing' of shared beliefs. This might mean creating a reflective space in which people can discover the new realities and recognise inwardly the defects of an entrenched culture. They may then move on to internalising a changed perception of their environment and 'refreezing' the beliefs that will form a new culture.

By contrast, simple commands or exhortations passed down a hierarchy may lead to modified behaviour, but leave the essential culture unchanged. This is the likely to undermine the intentions

Sears

In the early 1990s Sears, the famous chain of American department stores, was in trouble. Excessively decentralised (the territory managers 'ran the stores like barons'), the company faced falling customer interest, intensifying competition and low staff morale. Radical streamlining by the CEO Ed Brennan rebalanced the organisational structure and greatly improved efficiency. Unfortunately, the culture remained inward-looking, conservative and defensive. Managers were compliant, avoiding disruptive innovation and protecting their own interests.

Then a new CEO, Arthur Martinez, took over. At once he set discontinuously higher targets and began pushing the organisation towards a new self-criticism, a tough honesty, an escalating vitality. 'Yesterday's peacock is tomorrow's feather duster,' he observed wryly, as he outlined his vision of commitment to top executives. 'Phoenix teams' were formed from the ranks of senior management, who became innovators and drivers of new thinking.

But perhaps the greatest challenge was turning 300 000 demoralised sales personnel and stocking clerks into ambassadors for the new Sears. Day-long gatherings of staff called 'Town Hall meetings' were convened for all of the 800 stores. Here staff used learning maps – large visual devices that depicted the business realities of Sears – to recast their understanding of the company for which they worked. Over half a million staff suggestions were generated by this process and soon staff who had seen themselves as no more than tiny cogs in the corporate wheel were able to articulate a sense of business purpose.

Perhaps unsurprisingly all targets were surpassed. Martinez had disrupted the culture of complacency and resignation that had been for so long a dead weight.

of senior management as the new systems work against the cultural grain and staff seek psychologically to discredit the changes imposed.

An alternative approach is to recognise a culture as a living system that cannot be retooled like a machine, but can be encouraged and excited to emerge in a new direction (Pascale, 2000 refers to 'herding butterflies'). This does involve the presentation of compelling reasons for change, but it also waymarks the new path with emotional beacons signalling shared feeling alongside common cognition. And arching even above this picture is some shared directional energy, some vision of collective meaning that will guide the arrow of corporate intention along its new trajectory.

Culture can kill

We have seen the value of a strong fit between the culture of an organisation and its operating environment. Some business cultures directly reflect business reality: that is to say that the wavelength of the culture is the wavelength of the business and there is little distortion between the two. But it is very easy for an organisation, in terms of the McKinsey model, to develop a dissonant gap between the hard Ss of the cold triangle and the soft human Ss of the warm square.

Sometimes this is the result of problems between stakeholder interests. It can be that employees develop a defensive culture, buttressed by trade union support, that does not address market realities. Arguably this was quite common in Britain during the 1970s and 1980s. Conversely, a new management team may try to impose a shareholder value culture that is at odds with a company's traditions and the informal understandings and commitments that gave rise to staff loyalty and motivation.

A less obvious but equally lethal trap lies in the concept of the strong culture. During the 1980s many writers (notably Athos and Pascale, 1981; Deal and Kennedy, 1984) found strong, unitary cultures associated with long-term business success. These companies knew their own identity and each employee shared intimately in that knowledge. The strong culture theory is almost certainly valid, but only while culture and reality connect. Any significant disconnection should, of course, sound a strategic alarm and set off a process of cultural change. But confident, successful cultures can become inward-looking. Dangerous changes in a familiar picture become invisible though the lens of a strong culture. All the familiar routines, rituals and symbols remain as ever, even while the story of their collapse unfolds. Each strong culture believes it would never allow this to happen, an ironic ratchet upwards in the level of risk.

32 Change and transformation

Overview

Imagine a spring day with cloud formations moving busily about the sky, with patches of blue opening and closing like windows of opportunity. In a sense this is the reality of the business world. Organisations that stand sentinel on the high street or in business parks, whose credentials flash and glitter on websites are actually floating on hidden dimensions of strategic fit. What seems certain on one day may be uncertain on the next and history on the day after. Change in business is continuous, complex and compulsory.

Change is an energy that can destroy an organisation's fit, making its people and their mission redundant. Yet it can also be a force that powers an organisation from one peak of competitive advantage to another, accumulating vigorous assets of knowledge and distinctive capability. Firms can be victims or champions of change: stasis is an illusion.

Engines of change

Look at the following scenario. The Christmas merchandise sells less well than expected. The problem was lower spending on the high street/lack of advertising/supply failures/staff shortages/bad weather. Or was it actually the beginning of the end? Will that disappointing Christmas later be retitled 'the start of the import invasion'; 'the first time our products were outclassed?'; 'The moment the market moved away'?

There are three essential variables in this scenario: customers, competition and the firm itself. These are each connected to a multiplicity of other variables that form the interactive environment. Customer buying decisions to maximise utility represent the force of demand that drives the market system. The firm aims to add value by mobilising its resources to supply the products that are in demand. Competitors attempt to capture this flow of transactions by offering customers a substitute that they prefer.

This three-point relationship tends to be highly unstable. Both the budget and the preferences of customers are subject to continuous and uneven change. The cost and availability of resources to the firm change too, while the changes themselves alter the firm's systemic ability to add value. Meanwhile, changes in the market, changes in the firm and changes in other firms all affect the strategy of competitors who threaten constantly to disrupt every demand–supply relationship. And as the wider business environment changes, yet more instability is injected into the system scenario, until the only certainty confronting the strategist is uncertainty.

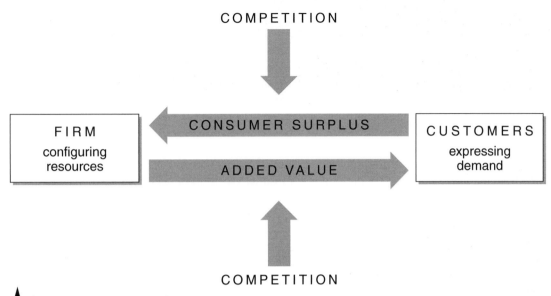

Figure 32.1 Firm, customers and competition

It is clear that change is not a choice, but a condition of doing business. Every firm is navigating through a storm where the wind can blow without warning from any direction.

For some firms, change is palpable and self-evident. The product range is replaced, the underlying technology is transformed, the target market is redefined, the name and logo are different. In other firms, the changes are hidden. The names are the same, the corporate DNA is still intact, but the reality is different.

Uniq

Better known as Unigate until 2000, the company had been a predominantly UK-based producer of dairy foods and provider of doorstep milk deliveries. It also owned a major pigmeat business in Yorkshire and the road haulage operator, Wincanton Logistics.

By 2001 the firm was renamed Uniq. It had sold its traditional dairy and cheese business, as well as the pigmeat and road haulage operations. Radically repositioned as a European specialist chilled foods supplier, the company has pushed its non-UK sales above 50 per cent of total turnover.

Woolworths

Woolworths is a general merchandise retailer of household goods, home entertainment, confectionery, children's clothing and toys. In 2001, the year of its demerger from the Kingfisher group, the company made an operating loss of £23.5 million or 0.9 per cent of sales value.

Led by a new CEO, the independent company is cutting back the multiple formats offered under the Woolworths name and concentrating on its 'mainchain' offering. Separate management structures are being removed, while the supply chain is simplified and made more flexibly reactive.

What guides firms in their continuous adaptation? Added value, whether taken as customer satisfaction or corporate profit, is like the magnetic north on a compass. Every organisation wants to add value. Every organisation must add value. Thus, no matter how pounded by the waves of change, an organisation paddles itself back towards the strategic fit that will maximise the generation of added value. Sometimes this effort is successful. Much of the time it is partially successful. Other times it is wrong. And the extent to which adaptation is inadequate and inappropriate is itself the initiator of more change as the firm conceives and implements corrective action.

Meanwhile, the changes that prompted the original imbalance or mismatch are succeeded by yet more change that often overtakes the response to earlier change. The whole palate of change is mobile and multilayered. Winning organisations are able to hold the best fit; suboptimal necessarily, but flexible, innovative and intelligent.

Incremental and step change

Often, change is incremental: it occurs continuously but almost invisibly when taken over a short timespan. The decline in the market for formal menswear, or the growth of car ownership come into this category. But change may also be in 'steps' – discontinuous in nature. Discontinuous change refers to variables or scenarios that change not in a progressive sequence, but through an abrupt transformation that cannot be anticipated through extrapolation from preceding events. Where change is discontinuous an unscheduled transition or 'Big Bang' changes everything. Examples include the arrival of a new technology such as the internet, the passing of a new competition law or the acquisition of another company.

The boiled frog

Charles Handy tells of the frog placed in a pan of water that is then gently heated. As the temperature begins to rise the frog swims around quite able to jump out and save itself. But as it allows the heating process to continue it starts to move more feebly. It is now too late for escape and the frog allows itself to be boiled.

Many firms take the role of the frog in the face of cumulative incremental change. Yet if they had detected the sequence of change earlier, their resources were quite sufficient for survival and perhaps even for reinforcement of their underlying competitive position.

The brick on elastic

A brick with a piece of elastic attached is placed on a table. The elastic is then pulled with a gentle but increasing force. The tension builds and builds until, without warning, the brick surges forward, often with damaging results.

If firms detected the pent up energy in frustrated change vectors, they might avert unplanned and violent change likely either to disrupt the business or deliver prime opportunity into the hands of a competitor.

Both types of change carry strategic traps. Incremental change is easily missed until competitive advantage is eroded or a competitor has seized the accumulated opportunity. By its nature, discontinuous change often strikes unexpectedly and the survivors are those with flexibility and creative powers of adaptation. Sometimes continuous and discontinuous change meet as pressure for change builds in a system until resistance finally gives and an immediate transformative change occurs.

Interactive change

The business world is a complex and highly interactive system. A change in one variable sets off cascades of changes in other variables, which trigger yet more changes – some known and some unknowable. A basic model of the firm in its environment indicates three basic drivers of change: demand, competition and access to resources.

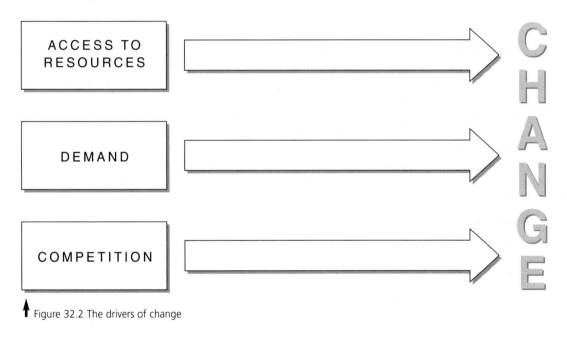

↑ Figure 32.2 The drivers of change

Inertia

In most organisations, a degree of inertia develops. This means that before any change can occur, an initial resistance must be overcome. In some organisations, inertia is no more than force of habit, but in others it can be so pervasive that a major restructuring and new leadership are necessary for any real movement to begin. Inertia among staff is typically caused by fear, lack of trust and uncertainty about the implications of change. Wider organisational inertia arises from the hardening constructs of reality that develop in organisations under stable conditions.

Lewin

Kurt Lewin (1951) saw organisations as existing in a dynamic equilibrium between driving and restraining forces. Taken together, these pressures form a 'forcefield' within which either driving or restraining forces may be ascendant. These forces are continuously interactive and increasing or diminishing in strength. The task of change management in planned situations is to weaken the restraining forces (e.g. explaining the need for change or reassuring those affected) and strengthening the driving forces (e.g. taking ownership for new objectives or offering inspirational leadership).

Lewin also describes the process of 'unfreezing', where old assumptions are dropped and a new frame of reference comes to be accepted. The next stage, 'moving to a new level', emerges as key decisions are made and the resulting changes become operational. The final 'refreezing' is said to occur as changes are 'locked in' and gradually become a new set of assumptions.

Although this can still be a useful model, it does treat changes as discrete events with phases corresponding to beginning, middle and end. This view is looking less realistic as change for many organisations becomes endemic. The appropriate imagery for today may be less a matter of unfreezing and refreezing and more a question of surfing successfully on one wave of change after another.

Isolated and systemic change

Change can be isolated or systemic. Where one variable changes with little if any connection to other variables then it is isolated in its effect and can be treated as a single issue. A failure in a piece of machinery or an insolvent debtor are possible examples. Much more complex to address are interfaces of change that are mutually dependent. What may initially look like one problem turns out to be a set of interactive problems where tackling one variable is pointless without tackling the others. The situation becomes even more complex if the map of interactivity is unknown in its connectedness or extent, or if the linkages change in response to any intervention.

Managers are highly prone to deciding that any change is isolated rather than systemic. This is because isolated change is largely non-threatening. Existing systems and strategy can continue to operate unscathed while the assumptions and culture of the organisation go unchallenged. But action taken under a misapprehension of this kind is likely to be wasteful and ineffective, while losing time in addressing the much more serious questions posed by systemic change.

Clearing Snow

Following a heavy fall of snow, two firms found themselves immobilised. One firm spent the next day digging themselves out. Eventually they had cleared an approach road but much of their transport fleet was still snowed in.

The other company raised the organisational temperature from minus one degree to plus one degree. All around them the snow melted and soon they were fully mobile.

Working hard to solve one problem at a time is a very slow and ineffective way to achieve a change for the better. Often this seems an attractive approach to managers because something can be done immediately with the benefit of tangible results. Systemic pan-organisational change may be slower, but it can make hundreds of small campaigns unnecessary while preventing any backsliding down the slope of the problem profile.

Compounding

Change can also be deceptive in the speed of its progress. There is a tendency to assume linearity in a pathway of change (profits are rising by 10 per cent year-on-year …) when the actual rate of change may decelerate or accelerate sharply. This leads to inadequate or overshooting reactions that are often further complicated by the phenomenon of compounding. This apparently simple idea means a rate of increase being repeatedly applied to a cumulative total, i.e. each one inclusive of the last increase. Even at low growth rates, compounding can produce rapid openings of threats or opportunities. At high growth rates compounding becomes an engine of change with awesome capabilities. For example, supposing a firm with £1m capital employed reinvests a 50 per cent ROCE for ten years. At the end of the period the value of capital employed will have grown to around £57.7m. The compounding principle has many applications. Quite small differences in performance spiral into huge gaps within a relatively short time. Aggregates can increase so quickly that timescales for their growth become deceptively compressed.

Compounding at 100 per cent

Gladwell (2000) draws attention to the counter-intuitive implications of compounding at 100 per cent. Consider folding a piece of paper (any size) 50 times. How 'thick' would the resulting 'bundle' be?

Most people make estimates that vary between the thickness of a telephone directory and the height of a house.

The actual answer is the approximate distance between the Earth and the sun – about 93 million miles.

Knock-ons

Within a system, any change in one variable is likely to cause 'knock-on' changes in other variables. Knock-ons can be defined as the indirect changes brought about by the subsequent interaction of variables stimulated by the initial change. Knock-on effects are highly significant even when they *lose* energy at each interaction. They become massively – even chaotically – powerful when *gaining* energy through a rapidly widening network of interaction. Once again a systemic reading of reality is required if organisations are to anticipate the effects of changes triggering changes.

However, the knock-on energy in systemic change can also assist an organisation that needs to achieve many changes across a broad front. For example, a business in a turnaround situation may find that the making of certain key changes will itself trigger a complex network of further change that reinforces the starting strategy. Where knock-on effects are self-amplifying or in positive feedback loops, the challenge becomes to select the correct triggering changes rather than the linear implementation of a conventional change agenda.

0.506127

In 1961 Edward Lorenz was a research meteorologist. Working with an early computer simulation of weather systems, he wanted to rerun a section of results. As a time-saver, he started the program in the middle of its earlier sequence and punched in the relevant number: 0.506.

Following a break for coffee, Lorenz looked at the print-out in amazement. It represented a whole new sequence of weather.

The reason? He had keyed in 0.506 as being virtually the same as the full number, 0.506127. Yet this apparently trivial difference in initial conditions had produced a vast difference in the emergent outcome.

Source: Based on Ziauddin Sardar and Iwona Abrams Introducing Chaos *(Icon Books, 1998)*

End of the straight line?

Chaos theory teaches us that straight linearity, which we have come to take for granted in everything from physics to fiction, simply does not exist. Linearity is an artificial way of viewing the world.

Real life isn't a series of interconnected events occurring one after another like beads strung on a necklace. Life is actually a series of encounters in which one event may change those that follow in a wholly unpredictable, even devastating way.

Michael Crichton Jurassic Park

Marginal change

Both compounding and knock-ons illustrate the importance of change at the margin. Marginal change means a change that represents a very small proportion of a total value. It can often carry the signal of a much more fundamental change that is approaching.

In 1998 Marks & Spencer misread trends in its own markets and underestimated its competitors. In the same period when Marks & Spencer foundered, Orange, the mobile phone operator, experienced explosive growth, well ahead of its own expectations. Not only had the industry reached a tipping point in the mass use of its product, but the Orange brand had become a key lifestyle choice.

The ability to identify marginal changes that are outriders of more fundamental change is a decisive advantage both in ensuring survival and in seizing opportunities. A business needs to use all of its experience and collective intelligence in reading these marginal changes.

Making marginal changes can also be a disproportionally powerful way of changing events that follow. Many variables in business have interactivity functions that include zones of extreme sensitivity. For example, each percentage point by which a firm cuts the price of a product causes an exponentially larger reduction in the profit margin. The marginal reduction that finally results in price being equal to cost will, of course, reduce the margin by 100 per cent.

Marks & Spencer

I am pleased to report a further increase in profits and a year of good sales progress, particularly in clothing and home furnishings.

The final dividend recommended by directors is ... an increase of 10 per cent, reflecting the underlying financial strength of the business and our confidence in the future.

Sir Richard Greenbury in Chairman, *reporting on the financial year ending 31 March 1998.*

In fact, the company was on the edge of a financial precipice. In the two years following Sir Richard's statement profits fell from £1.1bn to £450m, while the share price collapsed from 450p to 158p.

It is worth looking at the apparently innocent changes occurring between the financial years ending in 1997 and 1998.

Marks & Spencer	1996		1997		1998	1998*
Operating profit £m	937.4	1 037.9	1 116.7	1 063.5		
% annual change	+4.75	+10.72	+7.59	+2.46		

*After deducting an exceptional item (£53.2m) relating to VAT refund *from earlier years.*

Strip out the effect of inflation, and profits in 1997 were up to £1073.2m stated in 1998 terms. Real profit change between the two years now becomes *negative* at −0.9 per cent. The cracks in the M&S wall grow wider.

Similarly powerful ratios operate in costing. For example, suppose a firm manufactures small components at a unit cost of 25p and sells five million each month. Within a *kaizen* context (see Chapter 22), the production team finds a way to shave 0.2p off the unit cost. The implications of this marginal change are very significant, as seen below.

Unit cost	Saving		Output	Total saving
pence	*pence*	*%*		*£*
25	0.2	0.8	5 million	10 000

If the unit price of the components is 26p, then this saving has an even greater effect on profits, as shown on next page:

Selling price	Old profit	New profit	Profit change
pence	£	£	%
26	50 000	60 000	+ 20.0

Marginal changes in the design or quality of products can also yield hugely disproportionate increases in added value. These may take the form of fierce loyalty from devoted customers or rapid extension in market reach, moving out from a niche to a mass market. Such critical changes at the margin often carry a relatively low marginal cost. Simple examples include the quality of a zip fastener, the spice in a recipe or the design of a logo.

In broader and more strategic terms, the leverage of marginal change can be equally striking. We have seen (Chapter 10) how a small improvement in fit between a firm and its environment can be critical in gaining competitive advantage. By the same token, a small change in target market can increase sales by a very high factor. Marginality is written into the contours of demand. Aim in the wrong place and sales are negligible. Retarget and the firm struggles to meet orders. The landscape of demand has an alpine quality where peaks and precipices form and re-form and small changes in the accuracy of targeting are the difference between consistent success and persistent failure.

Highly leveraged margins are found in many other zones of business management. Small changes in context and conditions can bring huge changes in staff morale and motivation. In the same way, marginal changes in team membership can prompt profound changes in performance.

Complexity and chaos theory also point to some very important phenomena in the mechanics of marginal change. Consider the behaviour of water as temperature changes. Below zero degrees, water takes the form of a solid as ice. Only between 0° and 100° does water exist as a liquid. At temperatures above 100 degrees, water forms a vapour. But what happens at those critical temperatures? A radical system-wide change occurs that transforms the nature of water. If water is increased in temperature from, say, 50° to 51°, then the molecules in the liquid move slightly faster and the water is slightly warmer. But between 99° to 100° the sequence of progressive warming in the liquid is overtaken abruptly, as the water drastically changes its form from liquid into vapour.

This kind of 'phase transition' is common in the natural world. It can also be found in organisations as, for example, they reach a 'critical mass'. A small producer may be expanding but struggling to gain customer confidence and adequate distribution. Quite abruptly the size of the firm becomes large enough to interest national distributors. Its profile rises and customer confidence surges. New accounts are opened and the firm has made phase transition from the status of small local business to that of a larger national player. The same phenomenon can affect such factors as staff morale, quality performance or the rate of innovation. It also acts on the careers of individuals.

Managing change

The tendency towards acceleration in the flow of change has been running since the Industrial Revolution. Far from abating, the process of change has intensified and quickened in almost every dimension of the business world. It is not surprising that the ability to manage change successfully has become a central factor in sustaining competitive advantage.

In a bureaucratic organisation, change gets treated as an input into the decision cycles of senior management. Following appropriate analysis, a decision is fed down through the chain of command. In a stable environment that operates to shared rules, this approach safeguards continuity and avoids over-reaction. But in the near-chaotic, rapid-fire conditions of markets today, it is far too slow and overly mechanical; it lacks flair and on-the-ground intelligence; it has no ownership among the staff who count.

In less hierarchical organisations, there is a more open, flexible and networked approach to change. Authority and intelligence are more distributed in an organisation that treats change as an ongoing reality. Rather than a merely reactive relationship with change, a firm can be proactive and nurture change on its own terms. Indeed, anticipating or provoking change can be distinctive ways of sustaining or building a competitive advantage.

What makes change a creative and energising process and why is it so often experienced as a burden or a threat? When change is imposed by top management, it is usually perceived as a threat. Explanations of impending change become like helping turkeys to understand Christmas. Speculation and uncertainty feed on each other as staff calculate not how to further corporate interests, but how to protect their own. Instead of reaching out to the future for opportunities, individuals and groups hang on to the past and get ready to defend their turf.

Meanwhile, many organisations protect themselves from the outside world with the repetitions and rituals of their culture. Business as usual becomes a numbing state of mind. When external change bursts through the curtains of normality and threatens an organisation with events that it can neither prevent not control, a defensive reaction is inevitable. Staff usually feel helpless in the face of such events, or even deny that they are happening.

By contrast, an organisation that is change-hungry develops poise in the midst of turbulence and the discovers the art of redirecting negative force into a wave of positive energy. Like a team of commandos, the organisation is able and ready to respond at the first opportunity and to do so with a certain daring and élan.

Change ceases to be a threat once it is owned. Where a firm is changing its strategy, ownership can be engendered by engaging the whole staff in confronting the issues and making their own proposals. When the source of change is external, ownership springs from confidence in dealing with the unexpected and a repertoire of responses that make the firm feel able to sail in any weather.

33 Learning and creativity

Overview

In the simplest sense, a learning organisation is a group of people who are continually enhancing their capability to create their future.

Peter Senge The Fifth Discipline *(1990)*

The mechanistic paradigm that views a firm as a complex but inorganic piece of engineering is not designed or expected to learn. In this Fordist world, thinking is largely confined to senior managers who prescribe correct procedures for subordinates to follow. Although such a model is rarely endorsed today, it is still a mindset to be found deeply embedded in the culture and structure of many organisations.

Yet learning has become essential to every organisation if it is to compete effectively. A key trend of the late 20th century was towards flatter reporting structures, delegating decision making towards the point of its impact and getting closer to the customer. All this implied a more dispersed intelligence and a reflex among all employees to think and learn.

Learning adds value. It enables people to grow in their jobs and to find new ways of meeting their responsibilities more effectively. Learning progressively improves the cost–performance ratios on which the firm's competitiveness depends. Creativity can be triggered by learning. Original ideas for the reconfiguration of resources with the possibility of adding more value is the stuff of creative thinking. Discontinuous improvements in processes, products and positioning depend on creativity. This chapter explores how learning and creativity can be nurtured in every organisation.

A new paradigm for learning

When most organisations were run as mechanical devices for production, learning among employees involved little more than mastering a narrow set of specified skills. We saw earlier (Chapter 24) that many firms have been undergoing a fundamental change in the style of their organisation. This has progressed at different speeds and to different extents, but the trend is clear. Mechanical hierarchies are softening towards becoming more organic networks. Better management and better performance can be achieved by pushing many decision points downwards, nearer to the front line, nearer to the customer. Simultaneously, senior management need their staff to become the thoughtful agents of change, the creative conduits for added value.

Of course, there has always been learning in every organisation, through experience and through training, but much of it has been concerned with improving proficiency in a range of specified tasks. Learning in the new paradigm is different. It refers to an active process of treating all systems, all frontiers, all outcomes as contingent: statements of 'where we are now' that invite questions of 'where we might be'. Every employee at every level becomes a kind of scientist, a researcher, a thought adventurer who is constantly testing and remaking the boundaries of reality, no matter how mundane or well established they might appear.

Learning springs from curiosity. Curiosity is a state of consciousness, itself shaped by the prevailing culture. Learning also requires skills and tools for its pursuit, and the necessary discretionary space within which ideas and experiments are possible. And learning can be hugely amplified in its progress and value if it can be shared, sharpened and transmitted across an organisational network. Here, we reconnect with the structure and culture of the organisation.

Handy and the 3Is

Handy in *The Age of Unreason* (1989) argues that adding value will increasingly depend on the 3Is: intelligence, information and ideas.

> **The new organisation, making added value out of knowledge, needs also to be possessed with the pursuit of truth ...**

Handy proposes a collegiate culture governed by consent and not command. In old organisations, employees were paid not to think but to do; now, more and more, they need to do both. Thinking skills become the firm's most precious resource and depend on an organisational model that resembles a corporate university. Handy sees management becoming less the preserve of a hierarchical class and more an 'activity' for all core workers. Such staff will need specialist expertise and much broader business, human and conceptual skills.

The heroic leader, says Handy, 'knew all, could do all and could solve every problem'. By contrast, the post-heroic leader is talented not only in enabling other people to solve problems, but also in developing their capacity to solve such problems in the future.

The learning process

In this sense, the mechanical organisation is 'unnatural', often leaving its staff unable to learn or grow within the restricted space of a 'job'. What are the conditions that allow learning to happen – and keep it happening? At the pragmatic level, people learn in order to solve problems. Their lack of knowledge or skills prevents them from reaching their objectives. There is, therefore, a clear incentive to extend their knowledge and skills frontier.

At a deeper level, people are also driven to learn by their inner needs. These include a need to make sense of the prevailing conditions and a need to understand the human dynamics involved. People with a more introverted personality type tend to seek conceptual understanding, while those with a more extroverted personality often prefer an experiential understanding. Intelligibility may be cognitive or emotional, but it is a key source of identity and security.

Handy (1989) likens the mechanism of learning to the motion of a wheel. It starts its movement with a question springing from innate or aroused curiosity. This prompts the formation of theories that might provide an answer. These go through a process of testing by theoretical or practical experiment. The final phase is reflection. What worked and what did not work, and why? New questions form and the wheel continues to turn. The reasons why it might become stationary are discussed below.

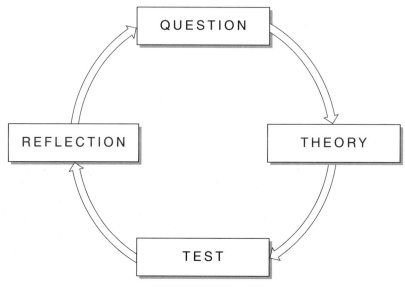

Figure 33.1 Learning: Handy's wheel model

How does learning add value?

Learning can add value at every level and in every function of the organisation. Staff can learn how tasks might be performed more efficiently. They can learn how to add more value in the process. Learning allows a broadening and deepening of context. Tasks can be understood in their interconnectedness with the richness of their implications exposed. And then people can learn how to shift perspective from an 'elevation' to a 'plan' view, how to fly above problems, spotting connections and possibilities not conceived before.

In practical terms, learning is essential to a philosophy of continuous improvement in the operations of a firm. It is vital to a marketing strategy of ever closer fit between the firm's resources and the demands of target customers. And learning drives innovation, creating new strategic space, new products and new ways of actualising the flow of added value. What is learned can form the basis of proprietary knowledge. Learning forms an invisible mesh of growing superiority in the design and configuration of the firm's activity. It is a formidable source of competitive advantage, resistant to being unpicked and likely to have changed its form and content ahead of being deciphered.

As Senge (1997) says:

> **People will talk about empowerment, they will talk about learning organisations but it will be mostly talk. Only a few will have the courage of their conviction and patience to move ahead. Those that succeed will, I believe, have unique advantages in the twenty-first century, because they will harness the imagination, spirit and intelligence of people in ways that no traditional, authoritarian organisation ever can.**

The firm as a living entity

Learning is natural. Not learning is unnatural, a kind of pathology that stunts human fulfilment and achievement. In both the brain centres of emotion and the intellect, people are hardwired to learn. Learning is a basic evolutionary propellant: elimination of options in favour of better options is the process by which species, societies and organisations progress.

It is easy to think of learning as the prerogative of individuals and to see organisations only as an assembly of individuals who may or may not learn. In the case of companies, we know that they have a legal identity in their own right. Do they have a social or an ethical identity? Could they have an existential identity? And can they also have a learning identity? De Geus (1997) explores this problem using Shell as an in-depth case study, and concludes that a corporation does indeed have a superordinate identity, relative to its employees and other stakeholders. While no one individual can *be* Shell, the entity 'Shell' has its own culture, it has a kind of collective consciousness and is regarded as carrying responsibility for 'its' actions. It is also capable of learning.

Say a team works together on a project that, over a period, involves research, learning and creative insight. During the project individuals leave the team so that by the time the original objectives are in sight, all team members have been replaced at least once. Yet the team that completes the project incorporates all the learning of the entire project. It is rather like the human body that, over five years, replaces every cell. When you meet someone after a five-year gap no physical part of the person you knew survives, yet it is still the same person – richer by five years' experience and learning.

People in organisations can be constricted, shrivelled, reduced by the circumstances of their work. But they can also be stimulated, empowered, even liberated by the experience of working with others. We are influenced in the ways in which we feel and think, respond and behave according to the human linkages we make and the dynamic culture that they represent. As all teachers know, learning speeds up or slows down depending on the shared resonance and energy of the group.

Organisational learning

The mechanical organisation may promote training (an essentially top-down process), but it does not facilitate learning. That is not to deny that people will gain experience and learn how to perform their specified duties to a higher standard. But learning in the sense of questioning, questing, experiment and discussion is against the engineering of a mechanical hierarchy.

Organisational learning depends on the connections and complexity in the 'organisational brain', and their flexibility to make innovative patterns. To learn, an organisation must be able to 'think', to connect its member individuals and groups so that they can share ideas and build critical awareness. For some limited purposes, this may only need effective cross-functional communications. But for a deeper, more pervasive capacity to learn, an organisation needs a network of communications that is more neural in nature.

Web-like networks allow 'conversation' to flourish. In this sense (de Geus, 1997; Pascale *et al.*, 2000), conversation means the exchange and interaction of thoughts, possibilities and methods of professional practice. Some conversations fall within the formal space created for that purpose, but many more occur within the informal space that forms and re-forms anywhere in the organisation.

Learning flourishes in a culture of curiosity, experiment and investigation. There needs to be an expectation of learning and an acceptance that failure is the inevitable precursor of success. Similarly, tolerance and respect are essential to effective learning. If people lose confidence in the organisation, their colleagues or themselves, then they stop learning and retreat into defensive postures that admit nothing new. This is all the more important given the need for the culture to be open, to avoid zones of secrecy and to minimise 'checkpoints' along lines of communication. Learning needs free pathways for its sharing and dissemination. Barricades, whether between strategic business units, departments or individual managers, greatly reduce the level and effectiveness of organisational intelligence.

Senge and the 'Five Disciplines'

Senge makes a clear distinction between receiving and possessing information and generating and sharing knowledge. He argues that the Western tradition of breaking knowledge down into its smallest constituent parts has powerful applications, yet loses the interconnectedness of complex systems that need understanding as a whole.

His book *The Fifth Discipline* makes its keystone a systems approach to knowledge.

THE FIVE DISCIPLINES

1 **Personal mastery** means dedication to the highest level of proficiency possible through lifelong learning. Work involves a long-term process of clarifying and deepening personal vision. This requires a focused energy and an almost spiritual commitment to growth. By contrast, Senge argues, many people close off the energy of their learning faculties once past the initial stages in their career.

2 **Mental models** means the hidden assumptions, structures and images that guide people's interpretation of the world around them and, more particularly, their place of work. These are embedded in the individual consciousness but are also widely shared. They deeply influence the perceptions and responses of everyone in an organisation. Senge stresses the need to expose and confront these models, which can become serious obstructions to new thinking.

3 **Building shared vision** means shared pictures of the future to which everyone is committed inwardly as well as outwardly. Effective leadership is based on developing a shared vision and not on imposing an individual vision. Senge emphasises the need for this shared vision to contain meaning and purpose that transcends pragmatic or instrumental goals.

4 **Team learning** refers to the synergies achieved through people working in teams, and to their accelerated growth as individuals. These do not occur automatically: teams can perform at a level well below the capabilities of any individual member. Open dialogue or 'thinking together' is essential to overcome defensiveness and accelerate learning.

5 **Systems thinking** is based on the recognition that phenomena in organisations are profoundly interconnected. Changes in one variable can have complex and far-reaching effects on other variables. The magnitude of these systemic effects can be amplified in transmission, sometimes discontinuously. Where systems thinking is absent, attempts to solve problems may prove self-defeating. Senge identifies archetypal patterns in systems behaviour that can be recognised and understood.

How do firms recreate themselves as communities of learning? The answer that Senge advocates is bringing together all five 'disciplines' with a particular commitment to a systems understanding of the organisation and its environment. Non-mechanistic, networked organisational structures are sympathetic to this vision of learning. Instead of attempting to impose linear order on a complex system, a non-linear structure can generate a flexible and evolving order of its own.

Knowledge management

'If only HP knew what HP knew.' This famous quote from Hewlett-Packard expresses the problem of capturing and managing knowledge. Unlike fixed assets that can be itemised, valued and placed on the balance sheet, knowledge is indeterminate, continuously changing its location, content and pattern. Even an individual can have difficulty in assembling and connecting their own knowledge resources in relation to a given problem. For an organisation, the task is incomparably more complex. As the competitive advantage of most firms has come to depend at least partly on the mobilisation of knowledge, so systems are having to be found for its storage and retrieval.

Hansen *et al.* (1999) argue that there are two distinct approaches to the management of knowledge. A codification strategy involves using information technology to collect and store knowledge. Custom-designed databases allow its multiple re-use by anyone in the firm. Staff are rewarded for their effective use of the resources available and for adding to the stock of knowledge. The contrasting personalisation strategy relies on identifying the expert individuals who hold knowledge relevant to a given problem. The accent is on sharing knowledge through direct personal contact. This puts a premium on the effectiveness of communications and suggests reward systems based on knowledge sharing.

The choice of strategy for knowledge management flows from the target market and those competences from which competitive advantage is derived. Generally, a faster-turnover business that is offering rapid customer solutions based on pre-existing building blocks of knowledge will use a codification strategy. But the slower-turnover firm that tackles unique problems with original solutions is likely to depend on the personalisation approach. Their overall returns will probably be supported by higher operating margins.

Ernst & Young

This global business consultancy has designed and built a large store of knowledge on electronic databases. Reports, detailed analysis and specimen documentation are carefully prepared for re-use and rapid retrieval. Partners can use the system to cut service times to customers and so pitch fees at competitive levels.

McKinsey

As a world famous consultancy, McKinsey emphasises the direct sharing of knowledge among its staff. A culture of reliable and intense communication is fostered with specialist knowledge brokers available to support project teams. New technology assists person-to-person communication but is not intended as a substitute.

Source: Hansen et al. 'Knowledge Management Strategy' (Harvard Business Review, March–April 1999)

Business and creativity

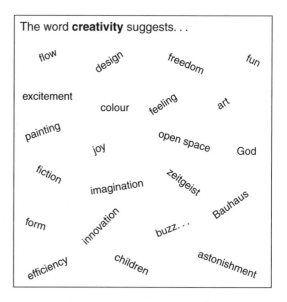

↑ Figure 33.2 Brainstorming associations

Source: Postgraduate students at University of Exeter

In what way is creativity different from learning? Successful creativity, like learning, adds to the available repertoire of knowledge and skills. But creativity involves a jump, a discontinuity, a making of something new that was not predictable from the move before. Creativity takes an idea, attaches it to another not obviously connected idea and reveals something different with unexpected value. Like a charge of electrical energy over the water of learning, creativity may be slow to flare and then very sudden.

The cost of creativity varies from the expense of elaborate and specialised R&D departments through to zero, as when a thought or a conversation triggers innovation. The gains may be modest but cumulative, or they can be colossal, a pole-vault of knowledge – and proprietary revenues. Creativity can be transformational in any kind of business. Hi-tech industries are just one setting. From catering to cosmetics, creativity is the engine of innovation.

Strategically, learning and creativity have different qualities. Learning usually spurs incremental improvements: ways of increasing efficiency, ways of adding new value. It builds expertise and improves decision making. Competitive advantage can be achieved through learning that is better directed or faster than the learning of competitors. The more complex the 'thinking network' required for learning, the more difficult it is to replicate.

Creativity is an almost impossible code to break. With its non-linear structure, no competitor can just copy or reverse engineer creativity. By jumping frontiers, creativity can yield a competitive advantage that is decisive and unique. When creativity becomes recurrent in an organisation, a phenomenon in its culture, the competitive gains compound. Usually, such creativity is only sustained for a limited period, but its effects can be seen in many companies, for example in Monsanto or Apple Computers in the USA and in ARM or Virgin in the UK.

Making waves

If creativity matters, what makes it happen? Equilibrium, stability and routine do not make the waves that spark creativity. Indeed, for creativity, life in the so-called comfort zone is anathema. It is perhaps ironic that managers so often make admiring references to 'keeping an even keel', 'a well-oiled machine' and 'a smooth pair of wheels'. Of course, every firm needs recurrent patterns and some underlying continuity, but the bias in many organisations is towards repetition, framing and self-regard. Harmony becomes not a transformational pitch of achievement, but the ostensible absence of dissent.

Despite a long history of interest in the phenomenon of creativity, the concept has made very limited inroads into writing and teaching about management. Rickards (1999) suggests that this arises from the uncomfortable relationship between the rationalist orthodoxy of management and the non-linear and intuitive ethos of creativity. Significantly, creativity lacks any generally agreed definition or test for its occurrence.

These problems are reflected in an early model for creative thinking offered by Graham Wallas at the beginning of the 20th century: preparation → incubation → illumination → verification. It is a useful taxonomy but only the first and last stages are 'scientific': incubation and illumination move outside the normal sequences of logical thought. The same tensions surface in the injunctions of Osborn (1953) in his brainstorming techniques: 'postpone judgement', 'freewheel' and 'hitch-hike'. The lateral thinking advocated by De Bono (see below) has a similar ring in its requirement to break away from the vertical chains of deductive thought.

The environment for creativity does matter. Tolerant, open and thoughtful cultures are fertile for the creative process. What De Geus calls 'conversations' or networks of communication within an organisation make creativity more likely. But arguably there is still a need for peturbation, challenge and discontinuity if creativity is really to begin, if the 'hot' psychological condition identified by Gordon (1966) is to release insight and trigger leaps in understanding.

Translated into the agenda of practical management, Sutton (2000) urges firms to recruit staff who do not fit the organisation's formal requirements. He stresses the need for creative personnel to work outside systems and to be allowed to make mistakes or follow (apparently) fruitless pathways. Attempting to back winners in the process of creative thinking is usually unproductive while the priority is 'big picture' commitment to the firm and its projects.

Xerox ←

Gary Starkweather was recruited by Xerox in 1968. Working in their New York research facility he argued that the new technology of lasers could offer greater speed and definition in the reprographic process. Xerox engineers rejected his ideas.

Starkweather ignored his line manager and persisted with his research. The conflict led to his relocation at the company's new research centre in Palo Alto, California. Soon, a workable product had been designed that countered the original criticisms. In 1977 Xerox launched the first laser printer – model 9700 – which became a huge success.

Out of the box?

There can be little doubt that people and organisations in any situation establish patterns in their responses and behaviour. Over time these patterns become a mindset: assumptions accumulate and harden; responses become conditioned; flexibility and experiment decrease. In today's world, these are likely conditions for strategic failure. We have seen (Chapter 10) that the need is to retain strategic fit in conditions of turbulence and unpredictability, and to innovate faster and with more originality than competitors.

This tendency towards repetitive stability can form a kind of 'box'. In this context, 'the box' means any restricting construct of awareness. The 'walls' of the box are limits to vision, thought, possibilities. We can imagine two types of box:

- **'Soft boxes'** are created by everyone at work (and in private life) – comfortable and made-to-measure. Repeated patterns of life form a cocoon or 'soft shell' to our behaviour – a kind of mould within which we repeat the 'castings'. In time this affects not only behaviour patterns but perceptual and response patterns – conditioned *not* to experiment.
- **'Hard boxes'** are formal and geometric, built by systems, rules, training, procedures, routines, times – all sharp angles with the planes of a 'box'. These boxes are ubiquitous: diaries, timetables, targets, budgets, job descriptions, committees, offices, gender roles – even relationships.

De Bono (1971) characterises the classical Western tradition of thought as vertical thinking in that it proceeds in linear, logical steps to prove what is right and expose what is wrong. This approach, he says, dominates education and is widespread in business. He does *not* condemn vertical thinking; on the contrary, he recognises its immense power, but he does also advocate an alternative: lateral thinking.

Very often, de Bono argues, business thinking enters a problem at the second stage – where logical techniques of analysis are applied, calculations made and proofs deduced. This misses what should be the first stage where the problem is framed, entry points to the problem are chosen, useful concepts are formed and selected, and weights of relative importance are assigned to the active variables.

As a self-organising system, the mind is prone to standard patterns of thought, response and behaviour that are reinforced and repeated. Critically for strategic thinking, patterns reduce reality to their own terms – and lose the richness of what is possible in the process. De Bono, through the lateral thinking process, recommends escape from clichés and fixed patterns by challenging basic assumptions and generating alternatives outside the arena of debate. Lateral thinking involves a readiness to find new entry points to problems and jump directly to ideas and scenarios without any pathway of supporting evidence.

Vertical versus lateral thinking: a summary

Vertical thinking	Lateral thinking
Analytical	Explanatory
Resolution-oriented; towards proof	No one solution
Stability	Change, movement
Yes/No – must not be wrong	No right/wrong
Continuity	Discontinuity
Avoid gaps	Use gaps
Evidence → conclusion	Conclusion → evidence
Relevance; no chance	Welcome chance; no relevance rules
Follow signposted pathway	Look beyond obvious
Start with where we are now	Start with where we'd like to be

Pascale (2000) urges the break from regularity and periodicity by moving towards 'the edge of chaos' – a narrow but rich and fertile strip of reality on the border between order and chaos. In this zone all kinds of unexpected ideas present themselves as the patterns of stability stop repeating and start forming novel configurations. If one firm does not learn how to 'surf the edge of chaos', then perhaps others will.

34 Emotion and passion

The idea

The title of this chapter sounds slightly peripheral to a book that aims to explain how business works. Significantly, neither economics nor business are particularly associated with feeling. Yet the value added by emotion is rising. A firm energised by passion is often hard to beat, while a product that is not energised by passion is often hard to sell.

As firms begin to take on the shapes and patterns of living organisms, their ability to manage feelings becomes a source of competitive advantage. Becoming a learning organisation means recognising emotions alongside cognition and the links between the two. When the value circuitry of firms is deconstructed, feeling can outscore function.

Emotional value

Unlike cost, value is dependent on personal judgement without any link to fixed standards or conventions. We have seen that consumer valuation is driven by both the product's objective qualities and by its emotional appeal (see Chapter 17).

Apple Macintosh

When Apple Macintosh introduced their revolutionary Apple II in 1984, it commanded a premium price because of its functional advantages such as the use of user-friendly icons. But by the time Windows 95 had arrived, PCs had eroded most of Apple's advantages.

Yet the launch of the i-Mac in 1998 revived Apple's fortunes not so much because of its respectable performance at a functional level, but more because of its innovative appearance and user 'feel'. No longer was a desktop simply hardware – now it was a designer's child, an essential piece of urban chic, a statement of sophistication about its owner.

The i-Mac had exceptional appeal in its target market and seemed to epitomise Apple's strapline: 'Think different'.

It usually takes a real breakthrough to increase customer valuation of a product's functional capabilities. Many failed new product launches have been based on claimed improvements in performance that in practice consumers hardly value. New products like the early Apple or the original Pentel R50 rollerball do create lift-offs in value. They are, though, prone to imitation by competitors so that only continuous innovation is likely to protect their competitive advantage. By contrast, surges in emotional value are harder to copy but vulnerable to their potentially fickle nature.

Swatch

We were convinced that if each of us could add our fantasy and culture to an emotional product, we could beat anybody.

Emotions are something that nobody can copy.

Nicholas Hayek, Chairman of Swatch

Tom Peters (1994) has observed how value can ratchet upwards when an emotional link is made between the customer and the product. When the general run of products are fairly close substitutes for one another, a product with which the customer feels a personal relationship can build and sustain a superior level of value – and profitability. It is its emotional rather than its functional strengths that make the product special.

Exploiting emotion?

Babyboomers want to feel that they have grown up, not old, and that they retain the childlike sense of wonder and enjoyment of their youth. Wise marketers can reinforce these deep desires to their advantage by wrapping promotional messages in the cosy warmth of some of boomers' most cherished memories.

Sid and Bruce Good in 'Boomers Need Security Blanket', Marketing News, *9 September 1996*

The culture of business has had a tendency to adopt language that is dry and rather cerebral when articulating the meaning of products. Even advertisers are prone to use clichés of the superlative and mainstream psychological imagery without exploring the secret recesses of feeling, memory and imagination where emotional relationships begin. The 'something' that makes a product adhere to the memory and form a desire is often simple and largely symbolic. It is usually inexpensive to provide.

The widely adopted tenets of market orientation have ensured a consensus around the idea of firms as servants of customer demand. No firm should think it produces anything except what customers want, and that is always provisional and subject to constant change. In this view, the firm is merely a productive conduit linking consumer demand to the factors of production. But closeness to the customer can mean something more. Firms can innovate to offer products that were hardly conceived before and that meet needs of which potential customers were totally unaware. Peters urges firms to 'dazzle' and 'bewitch' their customers with products that elicit the naïve but unpremeditated response: 'Wow!'

Modern asset-led marketing avoids any open-ended promise to meet customer demand, and concentrates instead on using distinctive capabilities to best innovative effect. This usually implies developing products that are related to existing success stories, building on the foundations of reputation and customer loyalty. Brands are often a key factor with their implicit elevation of customer value.

During the 1990s, interest shifted from the traditional notion of 'satisfying the customer' to the new goal of 'exceeding customer expectations'. This suggests that the firm's products will deliver fully on the sources of satisfaction normally expected, plus a kind of bonus in terms of quality or quantity that will represent a favourable surprise. In analytical terms, customers are being advised to revise their estimates of product value sharply upwards towards an unknown ceiling. The firm is attempting to give its demand function an abrupt push to the right. This will only occur if its claim is credible and if a cost-effective way has been found to fulfil the promise sustainably.

An emotionally more potent form of exceeding expectations is the concept of 'customer delight'. This captures the emotional, unpredictable and transformative quality that can lie in the experiential unfolding of a product.

┌ Kwik-Fit ◄

Kwik-Fit, the UK tyre, exhaust and battery chain, adopted the slogan 'Committed to 100% customer ~~satisfaction~~ delight' in 1989. This projected the idea of customer service beyond notions of competence and reliability and towards new standards. A product that was bought for essentially negative reasons could become a positive experience.

The experience of so many products is merely adequate: they succeed in fulfilling their basic function but fail to rise above the ordinary. The idea of 'delight' taps into the emotional springs of experience, promising the possibility of discontinuously better value.

Peters (1994) takes this idea further when he talks of products that 'redefine expectations'. No longer is the firm's task to deliver an experience that corresponds with the customers' hopes, even their highest hopes. The product actually demonstrates to customers the possibility of hopes never entertained yet now demonstrably fulfilled. Setting new rules for the game is a highly effective route to competitive advantage, where the products of other firms are not merely surpassed but made redundant by a new genre of experience. Crossing from the old to the new product categories is not easy for competitors: the pioneer holds emotional as well as functional capital.

Products as experience

Customers value a product because they believe that it will yield them a stream of satisfaction or utility. We have seen that this may be essentially functional or emotional in character (see Chapter 17). These sources of value are unified in the concept of *experience*. It has always been obvious that many service products represent an experience – a visit to the theatre, for example. Yet other services are ultimately no different.

Consider insurance. What is the product? An insurance certificate? Peace of mind? The possibility of a claim and pay-out? In complex ways it is all of these. The certificate may meet legal or contractual obligations. As a document it also suggests the purpose of insurance cover, which is affordable protection against misfortune. And the thought of a pay-out is undeniably attractive. These and other sources of value from insurance form a web of experience that links and makes an affirmative connection with other linked webs, such as driving a car or home ownership.

Are manufactured products any different? The old Coca-Cola strapline suggests the answer: 'You can't beat the feeling'. Is Coke a fizzy drink or a feeling? The answer, of course, is both – or rather, beyond both. Coca-Cola is a complex experience that includes taste, the quenching of thirst and personal identification with a brand that speaks of youthful freedom, rugged style and American values.

Cadbury-Schweppes ◄──────────────

WE ARE *passionate* **ABOUT WORKING TOGETHER TO CREATE BRANDS THAT PEOPLE** *love*. **BRANDS THAT BRING THE** *world* **MOMENTS OF** *delight* **AND A SPLASH OF** *colour* **ON A GREY DAY.**

Source: (as printed here) Cadbury-Schweppes Annual Report, 2002

Once a product is deconstructed in this way, we can begin to see the circuitry of its value. Building on the concept of the value chain as described by Porter (1985), the elements of the product as experience can be identified and evaluated. This is arguably not quite as simple as Kim and Mauborgne (1999) imply. In deconstructing a product's value we are exploring an interactive system. Changing one source of value may have unexpected effects on other sources. Optimisation of the value circuit is a tuning process that forms a core competence. Being the secret of differentiation, it is a source of competitive advantage that other firms find difficult to replicate.

Pine and Gilmour (1999) view experiences as a distinct category of economic offering now finding an identity beyond the service sector (see Figure 34.1 overleaf).

Each category carries greater potential for differentiation than the one before, allowing correspondingly greater leeway for premium pricing. Experiences can either be sold as such (e.g. Disney) or be 'wrapped around' other products (e.g. Hard Rock Café). The key features of an experience are that it is unique to the individual, that it can engage with all the senses and that it is memorable.

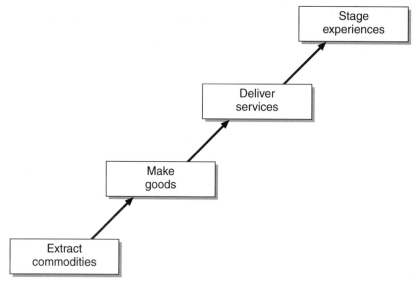

Figure 34.1 Pine and Gilmour's progression of economic value

Reprinted by permission of Harvard Business Review.
Adapted from 'Welcome to the Experience Economy' by B. J. Pine and J. H. Gilmour, July/August 1998.
Copyright © 1998 by the Harvard Business School Publishing Corporation; all rights reserved.

Emotional intelligence

When Nguyen Huy (2000) says 'Work is inherently an emotional experience', he is affirming the intuitive knowledge of almost everyone. Places where people work are usually portrayed as rational systems, but are actually stages of high drama where intense human feelings are aroused. Emotions are the unofficial subscript of business reality – and always have been. Yet only recently has serious attention been focused on how emotions infuse every functioning feature of an organisation: for example, the energy of a unit, the effectiveness of a leader, the interactivity of a team. The old assumption that people save their emotions for their private life and bring only their cognitive and technical skills to work is a myth. But still the failure by many companies to recognise and mobilise the emotional skills of their staff is the cause of untold conflict and underperformance.

What Goleman (1998) calls emotional intelligence is, he argues, a vital, even decisive element in the development and exercise of organisational competence. Recent advances in neurobiology show that the intellect and the emotions do not inhabit separate worlds but are actually interactively 'wired' with the proper functioning of cognition dependent on appropriate emotional responses. Studies have been made of patients with severance between their amalgyna (seat of key emotions) and frontal lobes (seat of cognition). These show that while formal reasoning may still operate normally, the application of intellect to real-life problem solving is hugely impaired.

Goleman's research findings indicate that while intellectual and technical capabilities are important in many jobs, the decisive driver of high performance is usually emotional intelligence. Indeed, cognitive abilities are often the threshold qualities required, and star performers rise primarily on their addition of acute emotional skills. The particular emotional competencies identified by Goleman as crucial are shown opposite.

The Emotional Competencies Framework ←

Personal competencies of self-management

Self-awareness

- emotional awareness
- accurate self-assessment
- self-confidence

Self-regulation

- self-control
- trustworthiness
- conscientiousness
- adaptability
- innovation

Motivation

- achievement drive
- commitment
- initiative
- optimism

Social competencies of relationships

Empathy

- understanding others
- developing others
- service orientation
- leveraging diversity
- political awareness

Social skills

- influence
- communication
- conflict management
- leadership
- change catalyst
- building bonds
- collaboration and co-operation
- team capabilities

Source: Daniel Goleman Working with Emotional Intelligence *(Bloomsbury, 1998)*

Although traditional hierarchy is hampered by its lack of emotional intelligence, its derivation of value from predictable, mechanistic activity allows it to function with the appearance of effectiveness. Since the late 20th century a number of trends have placed a growing premium on the individual and corporate exercise of emotional intelligence. The new leadership (see Chapter 26) and dependence on teamwork have made lack of emotional intelligence a serious liability in the performance of almost all job roles. Meanwhile, as the service sector expands (see Chapter 35), more firms depend on a direct staff interface with customers. Increasingly, added value is derived from the emotional qualities of interpersonal experiences. Finally, the ability to cope with rapid change and organisational transformation (see Chapter 32) is crucially dependent on both social and personal competencies.

Passion

Nothing great in the world has been accomplished without passion.

Georg Hegel, German philosopher (1770-1831)

A fundamental shortcoming in much of business today is that the leadership lacks vision and passion – the two most important ingredients to inspire and motivate.

Anita Roddick Body and Soul *(Ebury Press, 1991)*

Visions are aesthetic and moral – as well as strategically sound. Visions come from within – as well as from outside. They are personal – and group-centred. Developing a vision and values is a messy, artistic process. Living it convincingly is a passionate one, beyond any doubt.

Tom Peters Thriving on Chaos *(Pan, 1989)*

The power of passion

The dictionary definition of passion is 'strong emotion'. More telling are the synonyms offered, which include 'feeling, ardour, fervour, warmth, heat, spirit, intensity, vehemence'. These words do not suggest the cerebral and monochrome images of business that seem to inhabit most boardrooms and the City pages. But they have always been there, hiding in a sense behind the textual surface of prices and profits, costs and competitiveness. Dreams and conflict in the boardroom, pride and anger on the shopfloor, delight and dismay in the customer's carrier bag – passion pulls away from the normal zone and trips every gauge to 'danger'.

Yet it is this fire, this temperature, this turbulence that can carry a business into the realms of exceptional performance. Any number of firms can be well managed and efficient, with a sound product range and generally satisfied customers. Such enterprises are not characterised by passion. Like a combustible fuel, passion is usually fenced off in safe compartments beyond the reach of the sparks thrown up by the everyday energy of business. This is understandable since passion can be negative as well as positive, chaotic as well as creative. But it may also be wrong.

The challenge of dangerous energy is its disciplined release in work of originality and inspiration. This often requires certain structures and protocols to protect all involved and to concentrate energy where its action has most value. Openness in communication between people is particularly important. It must be possible to express conflicting views without the outbreak of acrimony.

What can passion do for the performance of a business? First, it can give a strategy pulling power that it would never otherwise have. Second, it can energise a workforce beyond the concept of motivation so that markers such as innovation, quality and customer service take discontinuous leaps. Third, it can be transmitted to the customers themselves, where liking a product becomes

The J Peterman Company

Peterman is an up-scale catalogue supplier of household goods. The difference is the engaging and quite complex stories behind the 'discovery' of each product and the concern for high quality in the manufacturing and presentational specification. The catalogue description for The Counterfeit Mailbag is very revealing and ratchets up value on the back of feelings that rise to passion:

> **The secret thoughts of an entire country were carried in leather bags exactly like this one. Except this one, a copy, isn't under lock and key in a museum. It's for sale.**

> **I borrowed an original from a friend, a retired mailman who, like thousands before him, was kind enough to test it out, for years, on the tree-lined streets of small towns everywhere. Before you were born.**

> **The test was successful; even though discontinued, it can't be improved upon. It's simply perfect as a device for carrying important ideas and feelings back and forth.**

Source: Tom Peters The Tom Peters Seminar (*Macmillan, 1994*)

loving a product and added value soars. Finally it creates a radiance in an organisation that is beyond the scope of conventional management but still absolutely real as a value transformer.

The richer possibilities for adding value in products through the in-building of emotional and experiential qualities have led the swing away from generic products. In consumer-led industries, most firms no longer offer their products in terms of simple descriptions or as a plain inventory. Instead, products are fires of feeling with a marketing mix that is designed to kindle passion. The flight away from product-as-commodity continues unabated.

35 Weightlessness and postmodernity

Overview

In advanced economies, the physical weight of output relative to its value is falling, in some industries heading towards zero. The old distinction between 'heavy' and 'light' industry is now joined by the category 'weightless'. The value added by knowledge, design, brands and even emotion is also becoming the key source of competitive advantage for more and more companies.

This trend has sent much of the Western world's manufacturing base to the Far East, yet living standards in the low-weight economies continue to rise.

Meanwhile, our traditional notions of 'firms' and 'products' have begun to dissolve. Fixed assets such as factories and offices give way to the intangible value of teams and capabilities, while products become whatever the customer wants them to be. In a postmodern world, it is argued, reality is defined by the observer.

The weightless economy

When Bell (1973) first used the term post-industrial, he was referring to a society that no longer drew its major source of wealth from such industries as iron and steel, coal, shipbuilding, textiles, mechanical engineering and railways. Since then, service industries have continued to grow rapidly, while the extractive and manufacturing sectors have lost further ground. Most developed economies are reaching a 75/25 or even 80/20 relationship between the output value of their service industries and the extractive, manufacturing and construction sectors combined.

A different, and in some ways more illuminating, perspective on this trend is offered by analysing the 'weight' of industry or, more particularly, the physical weight of its products. Alan Greenspan, recent Chairman of the US Federal Reserve Board, made the telling observation that the output of the USA in the 1990s was hardly any heavier than it had been 100 years earlier, yet its value had, in real terms, increased twenty-fold.

This dramatic loss of weight reflects the diminishing relative importance of extractive and manufacturing industries and the corresponding rise in the proportional value of the service sector. Pure services, such as banking or hairdressing, are clearly weightless. Many other services are not weightless but have a low weight–value ratio (e.g. catering or transport). Then there is the emergence of the 'new economy' – the high-tech or quaternary sector. In the world of computing, telecommunications, software, biotechnology and all the related services there is little or no weight produced but a huge amount of value.

The value chain in manufacturing is also deeply affected by the impact of new technologies. Often it is no longer the fabrication of the product that represents the bulk of final cost or value. Much more important is the patented design of the product and its microelectronic 'intelligence'. In many industries, added value has migrated far downstream or shifted beyond the end of the production process into distribution, branding and merchandising. As Ohmae (1990) points out, manufacturing costs have typically fallen to around 25 per cent of end-user cost, and are moving to even lower relative levels.

The commoditisation of all but the most advanced manufacturing is highly significant. Where once the only commodities were raw materials, the term may now include a vast range of components and finished goods. Many firms who saw their business as 'making a product' now outsource its manufacture (usually in China or the Far East) and confine themselves to the more profitable and highly downstream role of ramping up value through marketing.

All this represents a 'dematerialisation' of the economy in developed countries. Wealth is no longer created primarily by the physical process of extraction and manufacturing but by such relatively weightless activities as invention, design, problem solving and branding.

The new values ◄

The value in our economy – whatever it is we are willing to pay money for – has less and less physical mass. Whether it is software codes, genetic codes, the creative content of a film or piece of music, the design of a new pair of sunglasses or the vigilance of a security guard or helpfulness of a shop assistant, value no longer lies in three-dimensional objects in space. We will pay for amusement, for style, for convenience, for speed, for creativity, for beauty – but when it comes to things, commodities, we have turned into skinflints, and want the cheapest possible. We will buy either a cheap T-shirt made in Macau or Morocco, or we will buy a designer shirt for 20 or 50 times the price.

Diane Coyle The Weightless World *(Capstone, 1997)*

Of course, the issue is not unwillingness to pay for 'things', but the current competitive ability of a globalised economy to produce 'things' at very low cost. A textiles producer in Macau or Morocco may be paid no more than £1 for a T-shirt that may then be sold on at £3 if marketed as a generic, or £12 if emblazoned with a brand such as Adidas. These relationships are not irrational: they represent value that consumers acknowledge and the brand owner can add. They do, however, have ethical implications that are addressed in Chapter 38.

Weightless value

The key to understanding the new economic landscape lies in the theory of added value. We have seen that as a business adds market value to a product, the gravitational force of competition is brought progressively to bear on profit. All strategy has two fundamental purposes: to add value and to defend that value against competitors. The developed economies have spent 30 years losing the cost battle to retain basic manufacturing. In the end, low-wage producers had to win, and in doing so gain a modest slice of the value that is so much amplified after leaving their factory gates.

Most major firms in the USA, the EU and Japan use a culturally embedded knowledge base to sustain competitive advantage in their weightless additions to value. They are able to retain the larger part of a product's price tag because no low-cost producer can compete with their performance. This does not mean, though, that returns on capital are necessarily very high. Unless the firm has exceptional proprietary knowledge (such as Microsoft), the usual competitive forces will always be driving returns back towards the opportunity cost of capital (see Chapter 7).

In this dematerialised world, not only the products but also the assets of companies lose much or all of their weight. Traditional accounting is based on tangible assets such as buildings, plant and equipment. In an age of manufacturing, this made sense. It is only relatively recently that intangible assets other than goodwill, such as brands, have even begun to appear on the balance sheet. Talent, teams, culture or knowledge management systems do not even begin to figure among recognised 'assets'. Yet it is precisely assets such as these that have the power to add value and represent a competitive advantage.

The contradictions are apparent when comparing the capitalisations of companies (share price multiplied by number of shares issued) with the book value of their net assets. Many hi-tech firms have capitalisations many times greater than net assets and, for pure knowledge-based enterprise, the calculation is almost meaningless.

Capitalisation and balance sheet assets

Company	Capitalisation	Net Assets	Capitalisation/ Net Assets
Microsoft	$268 943m	$54 902m	4.90
Astra Zeneca	£46 109m	£13 361m	3.45
Psion	£320.4m	£185.6m	1.73
Logica	£1 228m	£783.7m	1.57

The weightless firm also faces problems in capturing the market value of its products. Quah (1995) points out that dematerialised products are infinitely expandable. The use of the product by one person does not preclude its simultaneous use by another. A film can be broadcast via satellite to few or many receivers at the same cost. Similarly, a piece of software can be installed on any computer at zero marginal cost. This makes important the policing of 'gateways' to the consumption of weightless products, as well as the protection of intellectual and other intangible property.

Weight and location

The physical presence of some firms is now very small indeed compared to the value of their sales, and it is a trend set to continue. The 'virtual firm' may have its main operations in cyberspace rather than a business park, yet it is no less real than a business with office blocks and factories. It is, though, incomparably more footloose, able to shift its location and national identity at very short notice. Already some weightless activities are starting to exploit the new communications technology and locating selected operations in low-wage parts of the world.

At the high added-value end of the weightless economy, the most powerful restraining factor on location is the benefit of 'clustering' (see Chapter 36) and its associated human 'infrastructure'. The Silicon Valley phenomenon in California dates from the 1970s and provides an unrivalled concentration of talent and experience in the computer and software industries. In the same way, London as a financial centre thrives on the proximity of people doing the same kind of work and forming a pool of expertise. Many smaller centres in the 'creative economy' (art, design, film, advertising, etc.) generate a locational value through their cultural synergies.

Weightless prosperity?

Back in the 1980s there was a widely held view that 'making real things' was the basis of a healthy economy, since manufacturing spawned home-based components and by-product industries while generating the exports that would enable the country to pay its way in the world. When, in 1985, the value of Britain's manufactured imports exceeded the corresponding value of exports for the first time, many commentators saw it as a sad comment on the one-time 'workshop of the world'.

Yet, more and more the economies of developed countries specialise in the conception, design and marketing of products, while what was once called 'production' is globally outsourced. Far from damaging living standards, the weightless economy has seen a steady rise in real national income (up by 51.5 per cent since 1985) and the export of invisible or weightless products.

It is not surprising that the search for competitiveness in developed countries has come to focus on education and the process of learning. However, in an environment where most firms want flexibility in the scale and nature of their operations, there are few jobs for life and investment in people offers uncertain returns. However, it is a measure of the need for an educated and trained workforce that some firms continue to fund often quite open-ended pathways to learning.

ARM ←

> ... we are in the midst of a digital revolution that is changing and reshaping all our lives. Its effects are comparable to the introduction of electricity over a century ago or steam a hundred years before that. Advanced digital technology is making the products we use every day more intelligent, more capable, more efficient and more affordable.
>
> Today, the world's leading 32-bit RISC architecture comes from ARM. ARM's processor designs have been licensed by over 50 semiconductor Partners and, last year alone, were used by them in over 400 million chips.

Source: ARM Report and Accounts

ARM chip designs are found in the products of Bosch, Texas Instruments, Sharp, Nintendo, Alcatel, Samsung and many other leading electronics companies. Net profit margins of over 30 per cent are achieved on sales, 70 per cent of which take the form of royalties and licensing revenue.

Making products 'mine'

More sophisticated market orientation has brought firms into closer and closer embrace with customers in their target markets, which are themselves becoming smaller and more intimately knowable. We have seen (Chapter 34) that value is added by injecting desire into products. This can be achieved weightlessly by projecting back to the customer some quality that feels authentically as if it comes from the realm of their own consciousness. Thus, the customer's perception of the product becomes less objectively 'it' and more subjectively 'mine'.

Marketing strategies of this kind often add value through customised design and differentiation. This is becoming available to firms at falling cost. Interestingly, it coincides with some decline of faith in objectivity and a growing interest in personal accounts of reality.

Business and postmodernity

The beginning in this respect can be traced back to Theodore Levitt's much quoted article 'Marketing Myopia' (1960). His advocacy of market orientation requires firms to abandon the idea that their purpose is the output of a definitive and objective product in favour of the idea that they sell customer experiences. This perspective enthrones the consumer in defining *their* product and *their* purpose. It also gives all firms and all products a plastic and contingent quality where their very nature is only ever provisional and in the service of changing customer wants.

We move from a world of 'how things should be' to a world of 'how things are', decided by 'how people wants things to be'. There is an intriguing irony that Levitt's article was published at the high water mark of scientific modernism in the study of business (e.g. Simon, 1960). A few years later the founding statements of postmodernity had been made by Venturi (1966). Soon it would be problematic to ask what was meant by 'a real job', 'a worthwhile product' or 'a good town centre'? No authoritative 'voice' could make judgements of these kinds: the only voice was the voice of customers as expressed by their purchasing decisions.

Meanwhile, as organisational structures softened, so their designs were becoming more contingent. The postmodern organisation loses the solidity and apparent permanence of the classic hierarchy. It is a conjunction of resources and managers configured to exploit a business opportunity. Firms grow, merge, split and grow again at a speed that makes their identity difficult to define. What *can* be evaluated is the performance of any aggregated resources, regardless of their name or formal ownership. Indeed, the 'pinning together' of trading units is itself an essential part of business strategy. Orchestrating potential synergies likely to arise from new patterns of ownership and management has become a real source of competitive advantage.

Technology and postmodernism

Technology was originally the language of modernism, but it has become a propagator of postmodernity. In the Fordist era – say, until the 1960s – the leading edge of technology was still about power and scale, not flexibility or intelligence. Mass production (see Chapter 21) required mass markets with standardised needs: that is, satisfaction from products that were an approximation to individual requirements but never an exact fit.

The micro-technology of post-Fordist times has allowed ever growing customisation in almost every product category. Individuals are encouraged to express and indulge their personal choices without regard to aesthetic standards, defining formats or product boundaries. All firms become architects or agents of experience.

Linking value chains vertically, and often horizontally, to form a contingent structure capable of adding value, intelligent networks continually adjust their offering to fit the environment, drawn as though magnetically to the contours of customers' desire. Meanwhile, new technology allows ever more complex patterns in the fulfilment of private choice.

Secure boundaries everywhere dissolve. Firms are facilitators, constructs of capability where products are evolving configurations of experience. The evidence is ubiquitous. Sub-brands within car marques proliferate as customers select specifications for their final vehicle. Satellite and cable TV offer multiple channels as opportunities for interactivity with the audience increase. Personal computers allow almost every kind of customisation, while the internet gives individuals as much right to a website as a global corporation. The idea of 'going *à la carte*' is now standard, from the international breakfast served in major hotels through to the choice of 'modules' making up an accredited course in higher education.

The end of serial narrative and prescribed form has widening strategic implications. Postmodernism as a cultural force is causing the fragmentation of products and markets. And as it dissolves boundaries, firms become brokers rather than producers: brokers of experience, brokers of feelings, brokers of dreams.

Any colour you like …

Firms who were once adamant about who they were and what they sold are now the compliant servants of customer choice. Building societies that once stood judgementally before members who wanted mortgages, are now banks eager to sell customised financial products to any creditworthy taker. Whitbread, a proud brewer from the 18th century, now brews no beer but purveys a multiplicity of entertainments. Schools, once receiving pupils by 'catchment area', are now interviewed and selected by increasingly discerning parents. *Big Brother*, Channel 4's runaway success of 2002, depends for its appeal on the audience making choices about who should remain on screen.

… as long as it is black

Henry Ford's purism with the Model T is not lost on the world's upmarket brands. Like anchorages in a sea of choice, classic products affirm their owner's discrimination and tacitly acknowledge ideas of 'taste' and style. BMW cars, Gucci bags, Beck's beer and the Swiss Army penknife are desired not for their readiness to customise but for their unyielding quality. They cause buyer passion not by moving closer to the customer but by standing their own ground.

Is Business Studies modernist?

The subject of 'business' or 'Business Studies' has an academic lineage that is distinctly 'modern'. During the first two-thirds of the 20th century, the field of business struggled to emerge as a distinct subject of academic enquiry. The chosen route for this emergence was through the adoption of scientific method and alignment with other more established social sciences. From FW Taylor's *The Principles of Scientific Management* (1911) to Herbert Simon's *New Science of Decision Making* (1960), a modernist mindset was in the making. This prizes reason and calculation over faith or intuition and gives automatic pre-eminence to that which is proven and demonstrable. Indeed, the Western approach to business has always tended to devalue that which cannot be measured (Pascale, 1981; Mintzberg, 1987).

Since the 1980s there has been much increased interest in the 'soft side' of business, with concepts such as organisational culture and knowledge management becoming legitimate areas for study. Even then there is a tendency to place these ideas within a mechanistic framework. Questions such as the nature of creativity and the applications of complexity theory remain barely on the boundaries of most mainstream studies.

Considering that business enterprise drove the Industrial Revolution, it seems surprising that scientific management was not invented until the 19th century was almost over. Indeed, although the Enlightenment of the 18th century was the making of the modernist worldview, most firms were run along pre-modern lines even as they helped construct the modernist vision. This reflects the delay in applying scientific method to human affairs: psychology and sociology were, after all, children of the 20th century.

What, then, is postmodernism and how does it help to explain the business world today? Postmodernism challenges the notions of certainty and progress that underpin the modernist paradigm. It questions why we should believe the account of reality provided by our dominant scientific culture and why we should not give equal credit to other accounts, currently marginalised or suppressed. Postmodernist commentators tend to see truth established only relative to the observer. They question systems of belief that claim wider or universal applicability.

This kind of thinking has some major cultural implications. The idea that society should have some shared agenda for improvement is rejected. 'Improvement' is a relative term that people will interpret in their own way. We cannot talk about a better society, only about people making what they think are better choices. In this frame, there is no definitive perception of the world, no 'good life' or 'good taste'.

Although many postmodern writers are deeply critical of capitalism for imposing its own totalising accounts of reality in the name of private gain, it is still arguable that business has been a key promoter of the postmodern condition. Meanwhile the validity of the postmodern perspective remains highly controversial.

36 Globalisation and localisation

Overview

Globalisation is the increasingly worldwide search by firms for their markets, inputs and places of operation. It is an emerging model that supersedes the old one of international trade. The difference lies in regarding the world as a more and more integrated system or network, where the processes of production and marketing are optimised without regard to nation states. This is a world where the production process can be disaggregated and dispersed to any part of the world, where markets are identified and targeted across frontiers and where the identity of the firm itself may develop multiple nationalities.

Principles of globalisation

What is the underlying rationale for globalisation? The basic goal of all business activity is to add value. National borders, insofar as they are obstacles to firms accessing inputs or marketing outputs, constrain the creation of value. In the absence of such barriers, firms can attempt to build the most effective possible value chains for maximised fit with the global market and its environment.

This means that patterns of national and regional specialisation are likely to become intense and more prominent. Counties will, over time, abandon the business activities in which they have no competitive advantage and concentrate instead on those industries and products where their capabilities are world class. Governments can obstruct or assist this process, but the more open and market-driven the world economy becomes, the more it will happen anyway.

Globalisation drivers

Internal

Globalisation is a phenomenon that reflects a number of long-term trends. Technology is clearly a prime factor. The falling real cost of transport has actualised countless flows of goods that would otherwise have been uneconomic. Information technology has made the management and co-ordination of global enterprise faster, more effective and far cheaper. Meanwhile, the development of mass tourism, together with the new telecommunications and media industries, has tended to homogenise consumer tastes and preferences. This in turn has opened numerous pathways for the development of global brands and transnational marketing.

Another major factor is the scale of production necessary to be competitive. In some industries, minimum efficient scale (MES) has fallen (e.g. brewing and baking), allowing entry of smaller competitors to the market. But in others MES values remain very high (e.g. cars, aerospace, bulk chemicals) and may be rising as improved management techniques delay the onset of diseconomies. This makes global markets essential.

As Ohmae (1990) points out, automation has drastically cut the variable costs of much manufacturing, leaving very high fixed costs that require a maximised contribution stream. Meanwhile, as the development costs of innovative products soar, R&D expenses have effectively become further fixed costs. And given the importance of advertising support and global brand recognition, a substantial part of a firm's marketing costs are also fixed. Recovery of these costs and the achievement of profitability necessarily imply high gross margins and, in many cases, worldwide sales.

External

Political and economic trends have operated closely together. Ever since 1945 there has been a trend towards trade liberalisation, and successive rounds of tariff reductions negotiated under GATT and (since 1996) the more globally titled World Trade Organisation (WTO), have greatly reduced the barriers to trade in manufactured goods. The formation of trade blocs including, most notably, the European Union (EU) have brought regional accelerations in the process.

The political barriers constraining the reach of firms in the free market economies have also crumbled. The end of the Cold War and the collapse of communism in most parts of the world have started to integrate large new markets with those of the capitalist West. The concurrent movement for privatisation and the contracting out of many services formerly in the public sector have stimulated further waves of investment and trade.

Meanwhile, real incomes have been rising across most parts of the world, albeit at very unequal rates. Significantly, the real value of world GDP has doubled since 1965. This has had a leveraged impact on the emergence of global markets. As incomes rise above subsistence level, so a household's disposable income that might typically be spent on traded products rises disproportionately. Whole economies that offered little real demand for, say, consumer durables can quite quickly become important markets.

Market size and growth indicators

	Population (millions)	GDP ($ bn)	GDP per capita ($)	GDP growth: average rate 1985–2002 (%)	GDP growth rate 2002 (%)
China	1 270	5 500	4 690	8·2	8·0
India	1 010	2 730	2 610	4·0	4·3
Indonesia	212	711	3 200	3·0	3·6
Republic of Korea	48	815	16 940	5·8	6·3
Thailand	62	406	6 920	5·0	5·2

Source: World Bank

Global strategy

In addressing global markets, the basic principles of business do not change. To be successful, a firm must add value through a sustainable competitive advantage. This will depend on achieving a strategic fit between the firm's capabilities and the market's requirements. Competing in worldwide industries presents a new layer of complexity in receiving and transmitting the strategic 'signals' that support a firm's manoeuvres towards optimum fit. In a purely national company the contest may be just as tough, but it is easier for managers to work together on interpreting strategic change and shaping their corresponding strategy. When managing across international frontiers, multiple time zones, different legal systems and cultural barriers, the lines of inward communication and outward implementation are more complex.

In analysing the strategies of worldwide business, Bartlett and Ghosal (1989) offer an important range of models. However, their use of terms such as 'multinational' and 'transnational' can be confusing in this context, and the simple generic term 'worldwide company' will be used where doubt might arise.

- **Multinational strategies** essentially reproduce national structures in different countries. This is facilitated by relatively low MES values and proportional fixed costs. Their intention is to offer brands and products that fit local preferences and exploit emergent opportunity.

- **International strategies** involve a highly centralised structure with all key functions in the home country. Only marketing, sales and limited production facilities are established in other countries. Such firms often have an international brand to exploit, such as Disney or McDonald's.

- **Global strategies** are based on designing standardised products and exploiting economies of scale to achieve lowest cost. Often selling industrial and other generic goods, firms of this type concentrate on the search for cost-minimising locations and sourcing channels. The essence of strategy is to achieve long production runs and to sell high volumes into an undifferentiated global market.

- **Transnational strategies** represent the emerging paradigm for the early 21st century. This is a more sophisticated model where the company attempts to achieve high performance in at least three major dimensions. These include responsiveness to local demand, minimised unit costs and the effective worldwide sharing of knowledge. This is a complex requirement since the desired performance criteria pull in different directions.

Organisationally, the transnational company will decentralise some of its functions while centralising others. Typically, it might localise sales and marketing functions so that they are in close touch with a national environment, and target segments of the market. Production and research functions might be concentrated at bases in each region of the so-called Triad – the Americas, Europe and Asia–Pacific. At the apex of the structure, overall strategy and issues of corporate identity could be lodged at HQ in the home country.

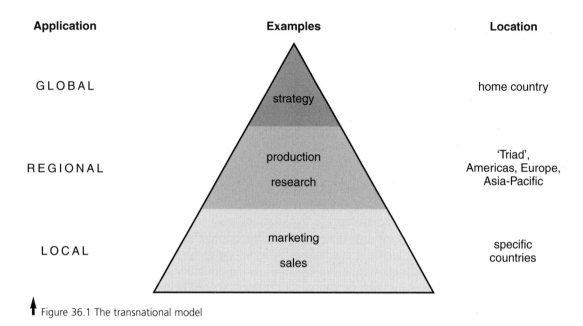

Figure 36.1 The transnational model

The principles of the transnational corporation were pioneered by Honda and Cannon, but have now been adopted by many major companies, including such giants as Nestlé and Unilever. To Bartlett and Ghosal, the first three strategic types – multinational, international and global – represent the old order that held sway in the second half of the 20th century. Multinational firms aimed to differentiate, global firms sought cost leadership and international firms used innovation to drive cost or value improvements. Today, the challenge is to build competitive advantage by managing all of these dimensions together as a self-reinforcing and knowledge-based system.

Building the transnational

The new model means that the generation and sharing of knowledge take on very special importance. As we have seen (see Chapter 33), the social architecture or 'wiring' of many firms is not at all conducive to this process. Inside the transnational model, there are two basic modes for learning. First, learning takes place in the decentralised local operations and is translated into innovation that can be applied across the whole organisation. Second, the capabilities and knowledge to be found in headquarters and at all levels in the structure are transformed into a stream of collaborative innovation that seizes business opportunity. We can see the outlines of an organisational intelligence emerging through this model.

Arie de Geus (1997) draws on experience at Royal Dutch Shell in indicating the cultural changes necessary to turn a worldwide company into a learning organisation. He observes that the vertical lines of authority in traditional organisations obstruct cross-functionalism and the social transmission of new knowledge. Instead, he stresses the value of informal 'conversations' within a company and 'organisational space' that deliberately allows experimentation with ideas and encourages 'flocking' or the social propagation of learning.

Also at Shell, Pascale (2000) tracks the empowerment of local frontline managers to offer real solutions to their customers' problems, and to develop entrepreneurial projects from which the organisation as a whole might later learn. Igniting entrepreneurial energy inside large organisations is a further objective in the new transnational model. Jack Welch, the former CEO at General Electric, famously stated: 'What we are trying relentlessly to do is get that small-company soul – and small-company speed – inside our big-company body.'

Asea Brown Boveri (ABB)

ABB was formed in 1988 from two large power equipment companies – one Swedish and one Swiss. With over-capacity and intense competition in the industry, ABB was barely profitable. Percy Barnevik, its new CEO, immediately embarked on a remarkable and successful turnaround programme of transformative change.

Radical decentralisation was the first step, as eight to nine level hierarchies were demolished in favour of a structure that placed only three layers of management between the CEO and a shopfloor worker. Thirteen hundred near-autonomous operating companies were created in 140 countries, whose managers were given two lines of responsibility: one to a geographical area and one to a business segment. Managing 210 000 employees, he more than decimated his headquarters staff to just 150.

The overriding goal was to turn each company into a real profit centre with a business culture that was 'spirited, obsessive, and energetic'. A uniform reporting and accounting system set out to 'democratise information' so that managers could take full, personal responsibility for their business objectives. These frequently involved discontinuous 'stretch', but trust in staff would be real and support made available.

The next phase – still incomplete – was to turn ABB into an intelligent, learning organisation where knowledge and experience connect across companies and countries with vigorous internal synergies.

Size and scale

During the late 20th century it was quite widely expected that larger and larger worldwide corporations would dominate global trade and that their products would be increasingly standardised, regardless of locality. In certain industries where MES values remain very high (bulk materials, basic components and commodity manufactures), this may be the case. Global brands where the product has universal appeal with little if any need for local adaptation are also likely to operate as very large units.

Otherwise the trend may be in the other direction. New technology is pushing down MES values across many manufacturing processes, enabling firms to set up local plants that lose little in unit costs but gain much in flexibility. While rising real incomes foster a taste for global brands, they also fragment mass markets, creating the kind of segmental complexity that small units are better suited to exploit. Meanwhile, the phenomenon of weightlessness (see Chapter 35) allows very small-scale enterprises to make themselves vital links in value chains almost everywhere.

Naisbitt (1997) argues that it is no longer the traditional concept of company size that matters, but the size of the networks into which real power is shifting. These are without any conventional headquarters yet every player is at the centre. Such networks, which carry complex interwoven flows of value, may grow larger but their nodes tend to become smaller. Much depends on our notion of the firm as a discrete entity. What, in the end, is the difference between a network of independently owned small firms linked together by tacit and contractual threads, and a constellation of relatively autonomous small business enterprises owned by a 'large' company that operates from a tiny HQ?

According to Naisbitt, 50 per cent of US exports are generated by companies with fewer than 20 employees. Meanwhile, the *Fortune 500* top US companies now only represent 10 per cent of the US economy, a proportion that has halved since 1970.

Joint ventures and strategic alliances

Many companies find that their existing internal resources are not sufficient to support their strategy. This is particularly the case for firms wishing to expand outside the home market. Typically they may need plant, distribution channels, brands and market access. Increasingly they may also need technical expertise and the services of key knowledge workers.

Where a global strategy confronts such a shortfall of necessary resources, it is not always necessary to gain ownership of the assets required. Although mergers and acquisitions remain a popular solution, it is often access to resources rather than their ownership that matters. Joint ventures and strategic alliances can be an effective and less risky way forward.

A joint venture is based on two companies combining complementary resources as the basis for a specific project or production facility. This is likely to need a formal agreement involving the ownership of assets and the sharing of profits (and losses). In some industries franchising avoids joint ownership of assets but involves a contractual agreement where the franchisee might typically provide production, distribution and selling functions, while the franchisor supplies the brand, the expertise and the training. Licensing in knowledge-based industries operates in a similar way: other companies pay fees to exploit a proprietory technology.

Looser alliances where companies typically agree to share specified types of knowledge or distribution networks are usually non-contractual. Mutual trust brings mutual advantage and such relationships often continue until overtaken by structural or strategic change.

National disparities

Porter (1990) aims to explain why some countries enjoy much greater concentrations of competitive advantage than others. In *The Competitive Advantage of Nations* he deploys a study of ten major economies to isolate the conditions that enable industries and firms to establish competitive advantage beyond their national boundaries. What emerges are four critical dynamics, said to form a national 'diamond'.

Porter's 'diamond'

1	**Factor conditions**	The availability of natural resources, infrastructure and knowledge/skills.
2	**Demand conditions**	The intensity and discriminatory quality of demand in the home country.
3	**Related and supporting industries**	The strength and international competitiveness of suppliers and related industries in the home country.
4	**Firm strategy, structure and rivalry**	The effectiveness and intensity of competition in the home market.

Earlier in the 20th century, when physical inputs were the key to competitiveness, it was indigenous raw materials, cheap labour or geographical location that mattered. But in terms of the new economics, competitiveness rests on the ability to add more value at relatively less cost to inputs of any kind. In the dynamics of the 'diamond', Porter is arguing that it is from rigorous, tough home markets that this wider competitive advantage springs. Undemanding, monopolistic or protected markets in the home country breed firms unable to reach the baseline requirements to compete in what Moss Kanter (1989) calls 'the global Olympics'. In this arena, she says, winning firms are 'focused, fast, friendly and flexible'.

Networks and clustering

While Ohmae was surely right to emphasise the declining importance of national borders, Porter notes the strikingly national basis of many world-class industries. Writing more recently (1998), he observes: 'the enduring competitive advantages in a global economy lie increasingly in local things – knowledge, relationships, motivation – that distant rivals cannot match'. While commodity-type industries are increasingly footloose in their search for low-cost locations, high added-value activities are often concentrated in 'clusters'.

What exactly are clusters? Porter writes:

> **Clusters are geographic concentrations of interconnected companies and institutions in a particular field. Clusters encompass an array of linked industries and other entities important to competition.**

Included within a cluster might typically be specialised suppliers and providers of customised infrastructure. There might also be a closely connected network of customers who occupy different points on interlinked value chains. Often found interwoven with the edges of the cluster are complementary industries and governmental agencies that assist or facilitate the cluster as a whole.

This new recognition of localisation as a foundation for competitive advantage runs contrary to some obvious arguments. In today's business environment, location might have been expected to matter less: transport costs are decreasing, the 'weight' of output is falling, while telecommunications links are cheap and ubiquitous. But as Kay (1994) points out, although financial information is instantaneously available anywhere in the world, 'the financial services industry remains concentrated in tiny areas of East London and Lower Manhatten'.

Kay's explanation echoes Porter's in the focus on localised networks, but he has significant observations to make about the cultural and psychological basis of these intangible entities. The effective transfer of skills and knowledge, and the building of trust between people and organisations are critical. So is tacit knowledge that may be industry- or culture-specific: insights and capabilities that are transferred without any act of discernible communication. Despite the new technology that seems to make distance irrelevant, people together have the capacity to create things that would never otherwise be – or, as Kay aptly puts it, 'there are still things that are done best by people who find themselves frequently in the same room'.

Toyota

At a time when the reputation of the British car industry was perhaps at its lowest point, Toyota ran the advertising strapline: 'Everything keeps going right'.

A key factor in the secret of Toyota's global success is its main location. The company is the downstream centre of a *kairatsu*, an associated network of independent suppliers localised around the car firm's main plant at Nagoya. Toyota's suppliers have not clustered in this way to cut the cost of transport – American car manufacturers actually drive down costs by having supply plants dispersed across huge distances. The *kairatsu* brings together managers of Toyota and its supplier firms in a web of relationships that are based on trust and mutual knowledge. It has formed a basis for the classic elements in lean production: right-first-time quality, just-in-time stock delivery, continuous improvement and shorter model development times.

Based on: John Kay ESRC Lecture, 1994

The future

In bulk and mass markets, globalised firms are likely to remain very large. It is also likely that more global brands will emerge and that the strongest of these will be largely standardised in all parts of the world. But small firms with global reach are exploiting the opportunites offered by cheap telecommunications and e-commerce.

It is highly probable that the world economy will become more integrated and that specialisation by countries, regions and cities will extend further. The internet and allied technolgy do not recognise national borders and cyberspace is stateless. But people do inhabit real places that sustain a distinctive culture. It is quite possible that as the borders of nation states become – in economic terms – less important, the demand for distinctively local products will increase. Ohmae's injunction to 'think global, act local' may take on a new meaning.

37 Stakeholding and accountability

Overview

It is clear that business activity incurs costs and confers benefits – typically social or environmental – that are not reflected in conventional management or accounting terms. The result is that business decisions and market verdicts are arguably based on incomplete evidence. This raises real problems regarding the ways in which these negative and positive flows of value should be brought inside the framework of a market economy.

The nature of business responsibility is also open to question. Generally responsibility is attached to ownership or control, yet these conceptual points of reference are increasingly difficult to locate in the business world of today. This raises the question of a firm's underlying purpose. In the traditional business worldview, it is always the interests of the owners or shareholders that are paramount. Challenging that view is the idea of stakeholding, where the firm's responsibilities are more complex and must be balanced across a range of interests. These are interactive and vary widely in their relative power to influence.

An increasing number of firms are considering not only the sustainability of their competitive advantage, but also the sustainability of their interaction with the natural and social environment. The emergence of reporting and auditing in this respect is an important development.

External costs and benefits

We have seen that if the operating profit arising from a business activity exceeds the opportunity cost of the relevant capital employed, then net value is being added and the activity is justified. But is it?

Profit ... or a loss?

Suppose that a company is producing AA size dry cell batteries for the budget end of the market. The unit cost of each six-battery pack is £1.10 and they sell for £1.25 each. Their production is therefore profitable on a 12 per cent margin. This gives rise to an overall rate of return that exceeds the opportunity cost of capital.

Meanwhile, research indicates that the environmental costs in production and eventual disposal of the batteries amount to 20p per pack.

Is production justified?

This simple example is a Pandora's Box for the market economy. The company's costs in this calculation are the usual accounting ones – the variable costs of production and the fixed costs of running the business. As such, these are costs that the company has legally accrued and arise from operations in its private domain. Any other costs associated with its product and incurred *externally* (e.g. relating to air and water pollution or waste disposal) do not enter its calculations. This is perfectly rational from the company's point of view; but from the perspective of society as a whole, it may make less sense.

All business activity, through its interaction with the world around it, continually generates external costs – and benefits. These costs include environmental impacts and many other social effects such as accidents, noise, congestion and stress. External benefits are equally absent from company accounts but might include recreational facilities, transport links or the social value of rural shops.

If we were to add social costs and benefits to private costs and benefits, it is clear that the 'profitability' of every product would be significantly different. Many goods and services would become more costly and their selling price would rise. The result would be a fall in sales and a reduction in output. Substitutes would be found for products carrying heavy external costs. Meanwhile, a few products carrying net external benefits would cost less and be consumed more. The market, in short, would be signalling different verdicts if it was connected to external as well as internal cost data.

A vast number of awkward questions move on to the agenda. For example, since air travel creates noise and air pollution among other external costs, are 'cheap' European air fares the bargain that they appear to be? If a bus can relieve the roads of up to forty vehicles, then should its fares not reflect some of the external benefits it is able to generate? If the petrol works out at less than the train fare, is it better value for one person to drive their large car from London to Birmingham and back or not?

In practice, many sources of the more serious external costs that might arise in a completely free market system are prohibited or regulated by law. This prevents offending costs from being incurred, but does not allow individual impacts to be considered on their merits. For example, tight controls on air pollution might be welcomed by the residents of a town until they discovered that a major local employer would be closing and moving abroad due to those controls.

The alternative is to find ways to internalise some of the external costs incurred by business activity. In a sense, taxation and business rates already perform this function, but they are blunt instruments in responding to external costs and benefits. No incentive is provided to consume less or more of one product relative to another. So far any exceptions are rather limited. The lower rate of duty on unleaded petrol and the more recent landfill tax are examples. Subsidies paid to some public transport operators recognise that they can generate external benefits.

In a wider context, the government provides certain services free (e.g. healthcare and education) or at substantially subsidised rates (e.g. the arts). 'Merit goods' of this kind have privileged status because their consumption is judged to have intrinsic value and to yield external benefits.

Meanwhile the external costs and benefits of most business decisions go unrecognised and uncalculated. However, major investment decisions in the public sector can be subject to a cost-benefit analysis. Introduced in the 1960s, this technique attempts to place money values on the social and environmental impacts of a given project. These are then combined with the conventional accounting costs and benefits to give a net outcome that reflects the project's overall worth to society.

Unfortunately, assigning values to external costs and benefits is very problematic. How do we place value on things of value that are not traded? Consider landscape, wildlife habitat or historic buildings, for example. These attract widely divergent valuations from different people. And can they be treated like a commodity available for sale? Do they have some intrinsic value?

Despite the problems, decisions about at least the relative value of non-traded assets still have to be made. Cost-benefit analysis at least has the virtue that it highlights external costs and benefits and stimulates a debate about their value.

Who is the business?

When a business starts life, the owner clearly represents its identity. In law, too, the sole trader *is* the firm. Incorporation as a private company marks a subtle change. Although a small family group typically owns the shares and continues to run the business, a company exists in its own right. 'The company' is a legal person: it owns property, enjoys limited liability and can sue and be sued.

Freeze-frame, for a moment, a private company of medium size. It might have 100 employees, and turn over £10 million on an asset base with a book value of £2 million. The equity stake is £1.5 million and the banks are owed £500 000.

To whom are the directors responsible? The conventional answer would be the shareholders or owners. But they have legal obligations to their creditors. They may well recognise moral obligations to their employees and customers. Many companies also acknowledge some sense of duty towards the communities in which they operate.

These are the elements of corporate responsibility. They are configured with more complexity if the firm expands and 'goes public'. The status of 'public limited company' means that the company's shares can be sold to the general public and to financial institutions. Who now 'is' this firm? To whom is 'it' responsible?

The shareholders do not expect to run the business and would be far too numerous to do so anyway. Instead, they elect a board of directors to manage the business and to represent their interests. Those directors then hire a team of managers who in turn appoint more managers who employ lower-level staff. Meanwhile, the shares are traded on the Stock Exchange and thus part of the firm's ownership constantly changes. Typically, three-quarters of the shares are owned by insurance companies, pension funds and investment trusts who are themselves represented by fund managers.

Perhaps further expansion gives the firm a worldwide presence. The company establishes registered subsidiaries in many other countries. Its shares are quoted on Wall Street. Turnover and assets are expressed in billions of pounds and dollars. The original founding family have sold their shares and the company changes its name. The question 'Who is the firm?' has retreated again.

Stockholders or stakeholders

If businessmen do have a social responsibility other than maximising profits for their shareholders, how are they to know what it is? Can self-selected private individuals decide what the social interest is?

There is only one social responsibility of business – to use its resources and engage in activities designed to increase its profits so long as it stays within the rules of the game, engages in open and free competition, without deception or fraud.

Source: Milton Friedman Capitalism and Freedom *(University of Chicago Press, 1962)*

Today companies must become more systemic in their outlook. Business is about relationships and most business decisions have implications for a variety of stakeholders whose support is essential for long-term prosperity. This means that all companies must focus on the protection of their employees and contractors, the needs of their local communities and the agendas of their host governments. It also dictates that they strive to minimise the environmental impact of their operations and activities.

Source: Annual Report (2002) of Invensys, multinational producer of power, control and automation systems

Friedman's view is the definitive argument for classic capitalism. The stockholders (or shareholders) are the owners of the company and carry the financial risk attached to their investment. Directors and managers should confine themselves to what they do best – namely, use of the firm's available resources in adding value. The basic legal constraints in this process and any ultimate redistribution of income and wealth are matters for government.

The contrasting view recognises that the modern company actually represents a complex and systemic coalition of interests. In this perspective the providers of capital are a legitimate interest group who take their place alongside others. Many individuals and organisations have some 'stake' in the firm's performance and are affected by its decisions. Meanwhile, the realities of competitive markets ensure that profitability and adding value must be the major priority. A basic stakeholder model is shown below:

Stakeholder groups

Stakeholder	Interest
Shareholders	Dividends; share price; ethical conduct
Directors	Remuneration; share options; personal careers
Employees	Job security; pay and rewards; career development; fair treatment; job satisfaction
Creditors	Prompt and reliable repayment of debt plus any interest
Suppliers	Future orders; related investment; cash flow

Customers	Good value; product availability; consumer rights
Community	Safety; local spending; sponsorship and donations
Society	Environmental protection; ethical standards
Government	Payment of taxes; employment and training; export sales

Social and environmental pressures

The relative strength of stakeholder groups varies widely between firms and over time. However, some important trends have emerged since the 1980s. Issues of social and environmental responsibility have moved up the agenda in most boardrooms. This has partly been driven by the activities of pressure groups. Although their membership is mainly relatively small, skilled use of media attention and latent public sympathy with their cause have often proved a powerful combination.

Larger groups, such as Greenpeace and Friends of the Earth have developed an influential voice in the public debate over corporate responsibility. Some firms, such as Shell, have entered into direct discussions with pressure groups. This followed international protest in 1995 over disposal of the Brent Spar oil storage platform. Ethical investment funds – in Britain alone, controlling the use of over £17 billion by 2001 – have also been vocal in urging firms to take responsibility for the wider implications of their competitive strategy.

The second factor in this trend has been the growing importance for many firms of reputation and brand equity. For some companies the capacity of names and brands to express moral as well as cultural meaning has become vital to every strategy for adding value. Major court cases have been fought in defence of reputation (e.g. Body Shop versus Channel 4, 1996; McDonald's and the 'McLibel' affair, 1994–96), and ensuring the probity of a brand has become essential. This has introduced the concept of traceability, where the upstream origins of a product are evaluated on environmental or ethical grounds. In these ways corporate responsibility now feeds directly into the value chain.

Employees, suppliers and customers

Until the 1980s, employees as stakeholders made their influence felt through trade unions or participative mechanisms within the firm. In many large firms there was a pluralist frame of reference, meaning an acceptance that different interest groups – including employees – would pursue different objectives. The HRM movement (see Chapter 23) has thrown the emphasis strongly towards a more unitary frame where all employees are expected to share the company's goals. Often the reciprocal expectation of employees has been the status of stakeholders in the enterprise. This has not always been fulfilled.

Meanwhile, the status and involvement of suppliers as stakeholders have been rising as supply chains become more collaborative. Working with a smaller supplier base to ensure just-in-time inventory cycles, quality standards and product development has implied a tacit partnership in which neither side wishes to be a defaulter.

Customers are also being drawn into a closer relationship with firms. The sharpening of strategic fit has meant getting closer to the customer base. Most firms no longer 'feed' output into a mass market, and an increasing number expect to customise their product on the basis of closely understanding the customer's needs. As these needs become more intangible and experiential, so this understanding needs to be more intimate and based on a degree of trust. Customers are increasingly being invited to get involved in the design and production process and are less often treated as the passive recipients of anonymous products.

Shareholders

The attitude of the shareholders themselves is changing too. Until the 1990s, the split between ownership and control had led to a fairly institutionalised disengagement of most shareholders from any levers of influence over the company's affairs. Change was stimulated by the ethical investment movement and the use of share purchase as a platform from which to criticise the directors of firms with a poor environmental or ethical reputation.

Potentially even more significant has been the tendency of fund managers to become more active in scrutinising and questioning the performance of the companies in which they invest. In most public companies a fairly small number of fund managers control overwhelming voting power, which they have often allowed to be used on a proxy basis in favour of the directors' recommendations. As fund managers start to have a higher profile in pursuit of better returns or reduced risk, so lines of accountability may strengthen and shareholders could become more effective in their 'ultimate stakeholder' role.

Directors

In theory, the directors of a company are appointed by its shareholders to run the business on their behalf. In practice, the board of directors is the defining power centre in a company. Although its authority is ultimately only licensed, the board is effectively autonomous in making most strategic decisions. Only in times of crisis and high-profile criticism of directors does shareholder power become a decisive factor. Even then the block votes of the institutions normally endorse the directors' decisions. Indeed, in many ways the board is often more accountable through the media than through the shareholders.

A basic problem is the extent of alignment between director and shareholder interests. Both groups generally share the broad objectives of profitability and growth, and the increased use of performance-related bonuses and share options encourage directors to focus on results. However, directors have careers to consider and may be motivated by the pursuit of personal power and the aggrandisement of status. This is often thought to be a major factor in corporate mergers, two-thirds of which, according to a US study (Ravenscraft and Scherer, 1987), actually lead to a deterioration in overall performance.

Following a spate of highly publicised corporate failures in the early 1990s and the discovery of major fraud at Maxwell Communications Corporation, the Cadbury Committee produced a report on corporate governance. This recommended that the positions of CEO and Chairman should not be held by the same person and advocated an enhanced role for non-executive directors. These part-time directors without an operating portfolio provide advice and guidance based on experience, and make independent judgements on such issues as directors' remuneration. However, many non-executives sit on a number of boards in a kind of interlocking network that arguably becomes too self-referential.

Meanwhile, the collapse of Enron and WorldCom in 2001 has brought renewed debate on corporate accountability and illustrated the lack of transparancy in the flow of information between directors and owners. Galbraith (2002) argues that complex modern corporations 'have grown out of effective control by the owners, the stockholders, into nearly absolute control by the management and the individuals recruited by the management'.

Stakeholding and society

┌─ Tesco ◄───

Founded in 1932 by Jack Cohen, Tesco has expanded rapidly over the last ten years, overtaking its greatest rival, Sainsbury's, and establishing an international presence.

	1994	1996	1998	2000	2002
Sales £m	10 101	13 887	17 158	20 988	26 337
Profit £m	617	774	965	1 174	1 484

Tesco is owned by its 240 000 shareholders, including the five major institutional investors who together hold 68 per cent of the issued shares. The company is run by 15 directors and about 700 managers. They in turn organise the work of 135 000 employees, a full 60 per cent of whom own company shares. Tesco buys goods from over 10 000 suppliers, while the store is the main source of food and household products for at least five million families. The business rates paid by Tesco are a major source of revenue for local authorities all over the country. In addition, the company has an active policy for assisting the communities in which it operates. Meanwhile, sales outside the UK were worth £1650 million in 2002 and growing rapidly.

In many cases, as at Tesco, stakeholder groups have overlapping identities. For example, an individual may be an employee, a shareholder and a customer. Indeed, Tesco is an illustration of how business organisations become embedded in the network of human and institutional relationships that make up a society.

Friedman's elevation of the shareholder interest to the exclusion of all others can be criticised on the grounds that in the modern public company, ownership has become too diffuse to support the classic notion of proprietorial capitalism. Not only are nearly 30 per cent of the UK adult population direct shareholders, but almost everyone has indirect investments through insurance policies, pensions and savings schemes. In effect, financial institutions have become a clearing house for wealth-creating investment that brings benefit to all in the form of direct returns, as well as providing employment, new technologies and better products.

On the other hand, there remains the argument that managers should confine themselves to the pursuit of business objectives since this is the subject of their expertise. This begs the question of how far the stakeholder model is valid. Insofar as it has validity, senior managers actually need the ability to resolve the competing claims of stakeholders and their representatives.

Towards sustainability?

Perhaps the clearest paradigm for long-term environmental and social responsibility is the concept of sustainability. This is based on the idea that business activity should generally be designed and managed so that its activities today do not jeopardise equivalent activities in the future. At the heart of the concept is the belief that business should not deplete its environmental capital. Any properly managed business expects to finance its productive process mainly from ongoing revenue. Inevitably it will also depreciate its capital stock, but will generally replace the resources consumed in this way through its programme of investment. To finance production mainly by running down capital assets would be unsustainable. As Pearce (1989) argues, the parallel need is to ensure that the economy of today at least sustains the stock of natural capital.

Business sustainability is a systems-led view of environmental and social responsibility. It stresses the interdependence between the economy and the natural and social environment within which that economic activity takes place. Business units are microsystems continuously interacting with this much more broadly defined macrosystem. It is argued that firms need a long-term strategy for their relationship with this wider environment that is inseparable from their corporate strategy as a whole.

Most major companies now have some written statement of environmental and social policy. A growing number publish regular reports on their environmental and social performance. These are usually based on an audit carried out by a specialist external agency. In this way accountability is more explicit and more transparent. It also makes it possible to analyse and evaluate progress towards declared objectives.

Looking to the future, we have seen that projections of complex phenomena are notoriously unreliable. Economic growth, globalisation and the spread of industrialisation could continue to place a spiralling burden on the natural environment. In the long run, for example, a rise in Chinese and Indian living standards, even to those of the West in 2000, would add an environmental burden equivalent to seven more US economies or 33 more UK economies at the same date.

On the other hand, there are also some emergent trends pointing in the other direction. New technology is improving efficiency in the use of resources and reducing the incidence of toxins in the cycle of production and consumption. The whole concept of quality is also beginning to embrace sustainable practices, driven by tightening regulation but also by markets. For a growing proportion of firms at all stages in the supply chain, brand equity is significantly dependent on environmental performance.

Finally, it is products and production processes with low environmental impact that are increasingly adding value. This rise of the weightless economy (see Chapter 35) is tending to reduce the environmental cost of new economic growth. The growing tendency to add value through micro-technology, personal service or managed experience all helps to reduce the ratio between economic growth and environmental cost.

38 Ethics and markets

Overview

The system of law provides a set of boundaries within which firms are obliged to operate. Many firms and individual employees apply their own ethical standards that are usually more exacting than the law. This may restrict commercial opportunity or it may establish higher standards of underlying quality.

Corporate ethics have a higher profile today in a climate of increased demand for accountability. Some organisations have responded with written codes of conduct, but it is usually the underlying culture that is most influential in setting ethical standards.

In conclusion, some strengths and weaknesses of a market economy are summarised. These highlight the importance of business ethics and the scope for intelligent regulation. The criteria for ultimate judgements about business are difficult to agree on, but the agenda for debate is likely to keep running.

Nature of business ethics

When Scrooge, in Dickens' *A Christmas Carol*, enforces the harsh terms of Bob Critchett's employment, there is no suggestion that he's breaking the law. He is only tightening the screw of his business to the legal limits in order to maximise, as he sees it, efficiency and profit. In his dreams that follow, Scrooge is put through a fantasy gala of business ethics. The ghosts that he is obliged to follow indicate how ethical awareness is a more demanding (and ultimately more rewarding) master than the law.

The law is the baseline for individual and corporate behaviour. Built above that in almost every organisation is a network of agreements and understandings, mostly unwritten and based on trust. Indeed, this is the basis of effective relationships among firms and individuals. It allows flexibility and discretion and expresses the goodwill that is the underpinning of loyalty and commitment.

Ethical standards of this kind are found in all stakeholder relationships. The framework of interaction between stakeholder and a firm is defined by the mutual establishment of ethical standards.

What is the origin, the ultimate justification, of ethical standards in business? There is a basic distinction to be made between ethics as a set of intrinsic values and ethics as a repertoire of instrumental behaviour (Chryssides and Kaler, 1993). When ethics are beliefs held for their intrinsic value, they guide decisions with no regard for repayment or gain. An ethical business of this kind protects staff from redundancy, pays suppliers promptly or refuses to use wasteful packaging not because it is good for the business or its reputation, even in the long run – it does these things because it believes they are ethically right.

By contrast, another firm might make exactly the same decisions (and might even go further in an 'ethical' direction), but its reasons are instrumental – it will attract loyal staff, it will gain creditworthiness, it will add value through environmental credentials. In practice, of course, most firms work with a mix of both motives. Does the Co-operative Bank uphold ethical standards because of its beliefs, or because such standards provide a value-adding source of differentiation? The difference matters. Instrumental standards in any business will usually be abandoned if their commercial value disappears or moves into reverse.

Development of business ethics

Ethical or religious beliefs have always been a force in business but have only been a defining feature of certain firms. They have been the basis of business philanthropy, and some famous firms have a long tradition of promoting social responsibility on such grounds. Cadbury's, Rowntree's, Pilkington's and Lever Brothers were typical of the large firms that built their business empires on strictly ethical foundations. Other firms, such as Marks & Spencer, Boots or Huntley and Palmer's became known as good employers and honest traders. These characteristics get deeply engrained in a firm's culture and survive through successive generations of management. The ability to infuse behaviour with ethical standards becomes a distinctive capability that, in the 'organisational fibre', can be a tough strand of competitive advantage.

Despite these examples, business ethics as a subject remained peripheral during the decades following the Second World War. 'Positive economics' and 'scientific decision making' made little if any reference to ethical behaviour. Business became an objective machine, the operation of which was to be optimised within legal and human 'constraints'. If anything, there was a view that personal and business ethics existed in distinct worlds and that trying to apply personal standards to business problems was naïve and unrealistic. Carr (1968) approvingly compares the ethics of business to a game of poker. Cheating or gaining unfair advantage are not acceptable, but:

> **No one expects poker to be played on the ethical principles preached in churches. In poker it is right and proper to bluff a player out of the rewards of being dealt a good hand. ... If one shows mercy to a loser in poker, it is a personal gesture, divorced from the rules of the game.**

Source: Harvard Business Review *January–February 1968*

During the 1980s a new mood developed. A number of serious accidents highlighted the issue of corporate responsibility. Major cases of fraudulent accounting and embezzlement had emerged. Criticism of large companies for the environmental damage that they were inflicting mounted steadily. Questions about multinational companies and human rights were being asked with a new insistence.

This was also a time of privatisation and contracting out of public sector services. Meanwhile, the state was moving back from the responsibility of macroeconomic management towards a more modest role of creating an economic climate favourable to business enterprise. With the private sector becoming responsible for many areas of national life that had been the responsibility of the state, there was arguably a new urgency about ethical standards.

Setting ethical standards

In recent years, many firms have adopted ethical codes of practice and formal statements about environmental and social responsibility. In practice, the firm's underlying culture is usually the most important determinant of actual behaviour. However, a written statement can signal an intention to bring about a change in culture (see Chapter 31). For companies operating worldwide, differing social and economic norms can pose real problems. What, for example, is the proper age definition of child labour? And what is a fair wage? Much has to be left to interpretation within the relevant context. Inevitably this allows some firms to take a weak or arguably negligent ethical stance on such crucial issues as basic human rights.

There is a growing argument that ethical standards can add value and are inherent in notions of excellence and quality. When, for example, customers make a buying decision in Boots, they are valuing the competence, security and ethical probity that they perceive as represented by the company. These intangible factors contained within a corporate identity become extremely valuable and an enduring source of competitive advantage. It is not surprising that firms vigorously defend such qualities and work hard to avoid the spotlight of negative media attention.

The ethical stance of a firm is greatly influenced by its top management, and in particular by the CEO. They in turn are often strongly affected by the norms of the industry, and especially by the assumptions of any dominant firms or market leaders. The intensity of competition in the industry can also be an important factor. Hartley (1993) stresses this point, particularly where a business cannot differentiate its products or is struggling to secure its place in the market.

Much also depends on the relative power of stakeholders and their own ethical positions. If end-consumers are placing an increasing value on ethical standards, then this influence is likely to spread up the relevant supply chains. On the other hand, if major institutional shareholders are demanding an early improvement in profitability and performance ratios, then the longer-term advantages of ethical standards can be sacrificed to short-termism.

Market myopia?

Markets do not make moral judgements. The price mechanism simply permits transactions to take place when both parties anticipate a net gain that exceeds the opportunity cost of their expenditure. The price charged by firms is built from market-determined costs and takes no account of ethical or human values.

Although markets are certainly very effective in responding to customer preferences, their allocation of resources reflects the inequality of incomes. The more that markets are left to take their own course, the more unequal the distribution of incomes tends to become. The result is an abundance of luxury goods and services but a relative shortage of generic necessities. Thus, the idea of 'consumer sovereignty' applies to a world where, as ever, only some are kings.

Markets enthrone individuals but not communities. As individuals people are at liberty to earn as much as they are able and to spend it how they wish. But to buy goods and services collectively with other people, and to share the benefits, requires a political process and not a market. The result has often been what Galbraith (1958) famously called 'private affluence and public squalor'.

As we saw in Chapter 37, non-renewable natural resources are treated by market economies as a current asset and not a capital stock. A resource such as oil, which took millions of years to form, is used at a price that takes no account of possible long-term shortages or the pollution caused by its conversion into energy. In any case, much environmental capital, such as animal habitats or the natural landscape, is unpriced and treated by firms as though it were 'free'. This leads to over-consumption, with negative consequences extending into the long-term future.

As Pearce (1989) points out, safeguarding the future is liable to be compromised by the logic of discounting (see Chapter 30) which can have some questionable implications. Suppose, for example, that spending just £1 million today on a safety device in nuclear waste disposal would avert a £1 billion problem in 50 years' time – strangely, the safety device would be uneconomic. Even at a 5 per cent discount rate, the present value of that future disaster is less than £1 million at current costs of capital. This heavy discount on the long-term future has problematic implications for environmental protection and the conservation of natural resources.

Reflections

Business organisations are probably about as fallible as human nature. When we hold up a mirror to business behaviour we may, perhaps, see ourselves – as consumers, as employees, as investors.

Free markets are wasteful and adversarial. They identify weaknesses in people and exploit them. They foster materialism and celebrate greed. They are essentially amoral. They wish to advance into every area of human desire and turn it into a commodity. They concentrate power. They shower winners with rewards and disburse to losers the absolute minimum.

Yet free markets have also raised living standards beyond the most optimistic projections of earlier generations. Remorselessly they stimulate efficiency and drive enterprise to match wants. They spur innovation in a permanent sponsorship of creativity. They require and energise political freedom. They generate fantastic cultural energy. They are a self-organising miracle directing myriad flows of resources with an effortless insight that no individual or organisation could ever conceive.

Business can never be fully explained but it will always be fascinating.

CITY OF WOLVERHAMPTON COLLEGE

References and further reading

Chapter 1

Kanter, R. M. (1989) *When Giants Learn to Dance*, New York and London: Simon & Schuster

Chapter 2

Drucker, P. F. (1954) *The Practice of Management* New York: Harper & Row

Fayol, H. (1949) *Industrial and General Management*, London: Pitman. Translated by Constance Storrs from the original *Administration Industrielle et Générale* (1916)

Handy, C. (1989) *The Age of Unreason*, London: Business Books; Arrow

Mintzberg, H. (1973) The Nature of Managerial Work New York: Harper & Row

Mintzberg, H. (1975) 'The Manager's Job: Folklore and Fact' Cambridge, Mass.: *Harvard Business Review* (July/August)

Pascale, R. T. and Athos, A. (1981) *The Art of Japanese Management*, New York: Simon & Schuster; London: Allen Lane, Penguin Books

Peters, T. and Waterman, R. H. Jr. (1982) *In Search of Excellence*, New York and London: Harper & Row

Taylor, F. W. (1913) *The Principles of Scientific Management*, New York: Harper & Row

Chapter 3

Peters, T. and Waterman, R. H. Jr. (1982) *In Search of Excellence*, New York and London: Harper & Row

Chapter 4

Chapter 5

Checkland, P. (1981) *Systems Thinking, Systems Practice,* Chichester: John Wiley

Peters, T. (1994) *The Tom Peters Seminar: Crazy Times Call for Crazy Organisations,* New York: Vintage; London: Macmillan

Porter, M. E. (1985) *Competitive Advantage*, New York: Free Press

Porter, M. E. (1996) 'What is strategy?' Cambridge, Mass.: *Harvard Business Review* (November/December)

Chapter 6

Friedman, M. (1962) *Capitalism and Freedom* Chicago: University of Chicago Press

Friedman, M. (1980) 'Freedom of Choice' *The Listener*, February 1980. BBC Publications

Kay, J. (1993) *The Foundations of Corporate Success*. Oxford: Oxford University Press

Chapter 7

Porter, M. E. (1980) *Competitive Strategy*. New York: Free Press

Prahalad, C. K. and Hamel, G. (1990) The Core Competence of the Corporation. Cambridge, Mass.: *Harvard Business Review* (May/June)

Mintzberg, H. (1991) *The Strategy Process: Concepts, Concepts, Cases* (with Quinn, J. B. and Ghosal, S.) 2nd edition Eaglewood Cliffs, NJ: Prentice Hall

Chapter 8
Prahalad, C. K. and Hamel, G. (1994) *Competing for the Future*. Boston: Harvard Business School Press
Hamel, G. 'Strategy as Revolution' Cambridge, Mass.: *Harvard Business Review*
Hamel, G. (2000) *Leading the Revolution*. Boston: Harvard Business School Press
Kay, J. (1993) *The Foundations of Corporate Success*. Oxford: Oxford University Press

Chapter 9
Ansoff, H. I. *Corporate Strategy*, New York: McGraw Hill
Chandler, A. D. (1962) *Strategy and Structure*, Massachusetts: MIT Press
Drucker, P. F. (1954) *The Practice of Management* New York: Harper & Row
Fayol, H. (1949) *Industrial and General Management*, London: Pitman. Translated by Constance Storrs from the original *Administration Industrielle et Générale* (1916)
Friedman, M. (1962) *Capitalism and Freedom*. Chicago: University of Chicago Press
Mintzberg, H. (1987) 'Crafting Strategy', Cambridge, Mass.: *Harvard Business Review* (July/August)
Mintzberg, H. (1989)*Mintzberg on Management*, New York: The Free Press; London: Collier Macmillan
Pascale, R. T. and Athos, A. (1981) *The Art of Japanese Management*, New York: Simon & Schuster; London: Allen Lane, Penguin Books
Peters, T. and Waterman, R. H. Jr. (1982) *In Search of Excellence*, New York and London: Harper & Row
Porter, M. E. (1980) *Competitive Strategy*. New York: Free Press
Porter, M. E. (1985) *Competitive Advantage*, New York: Free Press
Simon, H. (1960) *The New Science of Management Decision*, New York: Harper & Row

Chapter 10
Miles, R. E. and Snow, C. C. (1984) 'Fit, Failure and The Hall of Fame' *California Management Review* Vol. XXVI, No. 3 (Spring)
Peters, T. and Waterman, R. H. Jr. (1982) *In Search of Excellence*, New York and London: Harper & Row
Porter, M. E. (1980) *Competitive Strategy*. New York: Free Press
Porter, M. E. (1985) *Competitive Advantage*, New York: Free Press
Sull, D. N. (1999) 'Why Good Companies Go Bad', Cambridge, Mass.: *Harvard Business Review* (July/August)

Chapter 11
Deal, T. and Kennedy, A. (1982) *Corporate Cultures*, Reading, Mass.: Addison-Wesley
Porter, M. E. (1980) *Competitive Strategy*. New York: Free Press
Porter, M. E. (1996) 'What is strategy?' Cambridge, Mass.: *Harvard Business Review* (November/December)

Chapter 12
Keynes, J. M. (1936) *The General Theory of Employment, Interest and Money*, London: Macmillan
Ormerod, P. (1998) *Butterfly Economics*, London: Faber and Faber

Chapter 13

Chapter 14

Drucker, P. F. (1954) *The Practice of Management* New York: Harper & Row

Levitt, T. (1960) 'Marketing Myopia', Cambridge, Mass.: *Harvard Business Review* (July/August)

Chapter 15

Kotler, P. *et al.* (1980, 1996) *Principles of Marketing*, Eaglewood Cliffs, NJ: Prentice Hall; Hemel Hempstead, UK: Prentice Hall Europe

Ries, A. and Trout, J. (1981) *Positioning: The Battle for Your Mind*, New York: McGraw-Hill

Chapter 16

Chapter 17

Kotler, P. (1987) *Marketing – An Introduction,* Eaglewood Cliffs, NJ: Prentice Hall

McCarthy, E. J. (1960) *Basic Marketing: A Managerial Approach*, Homewood, IL.: Irwin

Chapter 18

Chapter 19

Kim, W. C. and Mauborgne, R. (1999) 'Creating New Market Space', Cambridge, Mass.: *Harvard Business Review* (January/February)

Ohmae, K. (1990) *The Borderless World*, London: Collins

Porter, M. E. (1985) *Competitive Advantage*, New York: Free Press

Chapter 20

Chapter 21

Crosby, P. B. (1979) *Quality is Free* New York: McGraw-Hill

Chapter 22

Peters, T. and Waterman R. H. Jr. (1982) *In Search of Excellence*, New York and London: Harper & Row

Prahalad, C. K. and Hamel, G. (1990) 'The Core Competence of the Corporation', Cambridge, Mass.: *Harvard Business Review* (May/June)

Schonberger, R. J. (1990) *Building a Chain of Customers*, New York: The Free Press; London: Business Books

Chapter 23

Handy, C. (1989) *The Age of Unreason*, London: Business Books; Arrow

Herzberg, F., Mausner, B. Snyderman, B. (1959) *The Motivation to Work*, New York: Wiley

McGregor, D (1960) *The Human Side of Enterprise,* New York: McGraw-Hill

Chapter 24

Handy, C. (1989) *The Age of Unreason*, London: Business Books; Arrow

Hammer, J. and Champy, J. *Reengineering the Corporation*, New York: HarperCollins; London: Nicholas Brealey

Kanter, R. M. (1989) *When Giants Learn to Dance*, New York and London: Simon & Schuster

Peters, T. (1987) *Thriving on Chaos*, New York: Alfred A. Knopf; London: Macmillan

Taylor, F. W. (1913) *The Principles of Scientific Management*, New York: Harper & Row

Chapter 25
Alderfer, C. P. (1972) *Existence, Relatedness and Growth*, New York: Free Press
Herzberg, F., Mausner, B. Snyderman, B. (1959) *The Motivation to Work*, New York: Wiley
Herzberg, F. (1968) One More Time: How Do You Motivate Employees? Cambridge, Mass.:
    Harvard Business Review (January/February)
Kanter, R. M. (1977) *Men and Women of the Corporation*, New York: Basic Books
McClelland, D. C. (1961) *The Achieving Society,* New York: Van Nostrand Reinhold
McGregor, D (1960) *The Human Side of Enterprise,* New York: McGraw-Hill
Maslow, A. H. (1954) *Motivation and Personality*, New York: Harper and Row
Mayo, E. (1933) *The Human Problems of an Industrial Civilisation*, New York and London: Macmillan
Mayo, E. (1949) *The Social Problems of an Industrial Civilisation*, Cambridge, MA.: Harvard
    University Press; London: Routledge and Kegan Paul
Ouchi, W. G. *Theory Z,* Reading, MA.: Addison-Wesley
Pascale, R. T. (1990) *Managing on the Edge*, New York: Simon and Schuster; London: Viking
Peters, T. and Waterman R. H. Jr. (1982) *In Search of Excellence*, New York and London: Harper &
    Row
Peters, T. (1987) *Thriving on Chaos*, New York: Alfred A. Knopf; London: Macmillan
Porter, L. W. and Lawler, E. E. (1968) *Managerial Attitudes and Performance*, Homewood, IL.:
    Irwin-Dorsey
Schein, E. H. (1980) *Organisational Psychology*, Englewood Cliffs, New Jersey: Prentice-Hall
Taylor, F. W. (1913) *The Principles of Scientific Management*, New York: Harper & Row
Vroom, V. H. (1964) *Work and Motivation*, New York: John Wiley & Sons

Chapter 26
Adair, J. (1973) *The Action-Centred Leader*, London: McGraw-Hill
Belbin, M. (1981) *Management Teams: Why They Succeed or Fail*, London: Heinemann
Bennis, W. (1989) *On Becoming a Leader*, Reading, MA.: Addison-Wesley; London: Business Books
Fiedler, F. A. (1967) *A Theory of Leadership Effectiveness*, New York: McGraw-Hill
Gladwell, M. (2000) *The Tipping Point*, London: Little, Brown & Co.
McGregor, D. (1960) *The Human Side of Enterprise,* New York: McGraw-Hill
Mayo, E. (1949) *The Social Problems of an Industrial Civilisation*, Cambridge, MA.: Harvard
    University Press; London: Routledge and Kegan Paul
Peters, T. (1987) *Thriving on Chaos*, New York: Alfred A. Knopf; London: Macmillan
Schonberger, R. J. (1982) *Japanese Manufacturing Techniques,* New York: The Free Press
Senge, P. (1990) *The Fifth Discipline: The Art and Practice of the Learning Organisation,* New York:
    Doubleday; (1992) London: Century

Chapter 27
de Geus, A. (1997) *The Living Company* London: Nicholas Brealey

Chapter 28

Chapter 29
Kaplan, R. S. and Norton D. P. (1992) 'The Balanced Scorecard: Measures that Drive Performance',
    Cambridge, Mass.: *Harvard Business Review* (January/February)
Kay, J. (1993) *The Foundations of Corporate Success*. Oxford: Oxford University Press

Kay, J. (2002) *The Financial Times*, 29 June

Chapter 30
Ross, S. A. (1976) 'The Arbitrage Theory of Capital Asset Pricing', *Journal of Economic Theory*, Vol. 13, No. 3

Chapter 31
Deal, T. and Kennedy, A. (1982) *Corporate Cultures*, Reading, Mass.: Addison-Wesley

Handy, C. (1976) *Understanding Organisations*, London: Penguin Books

Harrison, R. (1972) 'How to Describe Your Organisation' Cambridge, Mass.: *Harvard Business Review* (September/October)

Hofstede, G. (1991) *Cultures and Organisations: Software of the Mind*, Maidenhead, UK: McGraw-Hill

Lewin, K. (1951) *Field Theory in Social Science*, New York: Harper and Row

Miles, R. E. and Snow, C. C. (1978) *Organisational Strategy, Structure and Process*, New York: McGraw-Hill

Pascale, R. T. and Athos, A. (1981) *The Art of Japanese Management*, New York: Simon & Schuster; London: Allen Lane, Penguin Books

Pascale, R. T., Millemann, M. and Gioja, L. *Surfing the Edge of Chaos*, New York: Crown Publishing Group, Three Rivers Press

Peters, T. and Waterman, R. H. Jr. (1982) *In Search of Excellence*, New York and London: Harper & Row

Schein, E. H. (1985) *Organisational Culture and Leadership: A Dynamic View*, San Francisco: Jossey-Bass

Schein, E. H. (1991) 'What is Culture?' in P. J. Frost, L. F. Moore, M. R. Louis, C. C. Lundberg & J. Martin (eds.) *Reframing Organisational Culture,* Newbury Park, CA.: Sage

Stacey, R. (1996) *Complexity and Creativity in Organisations*, San Francisco: Berratt Koehler

Trist, E. L. and Bamforth, K. W. (1951) 'Some Social and Psychological Consequences of the Longwall Method of Coal Getting' *Human Relations* 4, pages 3-38

Chapter 32
Lewin, K. (1951) *Field Theory in Social Science*, New York: Harper and Row

Gladwell, M. (2000) *The Tipping Point*, London: Little, Brown & Co.

Chapter 33
De Bono, E. (1971) *Lateral Thinking for Management*, Maidenhead: McGraw-Hill; London: Penguin

De Geus, A. (1997) *The Living Company* London: Nicholas Brealey

Gordon, W. J. J. (1961) *Synectics: the Development of Creative Capacity*, New York: Harper & Row

Handy, C. (1989) *The Age of Unreason*, London: Business Books; Arrow

Hargadon, A. and Sutton, R. I. (2000) 'Building an Innovation Factory' Cambridge, Mass.: *Harvard Business Review* (May/June)

Hansen, M. T., Nohria, N. and Tierney, T. (1999) *What's Your Strategy for Managing Knowledge?*, Cambridge, Mass.: *Harvard Business Review* (March/April)

Osborn, A. F. (1953) *Applied Imagination, principles nad procedures of creative problem-solving*, New York: Charles Scribner's Sons

Pascale, R. T., Millemann, M. and Gioja, L. *Surfing the Edge of Chaos*, New York: Crown Publishing Group, Three Rivers Press

Rickards, T. (1999) *Creativity and the Management of Change*, Oxford: Blackwell

Senge, P. (1990) *The Fifth Discipline: The Art and Practice of the Learning Organisation,* New York: Doubleday; (1992) London: Century

Senge, P. (1997) 'Through the Eye of the Needle' in *Rethinking the Future* ed. R. Gibson, Sonoma, CA. and London: Nicholas Brealey

Wallas, G. (1970) 'The Art of Thought' in P. E. Vernon (ed.), *Creativity*, Harmondsworth: Penguin

Chapter 34

Gladwell, M. (2000) *The Tipping Point*, London: Little, Brown & Co.

Goleman, D. (1995) *Emotional Intelligence,* London: Bloomsbury

Kim, W. C. and Mauborgne, R. 'Creating New Market Space', Cambridge, Mass.: *Harvard Business Review* (January/February)

Nguyen Huy, Q. (2001) 'In Praise of Middle Managers', Cambridge, Mass.: *Harvard Business Review* (September)

Peters, T. (1994) *The Tom Peters Seminar: Crazy Times Call for Crazy Organisations,* New York: Vintage; London: Macmillan

Porter, M. E. (1985) *Competitive Advantage*, New York: Free Press

Pine II, B. J. and Gilmour, J. H. (1998) 'Welcome to the Experience Economy', Cambridge, Mass.: *Harvard Business Review* (July/August)

Chapter 35

Bell, D. (1973) *The Coming of Post-Industrial Society*, New York: Basic Books

Coyle, D. (1997) *The Weightless World*, Oxford: Capstone

Levitt, T. (1960) 'Marketing Myopia', Cambridge, Mass.: *Harvard Business Review* (July/August)

Mintzberg, H. (1987) 'Crafting Strategy', Cambridge, Mass.: *Harvard Business Review* (July/August)

Ohmae, K. (1990) *The Borderless World*, London: Collins

Pascale R. T. and Athos A. (1981) *The Art of Japanese Management*, New York: Simon & Schuster; London: Allen Lane, Penguin Books

Quah, D. (1997) 'Weightless Economy Packs a Heavy Punch' *The Independent on Sunday*, 18 May

Simon, H. (1960) *The New Science of Management Decision*, New York: Harper & Row

Taylor, F. W. (1913) *The Principles of Scientific Management*, New York: Harper & Row

Venturi, R. (1972) *Learning from Las Vegas*, London: MIT Press

Chapter 36

De Geus, A. (1997) *The Living Company* London: Nicholas Brealey

Ghoshal, S. and Bartlett, C. A. (1988) *Managing Across Borders* New York and London: Random House

Kanter, R. M. (1989) *When Giants Learn to Dance*, New York and London: Simon & Schuster

Kay, J. (1994) Economic and Social Research Council lecture

Naisbitt, J. (1997) 'From Nation States to Networks' in *Rethinking the Future* ed. R. Gibson, Sonoma, CA. and London: Nicholas Brealey

Ohmae, K. (1990) *The Borderless World*, London: Collins

Pascale, R. T., Millemann, M. and Gioja, L. *Surfing the Edge of Chaos*, New York: Crown Publishing Group, Three Rivers Press

Peacock, A. and Bannock, G. (1991) *Corporate Takeovers and the Public Interest*, David Hume Institute

Porter, M. E. (1990) The Competitive Advantage of Nations, New York: Free Press; London: Macmillan

Chapter 37

Friedman, M. (1962) *Capitalism and Freedom*. Chicago: University of Chicago Press

Galbraith, J. K. (2002) 'Shocked and angry: the prophet whose warnings over Wall Street were ignored', *The Independent*, 1 July

Pearce, D., Markandya, A. and Barbier, E. B. (1989) *Blueprint for a Green Economy*, London: Kogan Page, Earthscan

Ravenscraft, D. J. and Scherer, F. M. (1987) *Mergers, Sell-offs and Economic Efficiency,* Brookings Institution, Washington D.C.

Chapter 38

Carr, A. (1968) 'Is business bluffing ethical?' Cambridge, Mass.: *Harvard Business Review* (January/February)

Chryssides, G. D. and Kaler, J. H. (1993) *An Introduction to Business Ethics*, London: Chapman & Hall

Galbraith, J. K. (1958) *The Affluent Society* London: Hamish Hamilton Hartley (1993)

Pearce, D., Markandya, A. and Barbier, E. B. (1989) *Blueprint for a Green Economy*, London: Kogan Page, Earthscan

Index

Page numbers in italics refer to diagrams and charts.